CIMA Exam Practice Kit

Financial Analysis

CIMA Exam Practice Kit

Managerial Level

Financial Analysis

Paul Rodgers

AMSTERDAM • BOSTON • HEIDELBERG • LONDON • NEW YORK • OXFORD
PARIS • SAN DIEGO • SAN FRANCISCO • SINGAPORE • SYDNEY • TOKYO

CIMA Publishing
An imprint of Elsevier
Linacre House, Jordan Hill, Oxford OX2 8DP
30 Corporate Drive, Burlington, MA 01803

First published 2006

British Library Cataloguing in Publication Data
A catalogue record for this book is available from the British Library

Library of Congress Cataloguing in Publication Data
A catalogue record for this book is available from the Library of Congress

ISBN 0 7506 6934 9

For information on all CIMA Publishing Publications
visit our website at www.cimapublishing.com

Typeset by Integra Software Services Pvt. Ltd, Pondicherry, India
www.integra-india.com
Printed and bound in The Netherlands

Contents

About the Author

Paul Rodgers bridges the gap between knowledge and commercial application looking to promote value added for participants in an entertaining and interactive style. Paul trained as a chartered accountant before working in the computer industry. He subsequently moved into the training sector where he has specialised in financial and management skills for more than 14 years, whilst keeping in touch with the commercial world as a director of a large training organisation and its publication function.

Clients trained include participants from international accountancy practices, banks, government departments plus a wide range of retail and service companies.

The forthcoming introduction of international accounting rules has seen his skills in this area required by numerous organisations preparing for the transition, but he continues to provide a broad spectrum of training plus undertaking editorial projects for both professional bodies and private clients.

Introduction

Welcome to the new CIMA Exam Practice Kit which has been launched to coincide with a major change in the syllabus in which new examinations will take place from May 2005.

This kit has been designed with the needs of home study and distance education candidates in mind. It is also ideal for fully taught courses or for students resitting papers from the old syllabus.

These hints, question and answers have been produced by some of the best-known freelance tutors in the United Kingdom who have specialised in their respective papers. The questions and topics selected are relevant for the May 2005 and November 2005 examinations.

The Exam Practice Kits will complement existing study manuals with the Q & As from May 2005 examination published in the next edition of the CIMA study manual and the Q & As from November 2005 examination published in the 2006 edition of the Exam Practice Kit.

Good luck with your studies.

Syllabus Guidance, Learning Objectives and Verbs

A The syllabus

The syllabus for the CIMA Professional Chartered Management Accounting qualification 2005 comprises three learning pillars:

- Management Accounting pillar
- Business Management pillar
- Financial Management pillar.

Within each learning pillar there are three syllabus subjects. Two of these subjects are set at the lower "Managerial" level, with the third subject positioned at the higher "Strategic" level. All subject examinations have a duration of three hours and the pass mark is 50%.

Note: In addition to these nine examinations, students are required to gain three years relevant practical experience and successfully sit the Test of Professional Competence in Management Accounting (TOPCIMA).

B Aims of the syllabus

The aims of the syllabus are:

- To provide for the Institute, together with the practical experience requirements, an adequate basis for assuring society that those admitted to membership are competent to act as management accountants for entities, whether in manufacturing, commercial or service organisations, in the public or private sectors of the economy.
- To enable the Institute to examine whether prospective members have an adequate knowledge, understanding and mastery of the stated body of knowledge and skills.
- To complement the Institute's practical experience and skills development requirements.

C Study weightings

A percentage weighting is shown against each topic in the syllabus. This is intended as a guide to the proportion of study time each topic requires.

All topics in the syllabus must be studied, since any single examination question may examine more than one topic, or carry a higher proportion of marks than the percentage study time suggested.

The weightings *do not* specify the number of marks that will be allocated to topics in the examination.

D Learning outcomes

Each topic within the syllabus contains a list of learning outcomes, which should be read in conjunction with the knowledge content for the syllabus. A learning outcome has two main purposes:

1 to define the skill or ability that a well-prepared candidate should be able to exhibit in the examination; and
2 to demonstrate the approach likely to be taken by examiners in examination questions.

The learning outcomes are part of a hierarchy of learning objectives. The verbs used at the beginning of each learning outcome relate to a specific learning objective, for example, evaluate alternative approaches to budgeting.

The verb "evaluate" indicates a high-level learning objective. As learning objectives are hierarchical, it is expected that at this level, students will have knowledge of different budgeting systems and methodologies and be able to apply them.

A list of the learning objectives and the verbs that appear in the syllabus, learning outcomes and examinations follows

Learning objectives	*Verbs used*	*Definition*
1 **Knowledge**		
What you are expected to know	List	Make a list of
	State	Express, fully or clearly, the details of/ facts of
	Define	Give the exact meaning of
2 **Comprehension**		
What you are expected to understand	Describe	Communicate the key features of
	Distinguish	Highlight the differences between
	Explain	Make clear or intelligible/State the meaning of
	Identify	Recognise, establish or select after consideration
	Illustrate	Use an example to describe or explain something

3 Application *How you are expected to apply your knowledge*	Apply	To put to practical use
	Calculate/compute	To ascertain or reckon mathematically
	Demonstrate	To prove with certainty or to exhibit by practical means
	Prepare	To make or get ready for use
	Reconcile	To make or prove consistent/compatible
	Solve	Find an answer to
	Tabulate	Arrange in a table
4 Analysis *How you are expected to analyse the detail of what you have learned*	Analyse	Examine in detail the structure of
	Categorise	Place into a defined class or division
	Compare and contrast	Show the similarities and/or differences between
	Construct	To build up or compile
	Discuss	To examine in detail by argument
	Interpret	To translate into intelligible or familiar terms
	Produce	To create or bring into existence
5 Evaluation *How you are expected to use your learning to evaluate, make decisions or recommendations*	Advise	To counsel, inform or notify
	Evaluate	To appraise or assess the value of
	Recommend	To advise on a course of action

Learning Outcomes, Syllabus Content and Examination Format

Syllabus outline

The syllabus comprises:

Topic and study weighting

A	Group Financial Statements	35%
B	The Measurement of Income and Capital	20%
C	Analysis and Interpretation of Financial Accounts	35%
D	Developments in External Reporting	10%

Learning aims

Students should be able to

- prepare consolidated accounts and explain the accounting principles associated with this area, such as changes part-way through an accounting period and in the merger method;
- appropriately employ relevant accounting standards;
- evaluate a business entity's financial statements and provide analysis of performance;
- explain the problems of profit measurement and alternative approaches to asset valuations; and
- discuss and evaluate current developments in external reporting.

Assessment strategy

There will be a three-hour written examination paper, with the following sections.

Section A – 20 marks

A variety of compulsory objective test questions, each worth between 2 and 4 marks. Mini scenarios may be given, to which a group of questions relate to.

Section B – 30 marks

Three compulsory medium answer questions, each worth 10 marks. Short scenarios may be given, to which some or all questions relate to.

Section C – 50 marks

Two questions, from a choice of three, each worth 25 marks. Short scenarios may be given, to which questions relate to.

A – Group financial statements – 35%

Learning outcomes

On completion of their studies students should be able to

(i) explain the conditions required for an undertaking to be a subsidiary or an associate of another company;
(ii) explain and apply the rules for the exclusion of subsidiaries from consolidation;
(iii) prepare a consolidated income statement, balance sheet and cash-flow statement for a group of companies;
(iv) explain and apply the concepts of fair value at the point of acquisition and impairment of goodwill;
(v) identify the impact on group financial statements when a subsidiary is acquired or disposed of part-way through an accounting period (to include the effective date of acquisition and dividends out of pre-acquisition profits) and where shareholdings, or control, are acquired in stages;
(vi) explain the concept of an associate and a joint venture, and the principles of how they are accounted for;
(vii) explain the pooling of interests method of consolidation;
(viii) compare and contrast pooling of interests, acquisition and equity methods of accounting;
(ix) explain the principles of accounting for a capital reconstruction scheme or a demerger;
(x) explain foreign currency translation principles, including the difference between the closing rate/net investment method and the historical rate method; and
(xi) explain the correct treatment for foreign loans financing foreign equity investments.

Syllabus content

- Relationships between investors and investees, and the exclusion of subsidiaries from consolidation with reference to dominant influence, participating interest, management on a unified basis and significant influence.
- The preparation of consolidated financial statements (including the group cash-flow statement) involving one or more subsidiaries, sub-subsidiaries and associates, under the acquisition and pooling of interests methods (IAS 7, 22 and 27).
- The treatment in consolidated financial statements of minority interests, pre- and post-acquisition reserves, goodwill (including its impairment), fair value adjustments, intra-group transactions and dividends, piece-meal and midyear acquisitions and disposals to include sub-subsidiaries and mixed groups.
- The accounting treatment of associates and joint ventures (IAS 28 and 31) using the equity method and proportional consolidation method.
- The accounting entries for mergers, demergers and capital reconstruction schemes.
- Foreign currency translation (IAS 21) to include overseas transactions and investments in overseas subsidiaries.

B – The measurement of income and capital – 20%

Learning outcomes

On completion of their studies students should be able to

(i) explain the problems of profit measurement and alternative approaches to asset valuations;
(ii) explain measures to reduce distortion in financial statements when price levels change;
(iii) discuss the principle of substance over form applied to a range of transactions;
(iv) discuss the possible treatments of financial instruments in the issuer's accounts (i.e. liabilities versus equity and the implications for finance costs);
(v) identify circumstances in which amortised cost, fair value and hedge accounting are appropriate for financial instruments, and explain the principles of these accounting methods;
(vi) discuss the recognition and valuation issues concerned with pension schemes, and the treatment of actuarial deficits and surpluses.

Syllabus content

- The problems of profit measurement and the effect of alternative approaches to asset valuation; current cost and current purchasing power bases and the real terms system; accounting for changing prices (IAS 15) and hyperinflation (IAS 29).
- The principle of substance over form (IAS 1) and its influence in dealing with transactions such as sale and repurchase agreements, consignment stock, debt factoring, securitised assets, loan transfers and public and private sector financial collaboration.
- Financial instruments classified as liabilities or shareholder's funds and the allocation of finance costs over the term of the borrowing (IAS 32 and 39).
- The measurement and disclosure of financial instruments (IAS 39).
- Retirement benefits, including pension schemes, defined benefit schemes and defined contribution schemes, actuarial deficits and surpluses (IAS 19).

C – Analysis and interpretation of financial accounts – 35%

Learning outcomes

On completion of their studies, students should be able to

(i) calculate and interpret a full range of accounting ratios;
(ii) analyse financial statements (in the context of information provided in the accounts and corporate report) to comment on performance and position;
(iii) prepare a concise report on the results of an analysis of financial statements;
(iv) explain the limitations of accounting ratio analysis and analysis based on financial statements;
(v) prepare and interpret segmental analysis, interfirm and international comparisons.

Syllabus content

- Ratios in the areas of performance, profitability, financial adaptability, liquidity, activity, shareholder investment and financing, and their interpretation.
- Calculation of earnings per share under IAS 33, to include the effect of bonus issues, rights issues and convertible stock.

- Interpretation of financial statements via the analysis of the accounts and corporate reports.
- Reporting the results of analysis.
- Limitations of ratio analysis (e.g. comparability of businesses and accounting policies).
- The identification of information required to assess financial performance and the extent to which financial statements fail to provide such information.
- Segment analysis: interfirm and international comparison (IAS 14).
- Interpretation of financial obligations included in financial accounts (e.g. redeemable debt, earn-out arrangements and contingent liabilities).
- The effect of short-term debt on the measurement of gearing.
- The need to be aware of aggressive or unusual accounting policies "creative accounting" (e.g. in the areas of cost capitalisation and revenue recognition).

D – Developments in external reporting – 10%

Learning outcomes

On completion of their studies students should be able to

(i) discuss pressures for extending the scope and quality of external reports;
(ii) explain how financial information concerning the interaction of a business with the natural environment can be communicated in the published accounts;
(iii) identify those environmental issues which should be disclosed;
(iv) explain the process of measuring, recording and disclosing the effect of exchanges between a business and society – human resource accounting;
(v) identify the influences on financial reporting of cultural differences across the world; and
(vi) identify major differences between IAS and US GAAP.

Syllabus content

- Increasing stakeholder demands for information that goes beyond historical financial information and the model for an expanded Operating and Financial Review (OFR) proposed by the UK government.
- Environmental and social accounting issues, differentiating between environmental measures and environmental losses, capitalisation of environmental expenditure, and the recognition of future environmental costs by means of provisions.
- The Global Reporting Initiative [GRI]: non-financial measures of environmental impact.
- Human resource accounting.
- The influence of different cultures on financial reporting.
- Pressures for improved quality of financial reporting following large scale corporate collapses in the US and UK, and implications for corporate governance and external audit.
- Major differences between IAS and US GAAP.

Examination Techniques

Essay questions

Your essay should have a clear structure, that is, an introduction, a middle and an end. Think in terms of 1 mark for each relevant point made.

Numerical questions

It is essential to show workings in your answer. If you come up with the wrong answer and no workings, the examiner cannot award any marks. However, if you get the wrong answer but apply the correct technique then you will be given some marks.

Reports and memorandum

Where you are asked to produce an answer in a report type format you will be given easy marks for style and presentation.

- A *report* is a document from an individual or group in one organisation sent to an individual or group in another.
- A *memorandum* is an informal report going from one individual or group to another individual or group in the same organisation.

You should start a report as follows

To: J. SMITH, CEO, ABC plc

From: M ACCOUNTANT

Date: 31st December 200X

Terms of Reference: Financial Strategy of ABC plc

Multiple choice questions – Managerial level

From May 2005, some multiple choice questions will be worth more than two marks. Even if you get the answer wrong, you may still get some marks for the steps. Therefore show all workings on such questions.

Financial Reporting Frameworks

1

The international standard setting structure

- The organisational structure for international standard setting was headed by the International Accounting Standards Committee (IASC) Foundation.
- The IASC Foundation's principal activities include
  - appointing members to the IASB, IFRIC and SAC
  - promoting vigorous application of IASB standards
  - approving budget of IASB.
- Standards Advisory Council (SAC) advises IASB on its work agenda and provides feedback from members, organisations and individuals on standard setting projects.
- International Accounting Standards Board (IASB)
  - replaced IASC
  - key role is to drive and facilitate the convergence of national and international accounting standards.
- A problem faced by the IASB is that historically companies applying International Accounting Standards (IAS) did not always apply the rules stipulated therein fully; a tougher regime is to be implemented in the future.
- International Financial Reporting Interpretations Committee (IFRIC) reviews contentious accounting issues that might lead to unacceptable accounting practices unless addressed.

The IASB Framework

- Principal purpose is to assist the IASB with
  - development of international accounting standards
  - reducing the number of alternative treatments allowed by international standards.
- The framework helps ensure financial statements allow decisions to be made by different user groups.
- Seven distinct user groups are identified (investors, employees, lenders, suppliers, customers, governments and the public).

- The principal sections of the framework are:

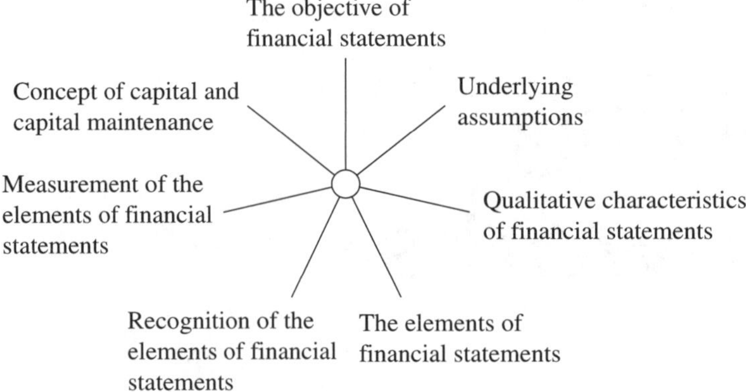

IAS 1 Presentation of financial statements

- Financial statements must contain the following
  - balance sheet
  - income statement
  - statements of changes in equity
  - cash-flow statement
  - accounting policies and explanatory notes.
- Financial statements should *fairly present* the position, performance and cash flows of an entity.
- Departure from international standards to give fairer presentation is very rare.

IAS 8 Accounting policies, changes in accounting estimates and errors

- When international standards do not give specific instructions, newly developed accounting policies should be relevant to user needs and reflect the attributes of reliability described in the framework (e.g. neutrality and completeness).

Structure and content of financial statements

- Balance sheet – minimum disclosure
  - property, plant and equipment
  - investment property
  - intangible assets
  - financial assets
  - investments accounted for using the equity method
  - biological assets
  - inventories
  - trade and other receivables
  - cash and cash equivalents
  - trade and other payables
  - provisions
  - financial liabilities

  - liabilities and assets for current tax
  - deferred tax liabilities and deferred tax assets
  - minority interest, presented within equity
  - issued capital and reserves attributable to equity holders.
- Income statement – minimum disclosure
  - revenue
  - finance costs
  - share of the profit or loss of associates and joint ventures accounted for using the equity method
  - pre-tax gain or loss recognised on the disposal of assets or settlement of liabilities attributable to discontinuing operations
  - tax expense
  - profit or loss
  - profit or loss attributable to minority interest.
- Statement of changes in equity – minimum disclosure relates to six specific requirements
  1 the net profit or loss for the period
  2 items of income, expense, gain or loss recognised directly in equity
  3 cumulative effect of changes in accounting policy and the correction of fundamental errors
  4 capital transactions and distributions to owners
  5 the balance of accumulated profit or loss at the beginning of the period, movements for the period and the balance at the end of the period
  6 a reconciliation between the carrying amount of each class of equity capital, share premium and reserves at the beginning and end of the accounting period.
- Notes to the financial statements.

Recent developments in international standards

- Improvements project – improvements made to 13 existing international standards to reduce choice and inconsistencies, and thereby help facilitate international convergence.
- IFRS 1 First-time adoption of International Financial Reporting Standard (IFRS).
- IFRS 2 Share-based payment – this addresses the difficult subject of share options being given in lieu of cash-based remuneration. Historically both recognition and measurement have proved contentious as there is no immediate cash cost and the value of the potential benefit is dependent upon the future.

  IFRS 2 solution – the standard identifies three types of share-based payment transactions
  1 equity-settled share-based payment transactions
  2 cash-settled share-based payment transactions
  3 transactions where one of the parties involved can choose whether the provider of services or goods is rewarded in cash (value based on equity prices) or in shares.

  A charge should be recognised against profit when the goods and services are consumed and measured at fair value.

- IFRS 3 Business combinations.
- IFRS 4 Insurance contracts.
- IFRS 5 Non-current assets held for sale and discontinued operations.
- IFRS 6 Exploration for and evaluation of mineral resources.
- Amendments to IAS 32 and IAS 39.

? Objective test questions

1.1 One of the four principal qualitative characteristics of financial statements as per the IASB Framework is reliability. Identify the remaining three characteristics and describe in a maximum of 50 words which one normally represents a trade-off against reliability when financial statements are prepared.

(3 marks)

1.2 The IASB Framework describes the elements of financial statements. Which of the following is the closest definition of an asset?

A A resource controlled by the entity as a result of a specific event and from which economic benefits are expected.
B A resource controlled by the entity as a result of a past event which can be accurately measured.
C A resource controlled by the entity as a result of past events and from which future economic benefits are expected to flow.
D A resource controlled by the entity arising from past events, legal or constructive, and from which economic benefits are expected to flow.

(2 marks)

1.3 A published set of financial statements comprises many components including

(i) Balance sheet
(ii) Chairman's statement
(iii) Operating and financial review
(iv) Income statement
(v) Statement of changes in equity
(vi) Director's report.

Which of these are stipulated disclosures under IAS 1 *Presentation of Financial Statements*?

A (i), (iii), (iv) and (v)
B (i), (iv), (v) and (vi)
C (i), (iv) and (v)
D (i), (ii), (iii), (iv) and (v)

(2 marks)

1.4 Describe in a maximum of 40 words how the operating cycle of a business might impact balance sheet disclosure under IAS 1 *Presentation of Financial Statements.*

(2 marks)

1.5 The IASB Framework specifies that losses constitute "decreases in ownership interest not resulting from distributions to owners". Why does this represent a dilemma when considering the issue of share options to a company director in lieu of cash remuneration? [60 words maximum]

(3 marks)

1.6 Under international accounting guidance financial statements are required to be fairly presented. Which of the following statements is not accurate with reference to the use of this term?

A There are rare circumstances in which a departure from international standards can be justified and the financial statements still be deemed to be fairly presented.
B Fair presentation implies full compliance with local legislation.
C Unacceptable accounting policies can never be rendered acceptable by way of full disclosure in the notes to the financial statements.
D Financial statements cannot be described as IAS compliant unless all the requirements of relevant international standards have been complied with in full.

(2 marks)

1.7 Selecting the most appropriate answer complete the following statement:
"IFRS 1 First time adoption of IFRS is to provide guidance when"

A IFRS are used for the first time in the preparation of the period end financial statements

B New IFRSs are issued and their implementation date reached

C An entity uses IFRSs for the first time and makes an explicit and unreserved statement of compliance with IFRS

D The national standard setting body dictates IFRS compliance

(2 marks)

1.8 IAS 1 Presentation of financial statements defines a current asset as one that is:

(i) expected to be realised in, or is held for sale or consumption in, the normal course of the entity's operating cycle
(ii) held primarily for trading purposes or for the short term and is expected to be realised within twelve months of the balance sheet date
(iii) Cash or a cash equivalent

A (ii) only
B (i) and (ii)
C (ii) and (iii)
D (i), (ii) and (iii)

(2 marks)

Objective test answers

1.1

(i) Understandability
(ii) Relevance
(iii) Comparability

Reliable financial statements are said to be free from bias and material error, whereas relevance implies that they meet the needs of users. This is inevitably a trade off as users want current information as a basis for decisions, but this involves greater estimation and uncertainty and hence is less reliable.

1.2 **C**

An asset is defined as "a resource controlled by the entity as a result of past events and from which future economic benefits are expected to flow to the entity". [IASB Framework paragraph 49]

1.3 **C**

IAS 1 stipulates that a complete set of financial statements comprises

- Balance sheet
- Income statement
- Statement of changes in equity
- Cash-flow statement
- Accounting policies and explanatory notes.

1.4 Current assets are represented by those that will typically be realised within 12 months of the balance sheet date, but if the business's normal operating cycle is greater than this then the asset will remain categorised as current.

1.5 If the market value of the company's shares exceeds the option strike price on the date of exercise, the director will convert the options into shares. If the shares are then sold the director will make a profit on disposal, but technically this does not meet the IASB Framework definition of a loss to the company as the ownership interest has not fallen.

IFRS 2 Share-based payment requires recognition of this concealed remuneration as an expense over the corresponding period of benefit gained from the directors' employment.

1.6 **B**

Fairly presented does not refer to local legislation relating to the preparation of financial statements.

1.7 **C**

Per IFRS 1 Appendix A.

1.8 **D**

For the majority of businesses the operating cycle, namely the period from the initiation of the transaction to the payment/receipt of cash, will be less than twelve months.

? Medium answer questions

Question 1 – Wels Ltd

You have recently been recruited by Wels Ltd, a fast growing food importation company. The senior management team has informed you that they are keen for the company to obtain a listing at the earliest opportunity, and as part of their preparatory work have decided to switch from UK GAAP to international accounting standards. It is their belief that this will make future funding more accessible.

Aware of your recent professional training, they asked you to give a brief presentation to the other members of the management team and have requested you to focus on two particular matters of confusion.

1 The status and purpose of the IASB Framework.
2 To improve the company's working capital, they are keen to maximise current assets; and have been previously informed that the concept of an asset needing to be recoverable in less than 12 months to be classed as current does not exist internationally.

You have been asked to prepare slides for the presentation and distribute them in advance of the meeting.

Requirements

(a) Prepare your lead slide for each of the matters raised (a maximum of four points on each), and briefly comment on the issues raised.

(6 marks)

(b) The IASB Framework identifies a range of stakeholder groups who could have an interest in the published financial statements of a company. Identify the likely interested parties, other than the shareholders, of Wels Ltd, and specify the cause of their interest.

(4 marks)
(Total = 10 marks)

Medium answer questions

Answer 1 – Wels Ltd

(a) Matters of concern

Slide 1 – Status and purpose of IASB Framework

- consistent development of new standards
- reduction in the number of alternative accounting treatments
- assist analysts and auditors.

The IASB Framework provides generic guidance relevant to the preparation of financial statements. It provides increased consistency between all newly developed accounting standards by defining key terms, such as asset and liability, and specifying criteria for both recognition and measurement.

This guidance plus the requirement to adhere to qualitative characteristics such as relevance, reliability, comparability and understandability allows less scope for diverse accounting policies of the same item. It is this consistency which in turn aids the reviewers of financial statements (e.g. auditors) as there will be fewer idiosyncrasies between different businesses and different accounting periods.

Slide 2 – Maximising working capital

A current asset is

- held for sale or consumption;
- expected to be realised within 12 months

unless

- operating cycle is longer.

With its intention to become listed, it is understandable that Wels Ltd wants to show its financial data in the best light. Transferring non-current assets to current assets will improve working capital and return on capital employed, but this is not an arbitrary decision and unless based on sound accounting reasons will be viewed as creative accounting.

To be classed as a current asset, the normal criteria are that it is held for sale or consumption and is expected to be realised within 12 months. However, if the operating cycle of the business exceeds 12 months then assets that meet the other criteria relevant to being classed as current will retain this classification.

In the case of Wels Ltd it seems unlikely that this will be relevant to a business involved in food importation.

(b) Stakeholder groups

Providers of long-term finance	To fund the company's growth and proposed listing, they will want to see evidence of assets that can be used to securitise their potential investment They will also be interested in both profitability and cash flows year on year as a platform to support repayments

Market analysts	Cash balances and "free cash" within the cash-flow statement will give evidence of ability to meet future funding costs Working capital balances will be reviewed to ascertain if the rapid growth of the company is based on overtrading
Potential investors	In anticipation of a listing, potential investors will want to evaluate potential for capital and income growth. Trends in earnings and dividends per share will be reviewed together with investment in the capital infrastructure of the business
Employees	Interest lies in profitability as a basis for remuneration levels, but will also look at indicators of long-term viability to ensure job security

The Consolidated Balance Sheet: The Basics

2

The conceptual background

- A *group* is a single cohesive unit of two or more legally separate entities where the legal status is overridden by the need to reflect commercial substance.

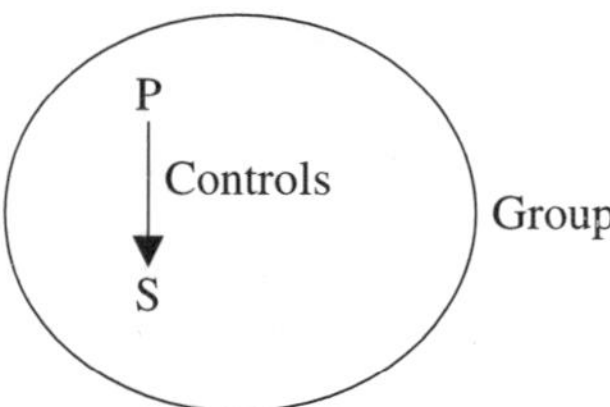

- A *subsidiary* is an entity controlled by the parent (IAS 27).
- Exemption from the need to produce consolidated financial statements
  - a parent that is itself wholly or, in some circumstances, partially owned and the owners allow non-consolidation
  - this exemption is lost if the shares or debt of the parent are publically traded.
- Exclusion of subsidiaries from the consolidation process
  - subsidiary acquired and held exclusively with a view to selling it.

The basic mechanics of consolidation

- The investment in S in P's balance sheet is replaced by adding S's net assets to P's line-by-line in the consolidated balance sheet to show group resources.

Ownership and control

- Ownership – minority interests should be given to that part of S's net assets not owned by P.
- Control – usually if P > 50% of S.

Key workings

- Group structure.
- Net assets at both the date of acquisition, needed for the calculation of goodwill, and at the balance sheet date, needed for the calculation of the minority interest.
- Goodwill – the difference between the cost of the investment and the fair value of the acquiree's identifiable assets, liabilities and contingent liabilities.
- Minority interest – their share of the net assets at the balance sheet date.
- Accumulated profits

	£
P (100%)	X
S (share of post-acquisition)	X
Goodwill impaired to date	(X)
	X

The treatment of goodwill (IFRS 3)

- Positive goodwill
  - no amortisation
  - tested annually for impairment.
- Discount on acquisition (negative goodwill)
  - written off immediately to the income statement.

Treatment of intra-group balances

- Current accounts between group members must agree before cancelling.
- Differences in current accounts due to
  - cash in transit
  - inventory in transit.
- Make balances agree by adjusting for in-transit items in the books of the receiving company.
- Cancel the intracompany balances.

Objective test questions

2.1 IAS 27 Accounting for Investments in Subsidiaries requires that a parent company should consolidate all subsidiaries other than those that meet specific criteria for exclusion.

The Duchy plc has three subsidiaries and has asked your help to determine which, if any, can be excluded from the consolidation process.

Crown Ltd – transferred to a new computerised accounting system during the year, which generated a severe delay in the production of year end financial information. This can only be curtailed by the recruitment of several temporary staff at a considerable expense.

Jewels Ltd – it is anticipated that this subsidiary will be sold in the next accounting period and a purchaser is actively being sought. The company has been a full group member for the previous two years.

The third subsidiary, Zastorian, is based on overseas. The local government has now imposed stringent exchange controls for the foreseeable future and is threatening to expropriate the assets of companies not locally owned.

The subsidiaries to be excluded from consolidation would be

A Jewels Ltd only
B Zastorian only
C Jewels and Zastorian
D Crown Ltd and Jewels Ltd

(2 marks)

2.2 Extracts from the financial statements of Drogba plc and its two subsidiaries as at 31 December 20X4 are given below

	Drogba plc	*Seel Ltd*	*Rindor Ltd*
	£m	£m	£m
Ordinary shares (10p each)	40	20	4
Accumulated reserves	395	90	10

At the date of acquisition, Seel Ltd had accumulated profits of £150 million and Rindor Ltd accumulated losses of £30 million.

Calculate the consolidated accumulated profits of Drogba plc on 31 December 20X4, and briefly comment on how this figure reflects the concept of control.

Drogba had acquired 180 million shares in Seel Ltd and 28 million shares in Rindor Ltd respectively. Both acquisitions were made on the same date three years previously, and no goodwill had arisen on either transaction.

(3 marks)

2.3 Wren plc purchased a 75% stake in the ordinary shares of Nest Ltd several years before. The purchase consideration comprised cash of £190 million and other assets with an additional fair value of £10 million.

On the acquisition date, extracts from Nest's balance sheet appeared as follows with all items believed to be at their fair value.

	£m
Non-current assets	520
Current assets	105
Non-current liabilities	(310)
Current liabilities	(35)

Nest Ltd has had 20 million £1 ordinary shares in issue since its incorporation.

Calculate the goodwill arising on Wren plc's acquisition of Nest Ltd and describe in 40 words or less the recommended treatment under IFRS 3 *Business Combinations*.

(3 marks)

2.4 Which of the following statements about the treatment of positive goodwill are true in accordance with IFRS 3 *Business Combinations*?

(i) If a definite useful economic life can be identified then amortisation should occur straight line over this period.
(ii) The goodwill should be reviewed annually for evidence of impairment.
(iii) Goodwill should be disclosed as a non-current asset.
(iv) The carrying value of goodwill should be revised annually to reflect all revisions in the fair value of assets existing at the date of acquisition and still held in the balance sheet.

A (i), (ii) and (iii)
B (ii), (iii) and (iv)
C (ii) and (iii)
D (i) and (iii)

(2 marks)

2.5 Romeo Ltd and Juliet Ltd have been wholly owned members of the same group for several years, and regularly trade between themselves. As at 30 September 20X4 the intercompany current accounts have the following balances:

	£'000
Romeo's Current account with Juliet	25 Credit
Juliet's Current account with Romeo	30 Debit

This difference is attributable to cash in transit.

The current accounts are held within the working capital balances of the two companies; details of which are given below

	Romeo Ltd	*Juliet Ltd*
	£'000	£'000
Current assets	127	82
Current liabilities	56	42

If the current assets and current liabilities of the parent company are £250k and £123k respectively, what are the consolidated figures for inclusion within the group financial statements at 30 September 20X4?

(2 marks)

2.6 In July 20X1 Repent plc purchased 7,000 ordinary shares in Rex Ltd for £200,000 when the reserves of the latter were £127,000. No further acquisitions have been made since this date, and as at 31 December 20X4 the individual balance sheets of the two companies were as follows

	Repent plc £'000	*Rex Ltd* £'000
Non-current assets	450	20
Current assets	125	160
	575	180
Ordinary shares [£1 each]	50	10
Accumulated reserves	455	145
Current liabilities	70	25
	575	180

Assuming no impairments have been identified, calculate the carrying value of goodwill and minority interests in the consolidated balance sheet at 31 December 20X4.

(2 marks)

2.7 The Mund Group comprises Mund plc and four subsidiaries none of which was purchased in the current year. Investment stakes range from wholly owned to 55%, and the purchase consideration given for each acquisition exceeded the value of the tangible net assets acquired.

The Chief Executive has asked you to briefly explain the composition of consolidated accumulated profits [60 words or less]. He is not interested in any financial data as this is the remit of the Finance Director.

(3 marks)

2.8 On 1 October 20X5 Lime plc acquired 100,000 shares in Lemon plc (issued share capital 125,000 $1 shares). For each share acquired the consideration given was $5 cash and one ordinary share in Lime plc. Additionally legal fees of $50,000 were incurred as part of the acquisition.

At 1 October 20X5 Lime plcs shares were trading at $2.50 each, but this had risen to $3 at the financial year end; 31 December 20X5.

What is the fair value of Lemon plc's net assets at acquisition if a discount on acquisition of $160,000 arose on the transaction.

A $1,200,000
B $1,137,500
C $960,000
D $910,000

(3 marks)

✓ Objective test answers

2.1 **B**

Zastorian is the subject of long-term restrictions that are likely to hinder the ability of the parent company to exercise control.

Jewels cannot be excluded as it has been previously consolidated and undue expense incurred by Crown Ltd is also not a permitted exclusion under IAS 27.

2.2 The consolidated accumulated reserves are

	£m
Drogba plc	395
Seel Ltd [90% × (90 − 150)]	(54)
Rindor Ltd [70% × (30 − 10)]	14
	355

Percentage stakes in excess of 50% indicate that Drogba plc has control of both Seel Ltd and Rindor Ltd which should be treated as subsidiaries. However, this control can only be exercised from the acquisition date, and Drogba plc cannot claim that its management was responsible for profits or losses earned by the other companies prior to this point.

2.3 Fair value of consideration = £200m
Fair value of net assets acquired [75% × £280m] = £210m
"Negative Goodwill" = £10m

IFRS 3 does not refer to this difference as negative goodwill. The £10 million will be written off directly to the income statement where it will be treated as gain.

2.4 C

IFRS 3 *Business Combinations* prohibits the amortisation of goodwill preferring an annual impairment review. It is not appropriate to revise the fair value of assets after acquisition.

2.5 Consolidated current assets [250 + 127 + 82 − 30 + 5] = £434k

Consolidated current liabilities [123 + 56 + 42 − 25] = £196k

2.6 Goodwill

	£
Consideration	200,000
Share of net assets at acquisition [70% × (127,000 + 10,000)]	95,900
Goodwill	104,100

Minority interest = 30% × 155,000 = £46,500

2.7 Consolidated accumulated profits comprise

- accumulated reserves of the Mund plc; the parent company
- Mund's percentage holding of the post-acquisition profits of each subsidiary
- any impairment of goodwill arising since acquisition.

2.8 **A**

(\$5 Cash + \$2.50 Share) × 100,000 =	\$750,000
Fees	\$50,000
	\$800,000
Discount	\$160,000
80% Net Assets	\$960,000

100/80 × \$960,000.

? Medium answer questions

Question 1 – Principles of group accounting

(a) Briefly explain the significance of the following terms in the context of the preparation of consolidated financial statements

(i) The single entity concept
(ii) Minority interest
(iii) Inventory in transit.

(6 marks)

(b) The following draft balance sheets were available for Round plc and its 80% owned subsidiary Oval Ltd as at 31 December 20X4

	Round plc	*Oval Ltd*
	£m	£m
Ordinary shares [50p each]	60	20
Accumulated profits	142	62
Non-current liabilities	200	31
Current liabilities	26	17
	428	130

The investment in Oval Ltd was made several years previously when Oval Ltd's reserves were £9 million. No goodwill arose on the acquisition.

Calculate the minority interest and consolidated accumulated profits to be shown on the consolidated balance sheet as at 31 December 20X4 taking into account the following issues.

1 During the year, Oval Ltd incurred surveyors fees of £400,000 but these are not reflected in the current liabilities and have not been paid.
2 During the current year goods purchased by Oval plc were sold to Round plc at their original cost of £5 million, and the outstanding liability settled prior to the year end. Also prior to the year end they were sold again to an external customer for £8 million. These transactions have been fully recorded in the books of each individual company.

(4 marks)
(Total = 10 marks)

Question 2 – Orchid plc

Orchid plc purchased 30,000 shares in Stick Ltd on 1 January 20X0 when the accumulated reserves of the latter were £76,000. This is Orchid plc's only investment.

On 31 December 20X4 the balance sheets of the two companies are as follows

	Orchid plc		*Stick Ltd*	
	£	£	£	£
Assets				
Non-current assets				
Property, plant and equipment		234,000		50,000
Investments		70,000		5,000
		304,000		55,000
Current assets				
Inventory	83,000			43,100
Receivables	56,500			28,000
Stick Ltd current account	12,000			–
Cash	28,000			9,000
		179,500		
Total assets		483,500		135,100
Equity and liabilities				
Capital and reserves				
Ordinary share capital [50p shares]		50,000		25,000
Share premium account		10,500		–
Accumulated profits		310,000		90,000
		370,500		115,000
Non-current liabilities				
Loan		25,000		3,000
Current liabilities				
Trade payables	88,000		8,100	
Orchid plc current account	–	–	9,000	
		88,000		17,100
		483,500		135,100

Notes

- All positive goodwill is reviewed for impairment at the end of each year. No falls in value had been identified until the current year when an impairment of £5,000 was deemed necessary.
- The disparity on the current accounts is due to cash in transit.

Requirement

Prepare the consolidated balance sheet of Orchid plc as at 31 December 20X4.

(10 marks)

✓ Medium answer questions

Answer 1 – Principles of group accounting

(a) Explanation of key terms

(i) *The single entity concept*: Under UK law, every company is a separate legal entity with the right to enter into transactions and contracts in its own capacity. Consequently all the individual assets and liabilities of a company vest in its own name, and not in the name of the shareholders who ultimately have control over its operations.

This creates a dilemma when one company takes a controlling stake in another. Legally the only recognition it can give within its financial statements to its new investment is cost . . . remember it does not legally hold title to the assets and liabilities of the subsidiary.

When shareholders of the parent company receive its statutory financial statements it would be helpful to see the assets and liabilities that lie behind investments made in other entities, but following strict legal form this would not be possible.

The single entity concept represents an example of commercial substance prevailing over legal form. Assets and liabilities of subsidiaries are added to those of the parent line-by-line as if all the companies were a single entity. This gives the shareholders a clearer representation as to the true nature of their investment.

(ii) *Minority interests*: When an investment is made to acquire a subsidiary company, it is not necessary to take ownership of 100% of the equity share capital to gain control. The latter is normally associated with a stake in excess of 50%.

The remaining shareholding is said to belong to the minority interest.

The consolidated balance sheet represents their interest by separately disclosing their percentage share of the net assets of the subsidiary at the balance sheet date.

(iii) *Inventory in transit*: When companies are members of the same group it is a common practice that inventory and cash will be transferred between them. Amounts payable and receivable are tracked via intercompany current accounts held within current liabilities and assets respectively.

When the consolidated balance sheet is prepared, these current accounts need to be eliminated as they do not represent amounts payable to or receivable from outside the group. Unfortunately when the volume of transactions is high it is common for the current account balances not to be equal and opposite due to cash or inventory in transit. These items will have been recorded by the company dispatching them but not the recipient.

To facilitate the correct elimination of the current accounts, amounts in transit must be "driven" to their destination and recorded. Failure to do this will lead to an understatement of inventory or cash in the consolidated accounts.

(b)

Minority interest = 20% × net assets at the balance sheet date
= 20% × (20 + 62 − 0.4)
= £16.32m

Consolidated accumulated reserves

	£m
Round plc	142
Oval Ltd [80% × (61.6 − 9)]	42.08
	184.08

The intercompany trading has no impact as the current accounts will have been eliminated on settlement, and the transfer was made at cost.

Furthermore the goods have been sold outside the group which constitutes a genuine sale for the group.

Answer 2 – Orchid plc

Consolidated balance sheet as at 31 December 20X4

	£	£
Assets		
Non-current assets		
Property, plant and equipment		284,000
Intangibles [W1]		4,400
Investments		5,000
		293,400
Current assets		
Inventory	126,100	
Receivables	84,500	
Cash (28,000 + 9,000 + 3,000)	40,000	
		250,600
Total assets		544,000
Equity and liabilities		
Capital and reserves		
Ordinary share capital [50p shares]		50,000
Share premium account		10,500
Accumulated profits [W3]		313,400
		373,900
Minority interests [W2]		46,000
		419,900
Non-current liabilities		
Loan		28,000
Current liabilities		
Trade payables	96,100	
		96,100
		544,000

W1:

Goodwill

	£
Cost of investment	70,000
Net assets acquired [60% × (25,000 + 76,000)]	(60,600)
	9,400
Less: Impairment	(5,000)
	4,400

W2:

Minority interests

40% × 115,000 = £46,000

W3:

Accumulated reserves

	£
Orchid plc	310,000
Stick Ltd [60% × (90,000 − 76,000)]	8,400
Goodwill impairment	(5,000)
	313,400

The Consolidated Balance Sheet 3

Investments by the parent in the borrowings of the subsidiary

- Cancel on consolidation.

Investment by the parent in the non-equity shares of the subsidiary

- Control is determined by equity shares only.
- Minority interest needs to be calculated in two parts:
  1 their share of the net assets financed by the non-equity shares
  2 their share in the balance of the net assets financed by the equity shares.
- Similarly goodwill will also be a two-part calculation.

The treatment of unpaid intra-group dividends and interest at the balance sheet date

- If fully accounted for in the books of the parent and subsidiary, simply cancel the asset and liability outstanding to the other group member.
- When the dividend/interest has yet to be recorded in the individual books then these entries must be made prior to cancellation.
- For example if S proposes a dividend but has yet to record it:

	£	£
Dr Accumulated profits of S	X	
Cr Dividends payable		X

- When the intra-group amounts are cancelled this will leave a dividend payable to minority interests in the consolidated balance sheet.

Treatment of unrealised profits

- Unrealised profits remaining at the balance sheet date need to be eliminated as they do not represent a genuine profit to the group, which must be viewed as a single entity.
- Inventory – eliminate the unrealised profit against the reserves of the seller, to ensure the minority interest bear their share, and from the inventory total in the consolidated balance sheet.
- Property, plant and equipment – adjust the reserves of the seller and deduct from the property, plant and equipment total in the consolidated balance sheet.
- The inflated transfer price of property, plant and equipment will also lead to excess depreciation being charged in the books of the recipient. This excess will need to be added back to the non-current asset carrying value and to the accumulated profits of the receiving entity.

Other adjustments

- Misaligned accounting policies need to be adjusted prior to the consolidation process (IAS 27).
- The net assets of the target company must be restated to fair value at the acquisition date (IFRS 3).

Objective test questions

3.1 Trident Ltd owns the entire share capital of Polaris Ltd, and regularly sells goods to the latter at a 25% mark up on cost. At the year end the inventory balances for the two companies were:

	£
Trident Ltd	323,000
Polaris Ltd	111,000

During the year, goods with a marked-up value of £75,000 were transferred between the companies of which £15,000 remains in the inventory of Polaris Ltd at the balance sheet date.

Calculate the value of inventory to be included in the consolidated balance sheet, and in less than 40 words explain the significance of goods transferred intercompany being sold on to third party customers.

(3 marks)

3.2 Rodeo plc has two subsidiaries, namely Sand Ltd [100%] and Rain Ltd [60%]. The inventory of these companies at the balance sheet date was as follows:

	£
Rodeo plc	725,000
Sand Ltd	101,500
Rain Ltd	67,000

The companies regularly transfer inventory intra-group, and the following information is available regarding the previous accounting period.

- Sand transferred items with an original cost of £32,000 to Rodeo plc at a mark up of 25%. Half of these remain held within Rodeo plc's warehouse at the year end.
- Rodeo plc sold inventory to Rain Ltd at a transfer value of £12,000. There was a 10% margin included within this sales value. None of these goods remain within the inventory of Rain Ltd at the year end.
- In addition to the transfer above, Rodeo plc had dispatched a further £4,400 of inventory (this is the transfer value) to Rain Ltd, but this had not been delivered by the balance sheet date.

Calculate the value of inventory to be included in the consolidated balance sheet.

(3 marks)

3.3 Rogue Ltd has held a 75% stake in Saone Ltd for several years. At the current balance sheet date Rogue Ltd had £13,000 of inventory that had been transferred from Saone Ltd at a mark up of 30%.

In the preparation of the consolidated balance sheet, what impact will this information have on the calculation of:

- Inventory
- Minority interest
- Accumulated profits

(3 marks)

3.4 Freedom plc specialises in the manufacture of moulding machines, which it produces at a cost of £80,000.

In 20X2 it sold two of these machines to Rabbit Ltd, a 60% owned subsidiary, for £200,000. The depreciation policy of this company is to depreciate straight line over 10 years with a full years' charge in the year of acquisition.

In preparing the consolidated balance sheet of Freedom plc at 31 December 20X4, what adjustment would be needed to non-current assets for the assets transferred.

A Decrease by £40,000
B Decrease by £28,000
C Decrease by £24,000
D Decrease by £16,800 **(2 marks)**

3.5 Alpha Ltd purchased a 90% stake in Tunney Ltd during the current period. The consideration comprised:

- 10,000, 50p ordinary shares with a market value of £3
- £7,000 cash.

At the acquisition date, the balance sheet of Tunney Ltd, which has an issued share capital of 2,000 £1 shares, comprised:

	£
Non-current assets	31,000
Current assets	19,500
Non-current liabilities	(7,500)
Current liabilities	(23,500)

Included in non-current assets are items with a fair value £4,000 in excess of their book value.

Historically Tunney Ltd has adopted a provisioning policy that is contrary to international accounting practice. At the acquisition date, its balance sheet included £3,000 of disallowable provisions.

Calculate the value of goodwill arising on the acquisition.

(3 marks)

3.6 Flighty Ltd has two subsidiary companies. It holds a 60% stake in Radar Ltd and a 75% stake in Holmes Ltd. The following additional information is available:

- Radar Ltd has made a £30,000 long-term loan to Holmes Ltd.
- In addition to its equity investment, Flighty Ltd has purchased from Radar Ltd £70,000 of 4% debentures. Radar Ltd has issued £100,000 of debentures in total.

Which of the following statements is correct?

A Non-current assets will not disclose anything for the loan or debentures as they are intra-group holdings that cancel on consolidation.
B Both the loan and the £70,000 of debentures will be disclosed as part of the groups overall long-term funding.
C Non-current assets will only reflect the £30,000 debentures held by third parties.
D The loan will not be disclosed, but the full value of debentures must be shown as they are negotiable instruments that can be traded on the commercial markets.
(2 marks)

3.7 Ewe plc has the following investments in Hen Ltd:

	Investment	*Total in issue*
	£	£
25p Ordinary shares	20,000	25,000
3% Irredeemable preference shares [£1]	10,000	100,000
5% Debentures	70,000	100,000

At the year-end date the accumulated profits of Hen Ltd are £420,000.

Calculate the minority interest to be disclosed in the consolidated balance sheet.

(2 marks)

3.8 Dover Ltd has a 75% stake in Dab Ltd and a 90% in Skate Ltd. During the current year both subsidiaries announced dividends of £50,000, but due to an administrative error the dividend receivable from Dab Ltd has yet to be recorded in the books of the parent company.

In the preparation of the consolidated balance sheet which of the following options summarises the adjustments necessary with respect to current liabilities and accumulated reserves?

A Accumulated reserves remain unchanged, and non-current liabilities show dividends payable of £100,000.

B Accumulated reserves increase by £50,000 and non-current liabilities show dividends payable of £17,500.

C Accumulated reserves increase by £37,500 and non-current liabilities show dividends payable of £100,000.

D Accumulated reserves increase by £37,500 and non-current liabilities show dividends payable of £17,500.

(2 marks)

Objective test answers

3.1

	£
Trident Ltd	323,000
Polaris Ltd	111,000
Mark up on goods transferred and remaining in inventory	(3,000)
	431,000

If goods transferred between group members have been sold to third party customers prior to the year end then there is no unrealised profit to eliminate. The profits are now "genuine" as they have been made outside the single entity.

3.2

	£
Rodeo plc	725,000
Sand Ltd	101,500
Rain Ltd	67,000
Mark up on Sand Ltd to Rodeo transfers [50% × ((32,000 × 125%) − 32,000)]	(4,000)
Goods in transit	4,400
Unrealised profit on goods in transit $\frac{4,400}{1.1}$ =	(400)
	893,500

3.3 Inventory: decreases by £3,000 [30% mark up on £10,000]

Minority interest decreases by £750 [25% of £3,000]

Accumulated profits decrease by £2,250

3.4 **B**

Unrealised profit on transfer was originally £40,000, but this is reduced by three years depreciation of £4,000 per annum.

3.5 Fair value of consideration [(10,000 × £3) + 7,000] = £37,000

Fair value of net assets acquired:

	£
Net assets per balance sheet	19,500
Fair value adjustment	4,000
Policy alignment for provisions	3,000
	26,500

Goodwill = 37,000 − 90% × (26,500) = £13,150

3.6 **C**

3.7 Minority interest stake in preference shares = 90% × £100,000 = £90,000

Minority interest in remaining net assets = 20% × (420,000 + 25,000) = £89,000

Total minority interest = £179,000

The debentures are not part of the equity and reserves of the business, but a component of non-current liabilities. This will disclose £30,000 of debentures held outside the group.

3.8 **D**

The accumulated reserves need to reflect the unrecorded dividend attributable to the parent company.

Non-current liabilities only disclose those dividends payable outside the group as intra-group dividends cancel on consolidation.

? Medium answer questions

Question 1 – Sconer group

(a) The Sconer group comprises three companies, the balance sheets for which are shown below

Balance sheets as at 31 December 20X4

	Sconer plc £'000	*Rak Ltd* £'000	*Cop Ltd* £'000
Assets			
Non-current assets			
Property, plant and equipment	234	56	81
Investment in Rak [160,000 shares]	120	–	–
Investment in Cop [450,000 shares]	300	–	–
Current assets			
Inventory	225	39	302
Receivables	56	39	58
Cash	10	8	17
Total assets	945	142	458
Equity and liabilities			
Capital and reserves			
Ordinary share capital [50p shares]	100	100	250
Share premium account	27	–	–
Accumulated profits	627	10	44
Non-current liabilities			
Loan	150	–	90
Current liabilities			
Trade payables	41	32	74
	945	142	458

Further information:

- At the date of acquisition the fair value of Rak Ltd's non-current assets was £8,000 in excess of their book value.
- The inventory of Cop Ltd includes items valued at £12,000 transferred from Sconer plc who charged a mark up of 20% on cost.
- At acquisition the accumulated profits of Rak Ltd and Cop Ltd were £2,000 and £15,000 respectively.

Calculate the following figures for inclusion in the consolidated balance sheet.

- Goodwill assuming no subsequent impairment
- Inventory
- Consolidated accumulated reserves.

(8 marks)

(b) Explain the impact on the consolidated figures if the transfer of inventory had been from Cop Ltd to Sconer plc.

(2 marks)
(Total = 10 marks)

Question 2 – Zand Ltd

The summarised balance sheets of Zand Ltd and Bleak Ltd at 30 June 20X4 were as follows

	Zand Ltd		*Bleak Ltd*	
	£'000	£'000	£'000	£'000
Assets				
Non-current assets				
Property, plant and equipment		1,400		120
Investments		600		–
		2,000		120
Current assets				
Inventory	150		42	
Receivables	56		17	
Bleak Ltd current account	17		–	–
Cash	28		1	
		251		60
Total assets		2,251		180
Equity and liabilities				
Capital and reserves				
Ordinary share capital [£1 shares]		50		25
Share premium account		5		–
Revaluation reserve		22		–
Accumulated profits		1,496		100
		1,573		125
Non-current liabilities				
Loan		400		–
Current liabilities				
Trade payables	278		41	
Zand plc current account	–		14	
		278		55
		2,251		180

Further information:

- Zand Ltd acquired 15,000 shares in Bleak Ltd when the accumulated reserves of the latter were £80,000.
- Goodwill has not incurred any impairment.
- The difference in the current accounts is due to cash in transit.
- Both companies announced a £10,000 dividend before the year end, but due to problems with the computerised accounting system no entries have been made to date.
- During the year Zand Ltd sold inventory to Bleak Ltd for £25,000 representing cost plus a mark up of 25%. Two fifths of this inventory remains in Bleak Ltd's warehouse at the year end.

Prepare the consolidated balance sheet as at 30 June 20X4.

(10 marks)

✓ Medium answer questions

Answer 1 – Sconer group

(a) Goodwill

	£'000
Rak Ltd – Consideration	120
Rak Ltd – Net assets at acquisition [100 + 2 + 8] × 80%	(88)
Rak Ltd – Goodwill	32
Cop Ltd – Consideration	300
Cop Ltd – Net assets at acquisition [250 + 15] × 90%	(238.5)
	61.5
Total Goodwill	93.5

Inventory

	£'000
Sconer plc	225
Rak Ltd	39
Cop Ltd	302
	566
Less: Unrealised profit	(2)
	564

Consolidated accumulated reserves

	£'000
Sconer plc per question	627
Unrealised profit adjustment	(2)
Rak Ltd [80% × (10 – 2)]	6.4
Cop Ltd [90% × (44 – 15)]	26.1
	657.5

(b) Intercompany transfer of inventory

If the direction of transfer had changed from Cop Ltd to Sconer plc it would still be necessary to remove the unrealised profits from the consolidated inventory figure.

However, as Cop Ltd is not a wholly owned subsidiary there would be an impact on the calculation of both minority interests and the consolidated accumulated profits.

The minority interest will be required to absorb their percentage share of the profit, and hence the minority interest in Cop Ltd would have been reduced by £200 [10% × £2,000]. The consolidated accumulated reserves would increase by a similar margin.

Answer 2 – Zand Ltd

Consolidated balance sheet as at 31 December 20X4

	£'000	£'000
Assets		
Non-current assets		
Property, plant and equipment		1,520
Intangibles [W1]		537
		2,057
Current assets		
Inventory [150 + 42 − 2]	190	
Receivables	73	
Cash (28 + 1 + 3)	32	
		295
Total assets		2,352
Equity and liabilities		
Capital and reserves		
Ordinary share capital [50p shares]		50
Share premium account		5
Revaluation reserve		22
Accumulated profits [W3]		1,496
		1,573
Minority interests [W2]		46
		1,619
Non-current liabilities		
Loan		400
Current liabilities		
Trade payables	319	
Dividends payable by Zand Ltd	10	
Dividends payable to minority interests	4	
		333
		2,352

W1:

Goodwill

	£'000
Cost of investment	600
Net assets acquired [60% × (25 + 80)]	(63)
	537

W2:

Minority interests

40% × (125 − 10) = £46

W3:

Accumulated reserves

	£'000
Zand Ltd	1,496
Less: Zand's own dividend	(10)
Add: Dividend receivable from Bleak	6
Less: Unrealised profit	(2)
Bleak Ltd [60% × (100 − 80)]	12
Less: Bleak's own dividend [60%]	(6)
	1,496

The Consolidated Income Statement and Statement of Changes in Equity

4

The principle

- Prepare the consolidated income statement on a basis consistent with the consolidated balance sheet.
- Show income generated from the net assets under P's control.
- Reflect ownership by deducting the minority interests share of S's profit after tax.
- Eliminate the effect on intra-group trading.

Investments in preferred shares and loans

- Intra-group borrowing will create an intra-group finance cost which must be cancelled on consolidation.
- An investment in the preferred stock of S has two consequences for the consolidated income statement
  1. Preferred dividends received or receivable from S for the period must be eliminated on consolidation.
  2. Minority interests must be calculated in two parts; separately identifying those components attributable to ordinary and preferred shares.

Intra-group trading and unrealised profits

- Intra-group trading must be eliminated in full.
- When goods sold intra-group remain within the inventory of the recipient group company, at the period end any unrealised profit must be eliminated from the books of the selling company.
- When there is a provision for unrealised profit brought forward from the previous period the adjustment to the current income statement will represent the movement on the provision.

Intra-group asset transfers

- Again consistency is needed with the balance sheet.
- Eliminate any profit or loss arising on the transfer of the asset, and adjust the depreciation charge to reflect a figure based on the original cost of the asset.

The impact of fair value adjustments and changes in accounting policy

- At the date of acquisition the assets of S are revised to their fair values – this has a knock-on effect for depreciation charges.
- Realigning the accounting policies of S to be consistent with those of P will frequently have a knock-on effect for the income statement.

Summary consolidation schedule

	P	*S*	*Adjustment*	*Consol*
	£	£	£	£
Revenue	X	X	Inter-co trading	X
Cost of sales	(X)	(X)	Inter-co trading	(X)
Unrealised profit adj. (to seller)	(X)			
Gross profit	X	X		X
Operating expenses	(X)	(X)		(X)
Goodwill impairment	(X)			
Profit from operation	X	X		X
Investment income	X	X		X
Eliminate intra-group dividend	(X)			
Finance costs	(X)	(X)	Inter-group interest	(X)
Profit before taxation	X	X		X
Taxation	(X)	(X)		(X)
Profit after taxation	X	X		X

MI based on their percentage of S's profit after tax

The statement of changes in equity

- Contains only the group share of the post-acquisition changes in equity of the subsidiaries.

Objective test questions

4.1 Trellis Ltd has a 75% stake in Wells Ltd; its only subsidiary. For the year just completed the cost of sales for each company is £12 million and £1.8 million respectively. During the period Trellis Ltd sold goods to Wells Ltd that it had purchased for £0.5 million, but transferred at a mark up of 20%. All of these goods remain within the inventory of Wells Ltd at the year end.

What is the consolidated cost of sales at the year end?

A £13.2m
B £13.3m
C £13.45m
D £13.7m

(2 marks)

4.2 Smith is a 60% subsidiary of Jones plc who purchased their stake eight months prior to the year end. Selling and administration overheads for the two companies for the full year were as follows:

	£
Jones plc	990,000
Smith Ltd	140,000

Included in the administration costs of Smith Ltd is a management charge from Jones plc of £20,000.

Calculate the figure for selling and administration costs to be included in the consolidated income statement, and briefly explain the logic of your approach.

(3 marks)

4.3 Alphabet plc has two subsidiaries, A Ltd and B Ltd, which were purchased several years previously. A Ltd is wholly owned whereas the holding in B Ltd is 80%.

During the year ended 31 December 20X4 Alphabet plc made sales to A Ltd valued at £50,000. In the same period B Ltd made sales to its parent valued at £20,000 which it had purchased for £16,000. Half of these items remain as part of Alphabet plc's inventory at the year end.

In the consolidated income statement for the year ended 31 December 20X4, calculate the reductions necessary to revenue and profit in respect of the information provided.

(2 marks)

4.4 At the date of its purchase of a 90% stake in Coker Ltd your client, Grim Ltd, had commissioned a due diligence report which indicated that the fair value of the tangible assets was £2 million in excess of their book values. How might this information impact on future consolidated income statements, specifically with regard to the treatment of goodwill? [maximum 40 words]

A Decrease by £40,000
B Decrease by £28,000
C Decrease by £24,000
D Decrease by £16,800

(2 marks)

4.5 Olice Ltd purchased a 90% stake in Lime Ltd several years previously. Extracts from the income statements of the two companies are shown below for the year ended 30 September 20X4.

	Olice Ltd	*Lime Ltd*
	£	£
Operating profit	549,000	99,100
Dividend income	26,500	–
Profit before taxation	575,500	99,100
Taxation	(123,000)	(14,000)
Profit after taxation	452,500	85,100

Lime Ltd has £100,000 of 50p ordinary shares in issue, and paid a dividend in the year of 10p per share.

Calculate the profit attributable to the shareholders of Olice Ltd to be disclosed in the consolidated income statement.

(2 marks)

4.6 Robust plc has invested in both the ordinary and preference shares of Timid Ltd as follows

	Issued	*Held by Robust plc*
£1 ordinary shares	1,000,000	850,000
£1, 4% irredeemable preference shares	500,000	300,000

During the year ended Timid plc declared and paid a dividend of 5p on each ordinary share.

If the profit after taxation for Timid Ltd was £100,000 what is the value of amount that will be shown for minority interests in the consolidated income statement?

A £32,000
B £21,800
C £20,000
D £15,500

(2 marks)

4.7 The following information is available regarding Rail plc and its 75% subsidiary, Motor Ltd:

- The opening provision for unrealised profits brought forward at the beginning of the financial year was £3,000.
- During the year Motor Ltd purchased goods for £40,000 which it sold on to its parent company for £46,000.
- One-third of these items remain within Rail plc's inventory at the year end.

Complete the following statement:

The revenue figure within the consolidated income statement will (increase/decrease) by £__________. A similar adjustment will be made to cost of sales, but this will also be (increased/decreased) by £__________ with respect to unrealised profits on inventory.

(2 marks)

4.8 Using a maximum of 50 words explain why it is necessary to eliminate trading between members of the same group.

(2 marks)

✓ Objective test answers

4.1 **B**

	£m
Trellis Ltd	12
Wells Ltd	1.8
Intercompany	(0.6)
PURP	0.1
	13.3

If goods transferred between group members have been sold to third party customers prior to the year end then there is no unrealised profit to eliminate. The profits are now "genuine" as they have been made outside the single entity.

4.2

	£
Jones plc	990,000
Smith Ltd	140,000
Eliminate intercompany management charge	(20,000)
Pro-rate remaining costs of the subsidiary	(40,000)
	1,070,000

The management charge can only relate to the period for which Smith Ltd was a subsidiary, and hence this fee should not be time apportioned as it must already relate to the final eight months of the year. The remaining costs must be time apportioned as Jones did not control Smith Ltd, and hence its revenues and costs, for the initial four months of the year.

4.3 Revenue reduction (50,000 + 20,000) = £70,000

Profit reduction (50% × 4,000) = £2,000

4.4 Increasing the value of assets acquired to fair value reduces the amount effectively paid for goodwill. This reduces the prospect of goodwill suffering an impairment and hence makes a reduction to consolidated profits less likely.

4.5

	£
Operating profit – Olice Ltd	549,000
Dividend income (external)	8,500
Less: Taxation	(123,000)
	434,500
Group share of Lime Ltd (90% × 85,100)	76,590
	511,090

4.6 **C**

	£
Share of preference dividend (40% × £20,000)	8,000
Share of ordinary profits (15% × £80,000)	12,000

4.7 The revenue figure within the consolidated income statement will decrease by £46,000. A similar adjustment will be made to cost of sales, but this will also be decreased by £1,000 with respect to unrealised profits on inventory.

4.8 If intra-group trading is not eliminated the revenue and cost of goods sold in the consolidated financial statements will be grossed up. This gives a false impression of group activity; particularly as a parent controls a subsidiary and hence could force it to buy or sell.

Medium answer questions

Question 1 – Ship plc

The income statements of Ship plc and its two subsidiaries for the year ended 31 December 20X4 were as follows:

	Ship plc £'000	*Kayak Ltd* £'000	*Barge Ltd* £'000
Revenue	750	460	400
Cost of sales	(150)	(80)	(120)
Gross profit	600	380	280
Selling and administration costs	(110)	(80)	(50)
Operating profit	490	300	230
Dividend income	60	–	–
Interest receivable	32	25	–
Interest payable	–	(30)	–
Profit before taxation	582	295	230
Taxation	(142)	(105)	(60)
Profit after taxation	440	190	170

Additional information:

- The investment in Kayak Ltd was acquired in 20X1 and consists of 160,000 50p ordinary shares. Kayaks issued share capital is £100,000.
- The investment in Barge Ltd represents a stake of 60% and was acquired on 30 June 20X4.
- There has been no goodwill impairment during the period.
- During 20X4 Kayak Ltd declared and paid a dividend of £75,000.
- Kayak Ltd has £1,000,000 of 3% debentures in issue. These are all held by Ship plc.
- In the final quarter of 20X4, a group reorganisation resulted in the commencement of intercompany trading. Ship plc sold £20,000 of goods to each subsidiary which included a one-third mark up on cost. Barge Ltd has already cleared its warehouse following a strong upturn in its markets, but Kayak Ltd retains 50% within inventory at the year end.

Prepare the consolidated income statement for the year ended 31 December 20X4.

(10 marks)

Question 2 – Reporting performance

(a) Trojan Ltd is a 75% subsidiary of Troy plc. The latter purchased its stake for £100,000 several years previously when Troy had a debit balance of £2,000 within its accumulated reserves and a £5,000 balance on its share premium account.

Based on the extract from Trojan Ltd's statement of changes in equity, calculate the amount paid for goodwill on acquisition, and the amount to be included in the accumulated profits for the year ended 31 December 20X4.

	Issued capital £	*Share premium* £	*Accumulated profits* £
1 January 20X4	100,000	30,000	25,000
Net profit for the period	–	–	12,000
Equity dividend paid	–	–	(4,000)
31 December 20X4	100,000	30,000	33,000

(4 marks)

(b) Outline the purpose of the statement of changes in equity, and briefly discuss any limitations that could diminish its effectiveness.

(6 marks)
(Total = 10 marks)

Medium answer questions

Answer 1 – Ship plc

Consolidated income statement for the year ended 31 December 20X4

	£'000
Revenue	1,370
Cost of sales	(252.5)
Gross profit	1,117.5
Selling and administration costs	(215)
Operating profit	902.5
Investment income	27
Profit before taxation	929.5
Taxation	(277)
Profit after taxation	652.5
Minority interest [W2]	(72)
Profit attributable to the shareholders of Ship plc	580.5

[W1] Consolidation schedule

	Ship plc £'000	*Kayak Ltd* £'000	*Barge Ltd* £'000		*Group* £'000
Revenue	750	460	200	(40)	1,370
Cost of sales	(150)	(80)	(60)	40	(250)
PURP	(2.5)				(2.5)
Selling and administration costs	(110)	(80)	(25)		(215)
Dividend income [60 – 60]	–	–	–		–
Interest receivable	32	25	–	(30)	27
Interest payable	–	(30)	–	30	–
Taxation	(142)	(105)	(30)		(277)
Profit after taxation	377.5	190	85		

[W2] Minority interest

Kayak Ltd = 20% × 190k = £38k

Barge Ltd = 40% × 85k = £34k

Answer 2 – Troy Ltd

(a) Goodwill

	£	£
Consideration		100,000
Net assets acquired		
Share capital	100,000	
Retained losses	(2,000)	
Share Premium	5,000	
	103,000	
at 75%		(77,250)
		22,750

Accumulated profits (£33,000 + £2,000) × 75% = £26,250

(b) The statement of changes in equity

Purpose

When a user of a set of financial statements reviews the figures contained therein, one of their expectations is that they will be able to navigate from the opening balance sheet to its closing equivalent. In a perfect world this would be achieved exclusively via the income statement that would disclose the performance of the business for the accounting period. This is often referred to as the "All Inclusive Concept".

However, trading activity and investment return are rarely the sole drivers of movements in net assets.

- Accounting standards require some items to be taken directly to reserves (e.g. revaluations).
- The issue of new equity or debt is associated with funding not performance.
- Dividends declared within the accounting period are not shown on the income statement as they represent an appropriation to shareholders rather than a cost against profit.

The statement of changes in equity aims to bridge the gap by requiring the disclosure of gains and losses not disclosed via the income statement; plus the effects of any changes in accounting policy or correction of errors relating to prior periods. It also discloses the net profit or loss for the period so that a link can be made to the income statement.

Limitations

In addition to the items already detailed, many companies provide additional disclosure within the statement of changes in equity. In particular:

- Capital transactions
- Distributions to owners
- The balance of accumulated profit or loss at the beginning of the period and at the balance sheet date, and the movements for the period.

Unfortunately these are discretional disclosures that can be relegated to the notes. This makes it more challenging for a user to understand the relationship between opening and closing net assets.

These issues are compounded by flexibility with regard to the layout of the statement of changes in equity, making direct comparability between companies more challenging.

Associates and Joint Ventures

5

The principle – associates

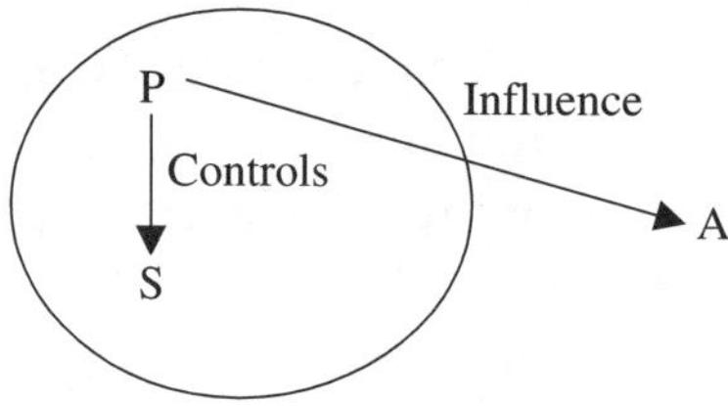

- An entity over which the investor has significant influence, and which is not a subsidiary of the investor.
- Normally signified by an equity holding between 20 and 50%.
- An associate is not deemed to be art of the single entity when considering the substance of the investment.

Equity accounting – the basics

- This is the method that must be used when an associate is being incorporated into consolidated financial statements.
- In the consolidated balance sheet the associate is disclosed as a single figure within non-current assets.
- The carrying value comprises P's share of the fair value of the associates net assets plus any goodwill not yet written off to the income statement.
- There is no minority interest.
- The consolidated income statement also discloses the interest in associates as a single figure representing P's share of the associate's profit or loss after taxation.

Equity accounting – intra-group issues

- In the consolidated balance sheet intercompany accounts are not eliminated, as the associate is not part of the single entity.
- Consequently the group can have receivables and payables with the associate, and sell to or make purchases from the associate.

- However, the ability of the P to influence the associate dictates that unrealised profits on inventory or non-current assets must be eliminated.
- Unlike a subsidiary only the group's share of the unrealised profit is adjusted as the balance sheet does not reflect 100% of the associates net assets.
- The consolidated balance sheet will disclose dividends receivable from associates separately as a current asset.
- The consolidated income statement must NOT include dividends from the associate as these will effectively be paid from the parent's share of the associate's profits. The inclusion of both profits and dividends would be double counting.

Joint ventures – the theory

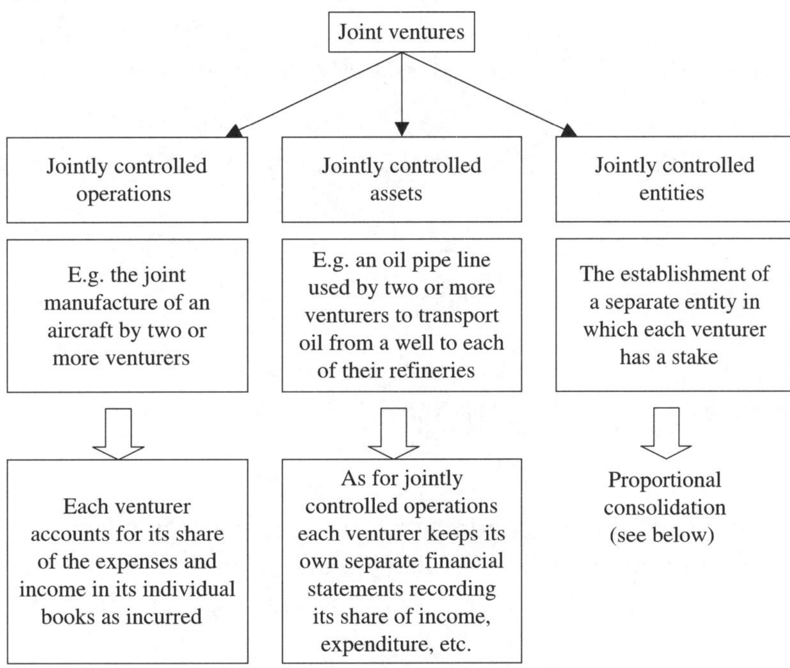

Proportional consolidation – the basics

- When a venturer sets up a separate entity with one or more other parties with whom they share control the consolidated financial statements need to reflect the increased influence over the assets compared to an associate, but it is inappropriate to acquisition account as full control is absent.
- Goodwill is calculated and disclosed as for a subsidiary.
- Assets and liabilities are added on a line-by-line basis, but unlike a subsidiary only the percentage held by the venturer is incorporated.
- Consequently there is no minority interest.
- Similar principles apply within the consolidated income statement.

Joint ventures – intra-group adjustments

- When using proportional consolidation for a jointly controlled entity, the prorated element of all intercompany transactions must be eliminated together with unrealised profits.

Objective test questions

5.1 For each of the situations described below, determine whether or not the investment would be classified as an associate based on the information provided, and briefly state your logic.

(i) The investor holds 18% of the share capital, and appoints three of the seven board directors.

(ii) The investor holds 45% of the share capital and appoints five of the seven board directors who each have one vote at the board meetings.

(4 marks)

5.2 Reels Ltd has a 50% stake in Float Ltd in the £10,000 share capital (£1 ordinary shares) for £20,000 and has always treated the investment as a subsidiary undertaking; an approach validated by the external auditors. At the date of acquisition the accumulated reserves of Float Ltd had been £17,000, and the goodwill arising has suffered no subsequent impairment.

Extracts of Float Ltd's balance sheet as at 30 September 20X4 are given below:

	£
Non-current assets	55,000
Current assets	9,000
Non-current liabilities	(16,000)
Current liabilities	(11,000)
	37,000

Calculate the value of the consolidated accumulated profits if the retained profits of Reels Ltd at 30 September 20X4 are £25,000, and explain any differences that would have arisen in this figure if Float Ltd had been an associate [assume the percentage stake remains at 50%].

(4 marks)

5.3 Three oil companies have collaborated in the construction of a single oil pipeline to transport oil from an undersea oil field to their individual refineries. In less than 80 words describe how you would account for the pipeline.

(3 marks)

5.4 Dream plc has a 60% investment in Cloud Ltd and a 30% in Nimbus Ltd. A review of their individual financial statements shows revenue and tax charges as follows:

	Revenues	*Taxation*
	£	£
Dream plc	120,000	24,000
Cloud Ltd	50,000	12,000
Nimbus Ltd	30,000	9,000

Calculate the amounts to be included in the consolidated income statement for revenues and taxation.

	Revenues	*Taxation*
	£	£
A	200,000	45,000
B	200,000	36,000
C	185,000	40,500
D	170,000	36,000

(2 marks)

5.5 During the year ended 31 December 20X4 Gof Ltd sold goods to Sawn Ltd, its 30% associate. The value of the sales was £50,000 and two-fifths of these remained within the inventory of Sawn Ltd at the year end.

If the intra-group sales were made at a mark up of 25% which of the following statements is correct with reference to the consolidated accounts?

A Consolidated inventory will be reduced by £4,000 and gross profit by a similar amount.
B Consolidated inventory will be reduced by £4,000 and gross profit by £10,000.
C No adjustment is required for unrealised profit as the associate is not part of the single entity.
D Gross profit will be reduced by £4,000 and the investment in Sawn Ltd by a similar amount.

(2 marks)

5.6 Angel Ltd purchased 25% of the ordinary share capital of Tomsk Ltd in 20X1 when the accumulated profits of the latter were £10,000. Further extracts from the balance sheet of Tomsk Ltd at the date of acquisition are shown below:

	£
Non-current assets	22,000
Current assets	11,000
Non-current liabilities	(7,000)
Current liabilities	(1,500)
	24,500

An assessment of asset values at the same date had revealed that the fair value of the non-current assets was £3,000 higher than that disclosed in the financial statements.

The purchase consideration given for the investment was £10,000.

Calculate the value of goodwill, and state how it will be disclosed in the consolidated balance sheet.

(3 marks)

5.7 Drum Ltd is a 40% associate of Yam Ltd, and during the last accounting period sold goods purchased for £80,000 to Drum Ltd for £95,000. At the balance sheet date 50% of these goods remain within the inventory of Drum Ltd.

Which of the following statements is false?

A Inventory within the consolidated balance sheet will be reduced by £7,500.
B Cost of sales will be reduced by £7,500.
C Share of profits in associates will be reduced by £7,500.
D Minority interests will not be affected by the unrealised profit.

(2 marks)

5.8 A client has approached you and asked for a brief outline of the different methods available for the implementation of proportional consolidation.

Briefly describe the options available. [50 words maximum]

(2 marks)

5.9 Toad plc has two subsidiaries, Frog Ltd and Newt Ltd, plus a 30% stake in Sala Ltd. The companies regularly trade with each other, and at the balance sheet date the following intercompany current account balances were recorded.

	Toad plc	*Frog Ltd*	*Newt Ltd*	*Sala Ltd*
	£	£	£	£
Toad – Frog	10,000	(8,000)		
Toad – Sala	(3,000)			3,000
Frog – Newt		2,000	(2,000)	
Frog – Sala		(5,000)		5,000
Newt – Sala			1,000	

Any disparities in the current accounts are due to cash in transit. When adjustments are made for these amounts what amounts relating to current accounts will be shown in the consolidated balance sheet?

(3 marks)

5.10 Z plc has three investments:

- A 25% stake in A Ltd [associate]
- A 50% stake in J Ltd [joint venture]
- 80% stake in S Ltd [subsidiary].

Z plc generated revenues of £100,000, which the individual financial statements for its investments highlighted revenues of:

	£
A Ltd	50,000
J Ltd	40,000
S Ltd	15,000

Sales between Z plc and S Ltd amounted to £6,000 during the financial year, and the transfers were made at cost.

Calculate the revenue to be disclosed in the consolidated income statement.

(2 marks)

Objective test answers

5.1

(i) Associate – The percentage holding is below 20%, but this is only an indicator level for associate status. With three of the board directors it is likely to have influence over the financial and operating decisions of the business.

(ii) Subsidiary – The percentage holding falls between 20 and 50% and taken alone this would be a strong indicator of associate status. However, with five of the seven board votes this suggests full control over the entity which will be categorised as a subsidiary.

5.2 Consolidated accumulated reserves

	£
Reels Ltd	25,000
Float Ltd 50% (37 − 10 − 17)	5,000
	30,000

If the investments were to be treated as an associate, the accumulated profits would be unchanged. As a subsidiary effectively 100% of net assets are consolidated to reflect control and then 50% removed as minority interests. As an associate, only the 50% we own is equity accounted for, but the net effect is the same.

5.3 The pipeline represents a jointly controlled asset. As such, each venturer will account separately for its share of income generated by the venture (less any joint costs), and also any individual costs it has incurred on the project. In the balance sheet each will show their share of the jointly controlled asset, their own liabilities and their share of any joint liabilities.

5.4 **D**

5.5 **D**

5.6

	£
Consideration	10,000
Net assets acquired [(24,500 + 3,000) × 25%]	(6,875)
	3,125

The goodwill is included within the carrying value of the investment in Tomsk Ltd, and not disclosed separately as an intangible asset.

5.7 **B**

5.8 Either

- Aggregate the appropriate percentage of net assets and net income with those of the group line-by-line or
- Disclose percentage of net assets and net income separately line-by-line.

5.9 Intercompany balances between the parent company and the subsidiaries will cancel on consolidation.

Balances relating to associates remain as associates are not deemed to be part of the single entity.

Consequently there is an amount due to associates of £8,000

5.10

	£
Z plc	100,000
A Ltd	–
J Ltd [50%]	20,000
S Ltd	15,000
Intercompany	(6,000)
	129,000

Medium answer questions

Question 1 – Hothouse plc

(a) Robert Snare the financial controller of Hothouse plc is under considerable pressure from the board of directors to improve the appearance of the financial statements which they feel are unnecessarily gloomy. The company has several investments in other entities and is also involved with a collaborative project with Turnmill Ltd; details are provided below:

Investment	*Further notes*
A 45% stake in the ordinary shares of Hobs Ltd	Hothouse plc is considering a further 75% investment in the irredeemable preference share capital of Hobs Ltd
A 45% stake in the ordinary shares of Furze Ltd	Hothouse plc has the right to appoint five of the six directors
A 75% stake in the ordinary share capital of Tease Ltd	
Hothouse plc shares its head office building with Retro plc	Retro plc occupies 50% of the office space, and the two boards of directors regularly meet to exchange ideas as both companies operate in the same commercial sector. Richard perceives this collaboration as a joint venture

Robert has been directed to "maximise" revenues and working capital as these are seen as the engine room of the business. Working capital comprises current receivables and payables plus inventory, but excludes cash.

The relevant figures for each of the companies are as follows:

	Revenue	*Working capital*
	£'000	£'000
Hothouse plc	670	346
Hobs Ltd	240	130
Furze Ltd	465	302
Tease Ltd	678	402
Retro plc	989	566

Identify the relevant accounting treatment for each of the investments in the consolidated financial statements, and comment on whether or not these will have the effect that the financial controller would like to achieve.

(10 marks)

Question 2 – Rainbow Ltd

Rainbow Ltd has investments into other companies which it has held for several years. The draft balance sheets for each company as at 30 June 20X4 are given below:

	Rainbow Ltd £'000	*Spectrum Ltd* £'000	*Scope Ltd* £'000
Assets			
Non-current assets			
Property, plant and equipment	666	310	150
Investment in Spectrum [800,000 shares]	330	–	–
Investment in Scope [480,000 shares]	160	–	–
Current assets			
Inventory	200	112	130
Receivables	165	88	60
Cash	25	–	15
Total assets	1,546	510	355
Equity and liabilities			
Capital and reserves			
Ordinary share capital [10p shares]	100	100	200
Accumulated profits	965	312	5
Non-current liabilities			
Loan	340	–	30
Current liabilities			
Trade payables	141	98	120
	1,546	510	355

The following information is available:

- The investment in Spectrum Ltd was purchased when the accumulated profits were £70,000.
- The investment in Scope Ltd was purchased when the accumulated reserves were £25,000.
- No impairments to goodwill have been recognised.
- Included within the current receivables and payables are intercompany current accounts.

	Rainbow Ltd £'000	*Spectrum Ltd* £'000	*Scope Ltd* £'000
Rainbow – Spectrum Ltd	20 Debit	15 Credit	
Rainbow – Scope Ltd	12 Debit		12 Credit

Any discrepancies are due to cash in transit.

Prepare the consolidated balance sheet as at 30 June 20X4.

(10 marks)

Medium answer questions

Answer 1 – Hothouse plc

(a) *Hobs Ltd*: The 45% stake in this company indicates that it is an associated undertaking, and should be incorporated into the consolidated financial statements using equity accounting.

If the additional investment is made in the preference shares this will not affect this decision as such shares do not carry the right to vote.

Under equity accounting rules, Hob Ltd's revenue and working capital will not be added to those of the group on a line-by-line basis, and hence will not increase these figures. Both income statement and balance sheet show a single figure for associates.

In the income statement a single line will reflect the share (i.e. 45%) of the results of the operations of the investee. The balance sheet will show a non-current asset investment comprising 45% of the fair value of the net assets of the associate plus any goodwill arising on its acquisition.

Furze Ltd: Although the 45% stake in this company suggests that it is an associate, the power of Hothouse plc to control the board of directors indicates more than significant influence.

This company is in reality a subsidiary and should be accounted for using acquisition accounting. Its £240,000 revenue will be added to the consolidated revenue line in full to reflect that in substance Hothouse plc has control over the assets. The 55% not legally owned will effectively be removed via minority interests.

Similarly the working capital assets and liabilities will be added line-by-line to those of the group.

Although the needs of the financial controller are being met he will need to take care not to inflate the numbers with intercompany trading and unrealised profits.

Tease Ltd: This investment represents another subsidiary and will be added line-by-line in both the consolidated income statement and the balance sheet.

As with Furze Ltd any intercompany trading will need to be eliminated from revenue, and any unrealised profits removed from inventory.

Retro plc: The arrangement with Retro has no direct impact on the financial statements other than Hothouse plc will treat its 70% share of the building running costs as an overhead within its income statement.

The two companies have not set up a separate entity in which they have joint control, and hence the concept of proportional consolidation does not apply.

Answer 2 – Rainbow Ltd

Consolidated balance sheet as at 30 June 20X4

	£'000	£'000
Assets		
Non-current assets		
Property, plant and equipment		976
Intangibles [W1]		194
Investment in associates		155.2
		1,325.2
Current assets		
Inventory [200 + 112]	312	
Receivables [165 + 88 − 20]	233	
Cash [25 + 5]	30	
		575
Total assets		1,900.2
Equity and liabilities		
Capital and reserves		
Ordinary share capital [10p shares]		100
Accumulated profits [W4]		1,153.8
		1,253.8
Minority interests [W3]		82.4
		1,336.2
Non-current liabilities		
Loan		340
Current liabilities		
Trade payables [141 + 98 − 15]		224
		1,900.2

W1:

Goodwill – Spectrum Ltd

	£'000
Cost of investment	330
Net assets acquired [80% × (100 + 70)]	(136)
	194

Goodwill – Scope Ltd

	£'000
Cost of investment	160
Net assets acquired [24% × (200 + 25)]	(54)
	106

W2:

Investment in associates

24% × 205 = 49.2 + Goodwill

= £155,200

W3:

Minority interests

20% × (100 + 312) = £82.4

W4:

Accumulated reserves

	£'000
Rainbow Ltd	965
Spectrum Ltd [80% × (312 − 70)]	193.6
Scope Ltd [24% × (5 − 25)]	(4.8)
	1,153.8

Complex Group Structures 6

The concept of the sub-subsidiary

- Illustration 1 – Company T is a subsidiary of the group as the control percentage exercised by the parent is 70%; although the effective stake is 56%.

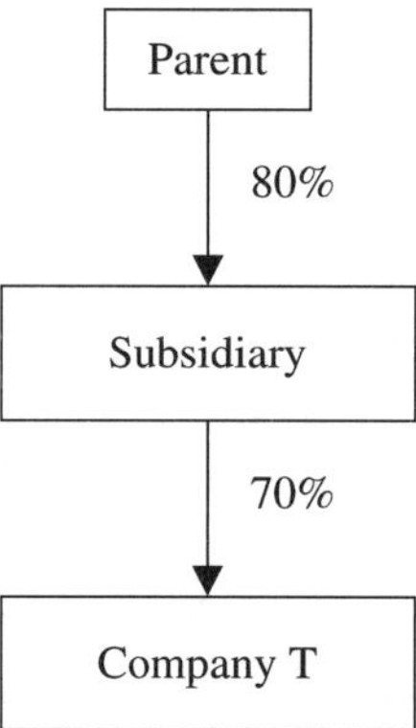

- Illustration 2 – Company T is a subsidiary of the group as the control percentage exercised by the parent is 60%; although the effective stake is 36%.

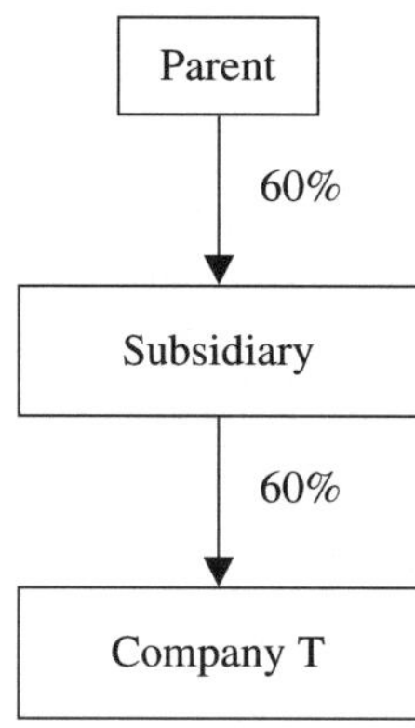

- When dealing with complex groups it is vital that a distinction is made between
  - Control percentage – used to determine the status of the investment, and hence the consolidation method is used; and
  - Effective percentage – used to actually perform the consolidation.

Key skills

- The fundamentals of consolidation remain the same.
- The calculation of goodwill for the sub-subsidiary.

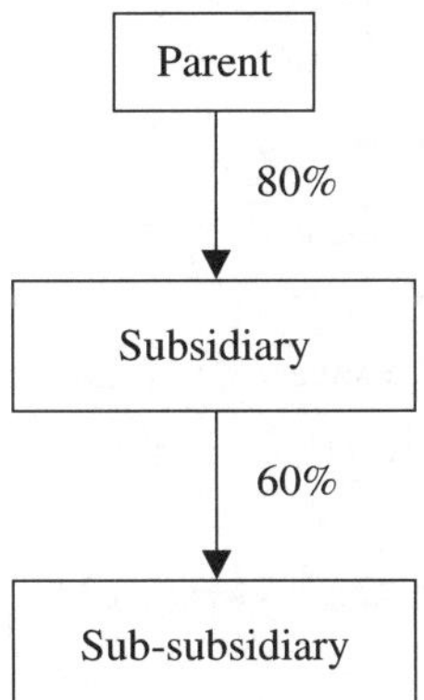

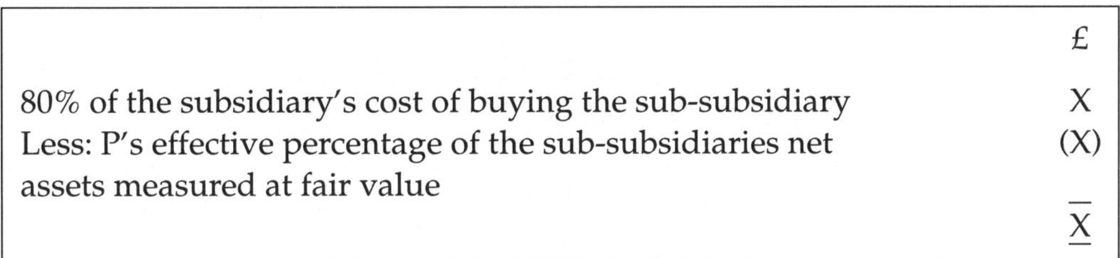

	£
80% of the subsidiary's cost of buying the sub-subsidiary	X
Less: P's effective percentage of the sub-subsidiaries net assets measured at fair value	(X)
	X

- The logic for this calculation is that as a shareholder of the parent company there is no reason why you should bear the full cost of the subsidiary's investment in the sub-subsidiary when you are entitled to only 80% of the subsidiary's post-acquisition return.
- The minority interest will be attributed with their effective percentage of the net assets and profit after tax of the sub-subsidiary.
- Acquisition dates

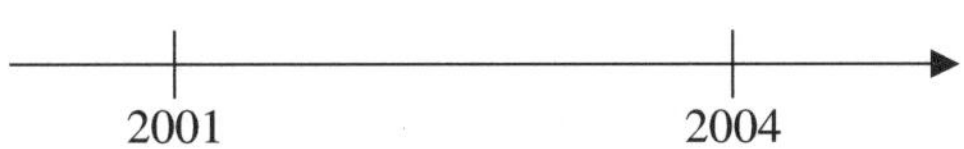

If the parent acquires a subsidiary in 2001 and the latter acquires its own subsidiary in 2004; the latter does not become part of the group until the later date.

- Beware dividends – a company cannot physically receive a dividend unless it has a direct stake.

Mixed group

- In these circumstances the parent company has both a direct and indirect stake in the sub-subsidiary.

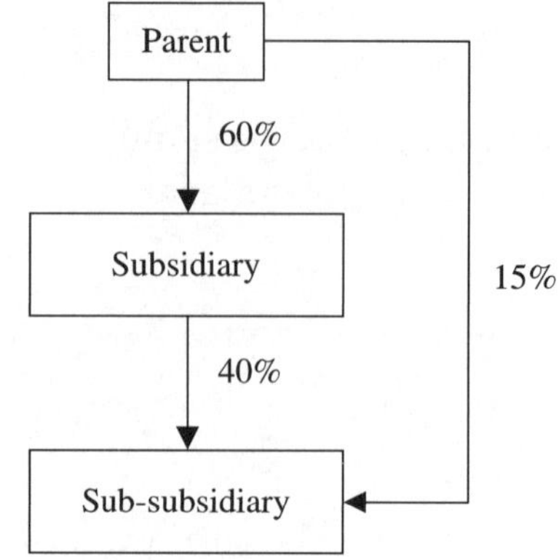

Control percentage = 55% (there a subsidiary)

Effective percentage = 39%

Indirect investment in associates or joint ventures

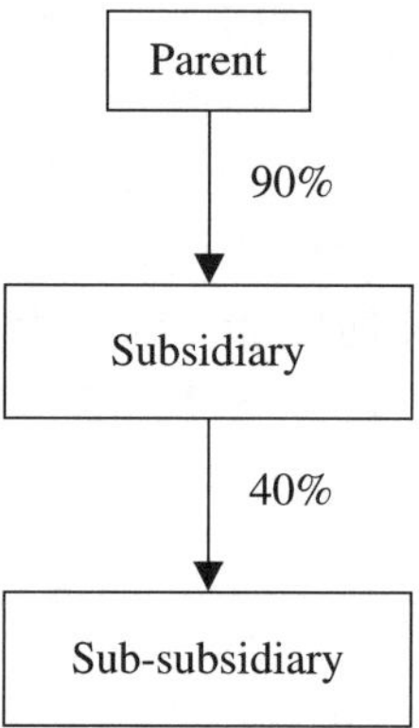

Control percentage = 40% (hence an associate)

Effective percentage = 36%

- The investment shown above will be consolidated using equity accounting as a 40% associate, and then 4% will be awarded to minority interests to achieve the lower effective percentage.

Objective test questions

6.1 Roberts plc has the following holdings in the equity shares of three companies.

Murphy Ltd	60%
Fjord Ltd	52%
Shah Ltd	35%

Additional information is available as follows

- Murphy Ltd owns 27% of Shah Ltd and 25% of Rowles Ltd.
- Fjord Ltd owns 26% of Rowles Ltd.
- Fjord Ltd has two classes of equity shares (voting and non-voting). As a consequence only 47% of Roberts plc stake in Fjord Ltd carries the right to vote.

Describe which companies are the subsidiaries of Roberts plc?

(4 marks)

6.2 XYZ plc purchased 70% of the share capital of Subalphabet Ltd on 31 May 20X2. Exactly one year later XYZ plc was itself the target of a takeover bid and became a wholly owned subsidiary of Ramiraz plc.

Describe the significance to Ramiraz plc of the acquisition dates to the preparation of the consolidated financial statements. [60 words maximum]

(3 marks)

6.3 As the newly appointed internal auditor of Bergin plc, you are trying to familiarise yourself with the company and its investments. The "group" structure diagram in your possession is as given below

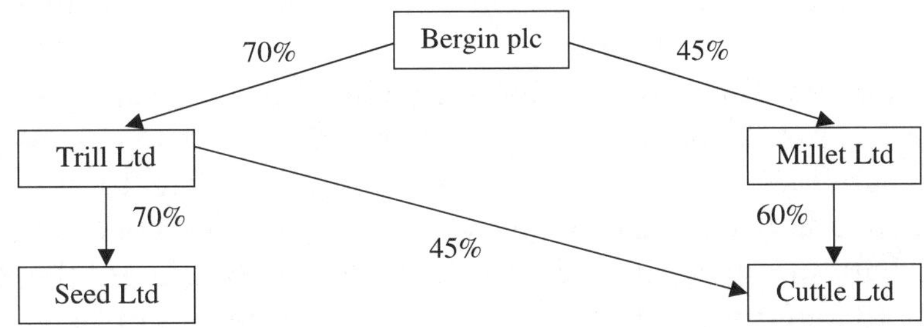

Identify those companies having subsidiary status.

A Trill Ltd only
B Trill Ltd and Seed Ltd
C Trill Ltd and Cuttle Ltd
D Trill Ltd, Seed Ltd and Cuttle Ltd

(2 marks)

6.4 Singh Ltd purchased 70,000 shares in Nylo Ltd for £90,000 when the accumulated profits of the latter were £25,000.

Nylo had a 60% stake in Tilt Ltd purchased for £75,000 when the accumulated profits of the latter were £10,000.

The share capital of all three companies comprises 100,000 £1 ordinary shares.

Assuming that no impairments have been recognised, calculate the value of goodwill to be included in the consolidated balance sheet.

(2 marks)

6.5 Master plc is the ultimate parent company to the following group

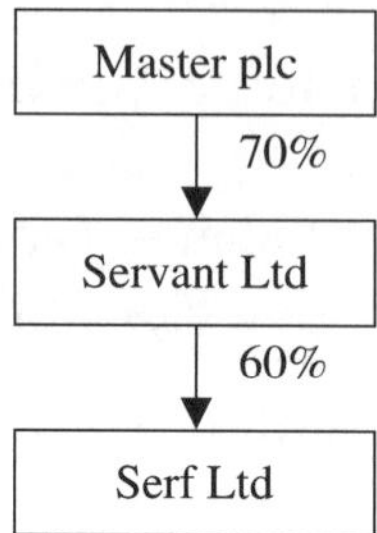

When the consolidated financial statements are prepared what percentage of the net assets of Serf Ltd will be attributed to the minority shareholders, and briefly explain why this might look unusual to a stakeholder with no accounting background.

(3 marks)

6.6 Twindle Ltd owns 80% of Round Ltd, which itself holds a similar investment in the share capital of Hex Ltd.

If each company declares a £10,000 dividend in the year and receives no other dividend income beyond amounts arising from these declarations, which of the following statements is correct?

A The consolidated income statement will show no investment income and only disclose the dividends payable by Twindle Ltd.
B There will be no disclosures in the consolidated income statement relating to dividends, and current liabilities will include only the dividend payable by Twindle Ltd.
C Current liabilities will include the dividend payable to the shareholders of Twindle Ltd and dividends payable to minority interests of £5,600.
D Current liabilities will include the dividend payable to the shareholders of Twindle Ltd and dividends payable to minority interests of £4,000.

(3 marks)

6.7 Zap plc acquired 80% of the ordinary share capital of Pow Ltd, which in turn acquired 60% of the ordinary share capital of Biff Ltd at a cost of £140,000. At 30 September 20X4 extracts from the individual balance sheets of each subsidiary company were as follows

	Pow Ltd	*Biff Ltd*
	£	£
Ordinary share capital	600,000	300,000
Accumulated profits	250,000	200,000
Dividend – proposed and declared	–	(20,000)
	850,000	480,000

The accounts of Pow Ltd have yet to record the dividend receivable from Biff Ltd.

In the consolidated balance sheet of Zap Ltd as at 30 September 20X4 the amount to be shown as minority interest is

A £404,400
B £432,400
C £402,000
D £404,080

(3 marks)

6.8 Able Ltd has owned 90% of the ordinary shares in Blend Ltd since its incorporation. Blend Ltd subsequently acquired a 30% interest in Bolter Ltd for £70,000 when the accumulated profits of the latter were £8,000.

All of the companies have issued share capital comprising 200,000 50p shares.

Calculate the carrying value of Bolter Ltd in the consolidated balance sheet assuming that any attributable goodwill has suffered a £5,000 impairment since the acquisition date and that the accumulated profits at the current balance sheet date are £65,000.

(2 marks)

✓ Objective test answers

6.1 Murphy Ltd: A subsidiary as Roberts holds majority of the ordinary shares.

Fjord Ltd: Not a subsidiary as the holding carries less than half the votes.

Shah Ltd: A subsidiary as Roberts controls 35% of the shares directly and 27% indirectly.

Rowles Ltd: Not a subsidiary as the indirect holding via Fjord must be ignored as the latter is itself not a subsidiary undertaking.

6.2 Ramiraz plc will consolidate the activities of both XYZ plc and Subalphabet Ltd from 31 May 20X3. If XYZ plc had acquired its stake in Subalphabet Ltd after being purchased by Ramiraz plc, the latter would not have consolidated the sub-subsidiary until it was brought into the group.

6.3 **B**

6.4 Goodwill – Nylo Ltd

	£
Consideration	90,000
Net assets acquired [(100,000 + 25,000) × 70%]	(87,500)
	2,500

Goodwill – Tilt Ltd

	£
Consideration [£75,000 × 70%]	52,500
Net assets acquired [(100,000 + 10,000) × 42%]	(46,200)
	6,300

Total goodwill = £8,800

6.5 Serf Ltd effective stake = 70% × 60% = 42%

Hence minority interest = 58%

This looks unusual as the minority interest have more than 50% of the net assets. This is because a distinction must be made between the effective interest in the company (i.e. 60%) which determines control and the interest which is consolidated.

6.6 **D**

Note: Dividends payable must be based on direct percentages and not effective stakes. A shareholder will only receive dividends in proportion to the share they directly hold.

6.7 **A**

	£
Pow Ltd [20% × (850 + 60% × 20)]	172,400
Biff Ltd [52% × 500]	260,000
Less: Cost [20% × 140]	(28,000)
	404,400

6.8 Goodwill

	£
Consideration [90 × 70,000]	63,000
Net assets acquired [(100,000 + 8,000) × 27%]	(29,160)
	33,840
Impairment	(5,000)
	28,840

Investment in associate

	£
Net assets [30% × 165,000]	49,500
Goodwill	28,840
	78,340

Note: The investment is based on a stake of 30%. The difference between this and the effective stake is adjusted via the minority interest. However, in accordance with IAS 22 the minority interest is not credited with any of the goodwill and hence this has been calculated using 27%.

Medium answer questions

Question 1 – Swain plc

(a) The Swain plc group structure is given below

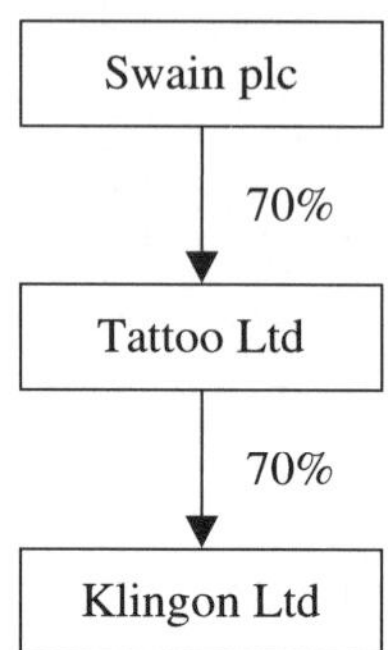

With reference to these companies highlight the treatment of the following items in the consolidated balance sheet and income statement

(i) Minority interests
(ii) Dividends receivable and payable
(iii) Goodwill.

(8 marks)

(b) Klingon Ltd is consolidated within the financial statements as a subsidiary undertaking. Briefly explain the theory behind this treatment given that the effective stake held by the ultimate parent company is less than 50%.

(2 marks)
(Total = 10 marks)

Question 2 – Tiger plc

The income statements of Tiger plc and its two subsidiaries for the year ended 30 September 20X4 are given below:

	Tiger plc £'000	*Platt Ltd* £'000	*Radcliffe Ltd* £'000
Revenue	910	350	270
Cost of sales	(210)	(90)	(110)
Gross profit	700	260	160
Selling and administration costs	(155)	(70)	(40)
Operating profit	545	190	120
Dividend income	85	–	–
Interest receivable	–	15	–
Profit before taxation	630	205	120
Taxation	(183)	(45)	(40)
Profit after taxation	447	160	80

Additional information:

- Tiger plc purchased 80% of the equity capital of Platt Ltd for £360,000 on 30 June 20X2 when the accumulated profits of the latter were £210,000.
- Platt Ltd purchased 60% of the equity capital of Radcliffe Ltd for £1,900,000 on 31 July 20X3 when the accumulated profits of the latter were £10,000.
- Platt Ltd declared a divided of £100,000 during the year, but Radcliffe Ltd did not pay a dividend.
- During the year Tiger plc sold goods costing £30,000 and £20,000 to Platt Ltd and Radcliffe Ltd respectively. These transfer prices were marked up by one third on cost. Half of the transfers to Platt Ltd remained in inventory at the end of the year.
- There has been no impairment of goodwill since the acquisition dates.
- The accumulated profits of each company at 30 September 20X4 were:

	£'000
Tiger plc	1,200
Platt Ltd	540
Radcliffe Ltd	40

Prepare the consolidated income statement for the year ended 30 September 20X4, and the closing accumulated profits at that date.

(10 marks)

✓ Medium answer questions

Answers 1 – Swain plc

(a)

(i) Minority interests

The minority interest in Tattoo Ltd is 30%. This will be represented on the consolidated balance sheet by a figure comprising their share of the net assets at the balance sheet date, whilst the income statement will disclose their share of Tattoo Ltd's profit after tax.

A similar treatment is adopted for the minority interest in Klingon Ltd, but comprises their effective stake in the company which is 51% [100% − (70% × 70%)].

(ii) Dividends receivable and payable

The consolidated income statement does not disclose any dividends paid or payable as these are an appropriation of profit rather than a charge against it. Details are disclosed in the statement of changes in equity.

Dividends received and receivable are reflected on the income statement as part of investment income. However, intragroup dividends must be eliminated as the single entity concept which underpins the consolidation process requires only income from outside the group to be included.

It is important to remember that for indirect subsidiaries such as Klingon Ltd it is inappropriate to use the effective stake for dividends as the amount received by other companies will be a direct proportion of the shares held. Swain plc will not receive any dividends from Klingon Ltd.

In the consolidated balance sheet, the current liabilities will reflect any dividends payable by Swain plc to its own shareholders plus any dividends payable to minority interests. Intragroup payables and receivables must again be eliminated as part of the consolidation process.

(iii) Goodwill

The goodwill calculation for Tattoo Ltd is calculated as the difference between the consideration given and the proportion of the fair value of net assets acquired. The resultant figure is disclosed as an intangible non-current asset and will be reviewed annually for impairment.

The goodwill calculation for Klingon Ltd will be derived by comparing 70% of the cost incurred by Tattoo Ltd with the effective percentage (49%) of Klingon Ltd's net assets. The shareholders of Swain plc do not bear the full cost as they only benefit from 70% of Tattoo Ltd's gains and profits. The balance 30% of the cost is attributed to the minority interest.

(b) Control percentage vs effective percentage

When deciding upon the accounting treatment of equity investments, the control percentage over that company must be identified. When the stake is a direct one this is relatively straightforward with stakes in excess of 50% indicating subsidiary status. In these circumstances the control percentage and effective percentage are the same.

When investments form part of a mixed or vertical group, the control and effective percentages diverge. It is important to establish the control percentage as the first step as this will determine the accounting treatment (i.e. acquisition accounting, equity accounting, etc.).

Swain plc controls Tattoo Ltd who in turn controls Klingon Ltd. Consequently Swain plc controls Klingon Ltd although it holds none of the shares directly. However, it would be inappropriate for Swain plc to consolidate 70% of Klingon Ltd as its own effective stake in the company is only 49%.

Answer 2 – Tiger plc

Consolidated income statement for the year ended 30 September 20X4

	£'000
Revenue	1,480
Cost of sales	(363.75)
Gross profit	1,116.25
Selling and administration costs	(265)
Operating profit	851.25
Investment income	5
Interest receivable	15
Profit before taxation	871.25
Taxation	(268)
Profit after taxation [W1]	603.25
Minority interest [W2]	(73.6)
Profit attributable to the shareholders of Ship plc	529.65

Accumulated profits as at 30 September 20X4

	£'000
Tiger plc	1,200
Less: PURP	(3.75)
Platt Ltd [80% × (540 − 210)]	264
Radcliffe Ltd [48% × (40 − 10)]	14.4
	1,474.65

[W1] Consolidation schedule

	Tiger plc £'000	*Platt Ltd* £'000	*Radcliffe Ltd* £'000		*Group* £'000
Revenue	910	350	270	(50)	1,480
Cost of sales	(210)	(90)	(110)	50	(363.75)
PURP	(3.75)				
Selling and administration costs	(155)	(70)	(40)		(265)
Dividend income [85 − 80]	5	–	–		5
Interest receivable	–	15	–		15
Taxation	(183)	(45)	(40)		(268)
Profit after taxation		160	80		603.25

[W2] Minority interest

Platt Ltd = 20% × 160k = £32k

Radcliffe Ltd = 52% × 80k = £41.6k

Acquisitions in the Accounting Period

7

Splitting the period

- The consolidated balance sheet is prepared based on the status of investments held at the period end date with consolidated accumulated profits including the post-acquisition profits of each subsidiary.
- The results of subsidiaries acquired in the year must be pro-rated in the consolidated income statement – this ensures that only the profits earned whilst under the control of the parent company are reflected therein.

Dividends paid out of pre-acquisition profits

- Dividends paid in the post-acquisition period are treated as income of the parent, and normal consolidation rules regarding intra-group transactions apply. Unless
  - The dividend is substantial and paid shortly after the acquisition date thereby reducing the value of the subsidiary; such payments should be accounted for as reduction in carrying value and not as income.
  - When a subsidiary pays a dividend before the acquisition date this cash flow must be accounted for as a reduction in the net assets of the subsidiary, and hence will impact the calculation of goodwill.

Piecemeal acquisitions

Scenario 1: Increasing a stake in an existing subsidiary

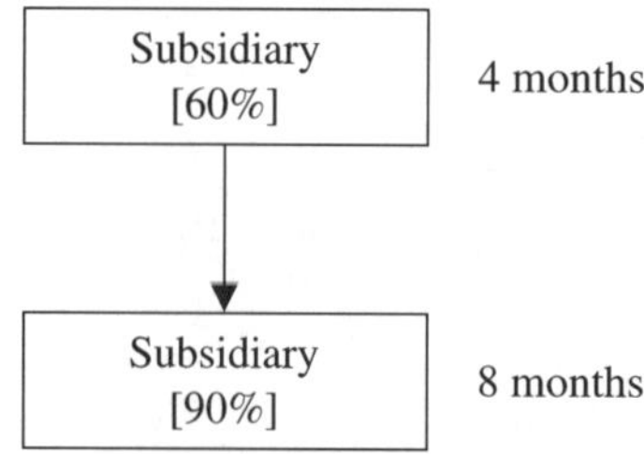

- Consolidated income statement – consolidate as normal, but calculate minority interests in two parts comprising 40% of PAT for 4 months of the year and 10% for the remainder of the financial period.
- Consolidated balance sheet
  – Minority interest comprises their closing percentage (10%) of the fair value of S's closing net assets.
  – Calculate goodwill and reserves at acquisition for each stage separately, that is, identify the net assets when 60% control is gained and again at the date of the second tranche.

Scenario 2: Increasing a stake in an associate such that it becomes a subsidiary

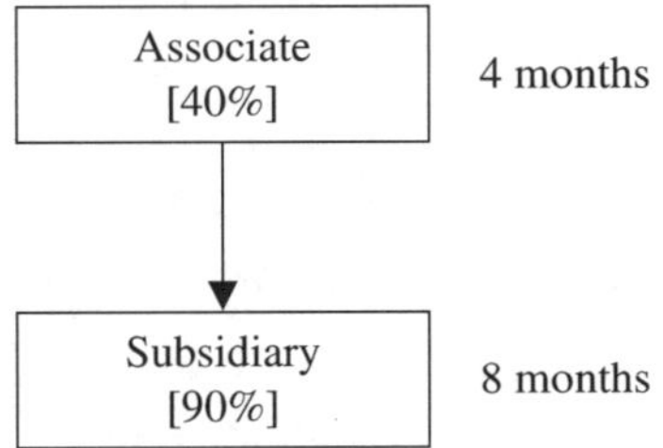

- Consolidated income statement – pro-rate the results for the year and equity account for the 4 month period when the investment stake constituted an associate (i.e. bring in a single figure representing the associates profit after tax), and acquisition account for the remaining 8 months.
- Consolidated balance sheet
  – Minority interest comprises their closing percentage (10%) of the fair value of S's closing net assets.
  – Calculate goodwill and reserves at acquisition for each stage separately, that is, identify the net assets when 40% influence is gained and again at the date of the second tranche.

Scenario 3: Increasing the stake in a trade investment so that it becomes a subsidiary

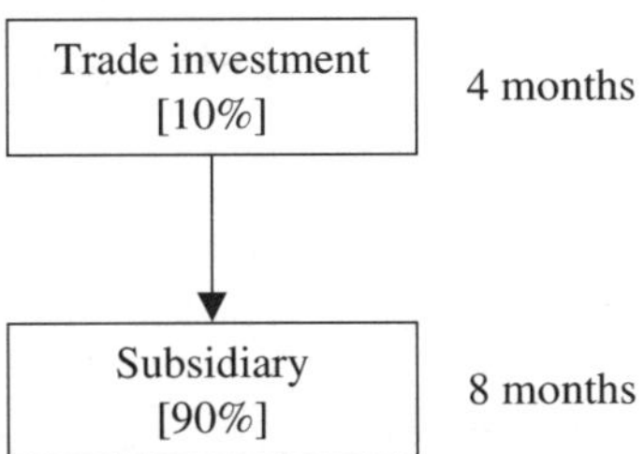

- Based on a 10% stake this investment will not have been previously consolidated.
- Consequently when the second tranche is acquired, it is as if a 90% subsidiary has been acquired.
- Goodwill will be calculated by comparing 90% of the fair value of the net assets at the date of the second purchase with the total consideration given (i.e. a one step calculation).
- Consolidated income statement – prior to the second acquisition only investment income will be recognised; thereafter the results for the remainder of the financial period will be pro-rated and consolidated.
- Consolidated balance sheet – minority interests will be attributed with 10% of S's closing net assets and consolidated accumulated reserves will reflect 90% of the post-acquisition profits of the subsidiary from the date of the second tranche.

Goodwill and the issue of fair value

- Goodwill – Difference between purchase consideration and the group's share of the fair value of the net assets acquired
- Fair value – The amount for which an asset could be exchanged or a liability settled between knowledgeable, willing parties in an arm's-length transaction
- The fair value of consideration includes cash given, but other consideration will include:

Direct costs	Costs uniquely incurred as part of the acquisition process
Shares	Published price on the date of exchange
Contingent consideration	Recognise those amounts that are probable and can be measured reliably

- Fair value of net assets acquired:

Property, plant and equipment	Depreciated market value
Specialised property, plant and equipment	Depreciated replacement cost
Inventory	Market value
Inventory (manufactured rather than purchased)	Current cost to the acquiring entity unless no current cost available when sales value should be used deducting – costs to complete – incidental disposal costs – a realistic allowance for profit
Listed investments	Quoted price on exchange date
Intangible assets	Recognised if it meets the definition of an intangible asset and can be measured reliably
Monetary assets and liabilities	Discount if long term
Restructuring provisions	Cannot anticipate future events
Contingent liabilities	These should be recognised if they can be measured reliably even if they are not currently recognised in the books of the entity being acquired

? Objective test questions

7.1 Gourmet Ltd acquired the entire share capital of Carrot Ltd for an immediate cash outlay of £500,000. However, there were other cost implications as follows:

- An actuary was employed specifically to value Carrot Ltd's pension scheme at a cost of 5,000.
- Peter Sand, the Commercial Director of Gourmet Ltd, estimated that he had spent one month of his time exclusively negotiating the purchase. His annual remuneration is £90,000 per annum.
- Gourmet Ltd will be required to pay a further £100,000 in two years if the annual profit after tax of Carrot Ltd exceeds £250,000 in both years. A downturn in the economic sector indicate that this return is now unlikely.

Calculate the fair value of the consideration given to buy Carrot Ltd.

(3 marks)

7.2 During the year ended 30 September 20X4 Ralph plc purchased a 75% stake in Joseph Ltd. Which of the following items would have been excluded from the fair value of consideration given in the calculation of goodwill?

A A professional fee paid to a surveyor who valued some of the assets of the target company.
B An additional fee payable if the earnings of Joseph Ltd exceed £50,000 for each of the next three years. Earnings are currently £60,000 and the latest forecasts predict this to grow.
C The administration department of Ralph plc worked predominantly on the acquisition for several weeks, and this has been costed by the finance director.
D Ralph Ltd will issue fixed rate bonds with a face value of £120,000 to the former shareholders of Joseph Ltd in two years.

(2 marks)

7.3 Serpent Ltd, a men's clothing manufacturer, is undergoing a due diligence review prior to its sale to Garden Ltd.

Its non-current assets comprise two processing machines on which the following information is available.

Machine 1 – This is a modern machine sold extensively across the UK and Europe by its supplier at £36,000 per unit. They can also be purchased second hand at the following prices:

Age of machine	£'000
3 years	22,000
6 years	11,000
9 years	3,000

Machine 2 – Serpent has a reputation for producing a specialist range manufactured using the original techniques employed in the 19th century. The machine used for this purpose had to be purposely built for the company.

Both machines are estimated to have a 12 year useful economic life, and were purchased on the same day six years previously. The cost of a new replacement of either machine is:

	£'000
Machine 1	36,000
Machine 2	42,000

Calculate the fair value of the two machines.

(3 marks)

7.4 Rog Ltd is acquiring a 70% stake in Grime Ltd for £1,000,000 in cash.

Grime Ltd has been poorly managed in recent years and needs new computer systems plus a complete reorganisation of its manufacturing division. Rog Ltd had been made fully aware of these issues during the negotiations, and priced the changes at £250,000.

In its year end consolidated accounts Rog Ltd has included the £250,000 as part of the purchase consideration creating positive goodwill of £20,000.

Briefly comment on the appropriateness of this treatment, and any consequential matters arising.

(3 marks)

7.5 Due to the long-term nature of its operating cycle a significant proportion of X Ltd's receivables will not be collected for three years. How might this information impact the calculation of goodwill by Y plc who has just purchased the entire share capital of X Ltd? [30 words maximum]

(2 marks)

7.6 On 1 April 20X4 Gel Ltd purchased the entire share capital of Agar Ltd following a very brief negotiation period.

Agar Ltd produces ice cream for the UK market, and two thirds of its annual sales are made between April and September inclusive. The total earnings for the year ended 30 September 20X4 was £270,000 before the deduction of dividends.

On 30 September 20X3 Agar Ltd had accumulated reserves of £400,000, and during the year the company declared and paid a £30,000 dividend [December 20X3].

When calculating goodwill arising on the acquisition what is the value of Agar Ltd's accumulated reserves?

A £505,000
B £520,000
C £535,000
D £640,000

(2 marks)

7.7 Rainbow Ltd purchased a 75% stake in Triad Ltd during the year ended 31 December 20X4. The finance director is now preparing consolidated financial statements, but is unsure the date from which Triad Ltd should be recognised as a group member.

Which statement most accurately describes the date he should select?

A The date on which the offer to acquire Triad Ltd became unconditional.
B The deadline date given to the 25% minority interest to lodge any objections to the acquisition.
C The date on which effective control is gained over Triad Ltd.
D The date on which the consideration was paid by Rainbow Ltd.

(2 marks)

7.8 During a recent board meeting the finance director of Tears Ltd was asked for her views on the timing of a potential acquisition. As part of her response she made the following comment:

"If a company is acquired three months prior to the date when we prepare consolidated financial statements then I am only interested in the dividends they pay from the acquisition date. There is no reason for me to be concerned about any dividend they might have paid the week before as none of that comes to me."

Briefly comment on the director's assertion. [60 words maximum]

(3 marks)

7.9 Rumble plc has acquired a substantial holding in Voce Ltd, and is in the process of preparing the consolidated balance sheet as at 31 December 20X4. The interest in Voce Ltd was acquired in two separate transactions:

- 55% on 30 April 20X1 for £3,000,000 when the accumulated profits of Voce Ltd were £1,200,000
- 35% on 31 October 20X2 for £1,700,000 when the accumulated profits of Voce Ltd were £1,650,000.

At the 31 December 20X4 the balance sheet extracts for Voce Ltd were as follows:

	£'000
Non-current assets	444
Current assets	2,666
Non-current liabilities	(324)
Current liabilities	(56)

Voce Ltd has one million £1 ordinary shares in issue.

Calculate the minority interest as at 31 December 20X4.

(3 marks)

7.10 DGH plc acquired 10% of Helm Ltd on 30 June 20X2 for £250,000 when the accumulated profits of the latter were £560,000.

Exactly two years later it has purchased a further 70% interest in the company at an additional cost of £1,700,000. At this time the accumulated profits of Helm Ltd were £1,100,000.

Helm Ltd has 1,000,000 50p shares in issue.

Assuming that there have been no impairments, what is the value of goodwill to be included in the consolidated balance sheet as 31 December 20X4?

A £824,000
B £670,000
C £580,000
D £280,000

✓ Objective test answers

7.1

	£'000	
Immediate payment	500,000	
Actuary	5,000	
Commercial Director	–	Not a direct cost as he would have been remunerated anyway
Contingent consideration	–	Payment now not probable and hence should not be provided for
	505,000	

7.2 **C**

7.3 Machine 1 – There is a ready market in this type of machine, and hence the depreciated market value can be used to represent fair value. As the machine is six years old it will be valued at £11,000.

Machine 2 – The specialised nature of this machine means there is no active market to gauge its current value. Consequently depreciated replacement cost can be used as an approximation.

Depreciated replacement cost = £42,000 × 6/12 = £21,000.

7.4 IFRS 3 does not allow the recognition of future costs as part of the purchase consideration as these do not meet the definition of a liability on that date.

When the £250,000 is removed from consideration then the goodwill arising changes from positive to negative. Unlike positive goodwill which is held as a non-current asset until it is impaired, negative goodwill would have to be recognised in the profit and loss immediately.

7.5 The receivables should be discounted to their present value to avoid distortion of goodwill by failing to reflect the time value of money.

7.6 **A**

7.7 **C** (the only date of significance is the date control passes to Rainbow Ltd)

7.8 The finance director has overlooked that dividends paid by a subsidiary out of preacquisition reserves immediately prior to the transfer of control may lead to an impairment in the carrying value of the investment. Additionally dividends post the acquisition date will cancel on consolidation.

7.9

	£'000
Non-current assets	444
Current assets	2,666
Non-current liabilities	(324)
Current liabilities	(56)
	2,730

Minority interest = 10% × 2,730,000 = £273,000

The minority interest would take their share of the closing net assets. Hence the dates of the piecemeal acquisition have no bearing on this calculation.

7.10 **B**

	£'000
Consideration (250 + 1,700)	1,950
Net assets [80% × (500 + 1,100)]	(1,280)
	670

Medium answer questions

Question 1 – PQR Group

(a) The PQR group has been expanding rapidly for several years after deciding to follow a policy of growth by acquisition. Their latest investment was a 75% stake in Juniper Ltd acquired on 30 June 20X4.

The balance sheet of Juniper Ltd at 1 January 20X4 was as follows:

	£'000
Non-current assets	550
Current assets	210
	760
Share capital [£1]	100
Accumulated profits	490
	590
Non-current liabilities	160
Current liabilities	10
	760

Additional information:

- The consideration paid for Juniper comprised:
  - £150,000 immediate cash payment
  - £100,000 in two years if the earnings of Juniper Ltd exceed £50,000 in both years; as is projected by the latest forecasts
  - 100,000 equity shares in PQR plc. The mid-market price of these shares on 30 June 20X4 was £4.20.
- Expert actuarial advice was taken to value Junipers pension scheme prior to the purchase. The actuarial fees were £10,000.
- Juniper Ltd has four operating divisions. It is the intention of PQR plc to reduce this to three at a restructuring cost of £25,000.
- The market value of Juniper Ltd's non-current asset at 30 June 20X4 was estimated to be £40,000 in excess of their carrying value in the accounts.
- Juniper Ltd earnings of £200,000 (post-dividend) accrued evenly over 20X4.
- On 28 February 20X4 Juniper declared a dividend of £20,000.

Calculate the value of goodwill arising on the acquisition of Juniper Ltd.

(6 marks)

(b) Comment on the consequences arising if the market value of the shares given as consideration had been £2.20.

(4 marks)
(Total = 10 marks)

Question 2 – Prime Ltd

(a) The management of Prime Ltd were always looking to expand the activities of the company, but wanted to remain true to their market sector. Consequently, they have always been interested in the acquisition of Target Ltd who manufactures complementary products.

Over recent years Prime Ltd has purchased shares in Target Ltd whenever the opportunity has arisen. Their investments to date have been as follows:

- On 31 March 20X0 acquired 10% for £75,000 when the accumulated profits of Target Ltd were £100,000.
- On 31 March 20X3 acquired 70% for £850,000 when the accumulated profits of Target Ltd were £150,000.

The balance sheets of the two companies as at 31 December 20X4 were:

	Prime Ltd £'000	*Target Ltd* £'000
Assets		
Non-current assets		
Property, plant and equipment	600	450
Investments	980	–
	–	–
Current assets		
Inventory	150	280
Receivables	20	150
Cash	10	40
Total assets	1,760	920
Equity and liabilities		
Capital and reserves		
Ordinary share capital [£1 shares]	100	100
Share premium account	30	–
Accumulated profits	1,320	200
Non-current liabilities		
Loan	250	490
Current liabilities		
Trade payables	60	130
	1,760	920

Further information:

- During 20X4 Prime Ltd sold inventory costing £40,000 to Target Ltd at a mark up of 25%. Half of this remains unsold by Target Ltd at the year end.
- Goodwill has suffered no diminution in value.

Prepare the consolidated balance sheet as at 30 June 20X4.

(8 marks)

(b) Comment on the potential impact on the consolidated financial statements if at the date of acquiring the 70% stake Target Ltd had been involved in a court case regarding potential environmental damage caused by its production process.

(2 marks)
(Total = 10 marks)

Medium answer questions

Answer 1 – PQR Group

(a) Goodwill

	£'000
Consideration	
Immediate cash payment	150
Contingent consideration (probable)	100
Shares at market price	420
Actuarial fees	10
[Ignore restructuring as this is a future event and hence these costs do not meet the definition of a liability at the acquisition date.]	
Total consideration	680

	£'000
Net assets at acquisition	
Share capital	100
Accumulated profits at 1 January	490
Profits to 30 June [(220,000/2) − 20,000]	90
	680
75% attributable to PQR plc	510

Goodwill = 680 − 510 = £170k

(b) Impact of changes to consideration

If the market value of the shares given as consideration had been £2.20 the total value of consideration would have fallen to £480,000.

This would have resulted in negative goodwill arising on the acquisition of £30,000, although under the rules of IFRS 3 the term negative goodwill is no longer used (now referred to as discount on acquisition).

Positive goodwill is included within the consolidated balance sheet as a non-current asset. It is not amortised, but must be reviewed for evidence of impairment. By contrast when the goodwill calculation generates a negative figure this must be validated by repeating the valuation exercise, and if confirmed the resultant figure is written off to the income statement immediately. Remember this will be treated as a gain.

Answer 2 – Prime Ltd

(a) Consolidated balance sheet as at 31 December 20X4

	£'000	£'000
Assets		
Non-current assets		
Property, plant and equipment		1,050
Intangibles [W1]		725
Investments		55
		1,830

Current assets		
Inventory [150 + 280 − 5]	425	
Receivables	170	
Cash	50	645
Total assets		2,475
Equity and liabilities		
Capital and reserves		
Ordinary share capital [£1 shares]		100
Share premium account		30
Accumulated profits [W3]		1,355
		1,485
Minority interests [W2]		60
		1,545
Non-current liabilities		
Loan		740
Current liabilities		
Trade payables		190
		2,475

W1:

Goodwill

	£'000
Cost of investment	925
Net assets acquired [80% × (100 + 150)]	(200)
	725

W2:

Minority interests
20% × (300) = £60k

W3:

Accumulated reserves

	£'000
Prime Ltd	1,320
Less: Unrealised profit	(5)
Bleak Ltd [80% × (200 − 150)]	40
	1,355

(b) Potential damages

The potential damages represent a contingent liability.

IFRS 3 requires that contingent liabilities should be recognised at fair value when calculating goodwill. Although it is a prerequisite that they can be reliably measured which is unclear from the information available on Target Ltd.

It should be noted that if Target Ltd believed that it could overturn the case, and win compensation this contingent asset would not be recognised by Prime Ltd at the date of acquisition.

Disposals in the Accounting Period 8

Complete disposals

Individual books of the parent	£
Sale proceeds	X
Less: Cost	(X)
	X
Less: Tax	(X)
Profit/loss on disposal	X/(X)

Consolidated financial statements	£
Sale proceeds	X
Less: Net assets at disposal	(X)
Less: Unimpaired goodwill	(X)
	X
Less: Tax	(X)
Profit/loss on disposal	X/(X)

- The income statement of the subsidiary disposed will have to be pro-rated and the activity prior to disposal consolidated using the normal rules of acquisition accounting.
- When pro-rating make a careful note of the date of any dividends paid by the subsidiary
  - If paid prior to disposal the whole dividend needs to be removed from the net assets at the date of disposal as this cash has been distributed.
  - If the dividend is paid after the disposal date it should ignored as net assets at disposal have not been diminished by this distribution.
- The consolidated balance sheet will not reflect the investment disposed as there is no control over its assets at the balance sheet date.

Partial disposals

Scenario 1 – after the disposal the remaining stake is sufficient to retain subsidiary status

Consolidated income statement

Consolidated using normal acquisition rules but calculate minority interests in two parts

Consolidated balance sheet

At the year-end subsidiary status is retained and hence consolidated using acquisition accounting

The figures should be prepared using whatever is the closing percentage stake held by the parent

Scenario 2 – partial disposal resulting in a drop to associate status

Consolidated income statement	*Consolidated balance sheet*
Consolidated using normal acquisition rules for the first part of the year for which subsidiary status is held This requires the results of the investment to be pro-rated For the remainder of the year equity account whereby only the parents revised percentage of the associates, PAT will be shown in the income statement	At the year end the investment should be accounted for according to its status at that time Hence equity account as if the investment had been an associate throughout

Scenario 3 – partial disposal resulting in a trade investment

Consolidated income statement	*Consolidated balance sheet*
Consolidated using normal acquisition rules for the first part of the year for which subsidiary status is held This requires the results of the investment to be pro-rated For the remainder of the year the remaining interest in shares represents a trade investment, and hence only dividend income would be recognised	At the year end the investment should be accounted for according to its status at that time However, it would be inappropriate to show the trade investment at its original cost as the group has been entitled to post-acquisition profits up to the date of the disposal Consequently the investment will be frozen at the parent's revised percentage holding of its net assets at the disposal date plus any unimpaired goodwill

Deemed disposals

- If a parent's percentage interest in an entity changes, although the absolute number of shares held remains the same, a deemed profit or loss on disposal will arise.
- An example would be a rights issue by the subsidiary when the parent does not take up its rights.

Objective test questions

8.1 Ceramics Ltd purchased 8,000 £1 ordinary shares in Flooring Ltd on 30 June 20X1, when the accumulated profits of the latter were £47,000.

Two years later Flooring Ltd sought additional finance via the issue of 5,000 additional shares at £4.20 per share, increasing its share capital to £15,000. Ceramics Ltd made a decision not to invest in this latest share issue.

Immediately prior to the issue the accumulated profits of Flooring Ltd were £90,000.

Calculate the deemed loss on disposal arising on the issue.

A £13,333
B £15,467
C £24,000
D £26,666

(3 marks)

8.2 The Rogere Ltd group owns 90% of the £1 ordinary share capital of Bamba Ltd, but is now in the process of selling half of this holding.

When recording the profit/(loss) on disposal arising in the consolidated financial statements what proportion of Bamba Ltd's net assets and goodwill will be included in the disposal calculation?

It should be assumed that goodwill on the original acquisition has not suffered any impairment since the acquisition date, and that Bamba Ltd's total issued share capital is £2 million.

	Net assets (%)	*Goodwill (%)*
A	45	45
B	50	45
C	45	50
D	50	50

(2 marks)

8.3 On 1 January 20X1 Vikmani plc acquired the entire share capital (2,000 50p ordinary shares) in Duff Ltd. The goodwill arising was £20,000, but it has proved necessary to impair this value by 20% in 20X3.

On 1 January 20X4 Vikmani plc sold all the shares in Duff Ltd for £260,000 when the reserves of the latter were £220,000.

What is the profit on disposal to be included in the 20X4 consolidated financial statements?

(2 marks)

8.4 Shiba plc has the following holdings in the equity of Timelord Ltd.

	Holding	*Total in issue*
£1 ordinary shares (purchased at 1 January 20X0)	90,000	100,000
£1 4% irredeemable preference shares (purchased at 30 June 20X2)	60,000	100,000

On 30 June 20X4 Shiba plc decided to dispose of its entire holdings in Timelord Ltd.

Additional information:

- On 1 January 20X4 the equity and accumulated profits of Timelord Ltd were £150,000.
- Profits after taxation, but before dividends and interest, for the year ended 31 December 20X4 were £48,000.
- Timelord Ltd has a seasonal business with two-thirds of its sales being made between 1 July and 31 December.
- An ordinary dividend of £5,000 was paid on 1 April 20X4.

What is the value of the net assets to be included in the calculation of the group profit/(loss) on disposal?

A £158,334
B £159,000
C £161,000
D £167,000

(4 marks)

8.5 Soldier Ltd disposes of one-third of its 90% in Najsport Ltd on 30 September 20X4. If the year end of Soldier Ltd is 31 December 20X4, briefly describe the impact of the disposal on the consolidated balance sheet and income statement. [Maximum 50 words]

(3 marks)

8.6 Swizzel Ltd acquired a 75% stake in Wheel Ltd on 30 September 20X4 for £100,000.

It has now decided to sell its entire holding on 30 June 20X4 for £180,000 when the accumulated profits of Wheel Ltd are £120,000.

If the tax rate is 30% what is the tax attributable to the profit on disposal to be incorporated into the consolidated income statement?

(1 mark)

8.7 Alpha plc has a 40% investment in Beta Ltd, but has decided to sell three quarters of its stake midway through the accounting period ended 31 December 20X4. There has been no impairment to goodwill since acquisition.

The finance director has asked you for a brief statement describing the repercussions for the accounting period. Outline the significant points to be included in your response.

(3 marks)

8.8 The finance director of Honey Ltd has recently been told by the board to increase the financing of the group by requiring the management of Toom Ltd, its 53% subsidiary, to make a 1 for 3 rights issue. The strike price of the issue is to be £1 below the current mid-market share price.

Honey plc does not intend to take up the rights itself.

The rights issue was perceived by the board of Honey plc as a "painless" way to raise cash as the company has a good reputation, and a full take up of the rights is expected by the shareholders. However the finance director is less certain and has asked for your advice before proceeding.

List the issues that might arise from action the proposal made by the board.

(3 marks)

8.9 Identify which of the following circumstances would not lead to a profit/(loss) arising on a deemed disposal.

A A 95% subsidiary makes a rights issue and the group does not take up its full allocation of shares.
B A 70% subsidiary makes a 1 for 5 bonus issue midway through the financial period.
C A 75% subsidiary issues shares at market value to a third party.
D Another party exercises options which give it an increased stake in your subsidiary.

(2 marks)

8.10 Rumble plc purchased a 70% stake of the £50,000 ordinary share capital of Court Ltd on 1 April 20X2 for £200,000 when the accumulated profits of the latter were £80,000.

The goodwill arising on the acquisition suffered a 50% impairment in 20X3.

In 20X4 the board of directors decided to dispose of the entire holding in Court Ltd for £160,000.

Describe the impact of the earlier impairment on the profit/(loss) arising on disposal both for the individual accounts of Rumble plc and the consolidated financial statements.

(4 marks)

8.11 Rotary Ltd has decided to dispose of three quarters of its 60% stake in Longines Ltd purchased for £1 million when the accumulated profits of the latter were £600,000.

At the date of disposal, extracts from the financial statements of Longines Ltd were as follows:

	£'000
Non-current assets	700
Current assets	450
	1,150
Share capital	100
Accumulated profits	750
	850
Non-current liabilities	80
Current liabilities	220
	1,150

On the basis that Rotary Ltd retains other investments in subsidiaries, calculate the carrying value of the remaining stake in Longines Ltd in the consolidated financial statements immediately following the disposal.

Assume there has been no impairment of the goodwill arising on the acquisition of Longines Ltd between the acquisition and disposal dates.

(3 marks)

Objective test answers

8.1 **B**

Before issue: 80% × (10,000 + 90,000)	£80,000
After issue: 8/15 × (10,000 + 90,000 + 21,000)	£64,533
Loss	£15,467

8.2 **C**

8.3

	£
Proceeds	260,000
Less: Net assets (1,000 + 220,000)	(221,000)
Less: Goodwill (20,000 − 4,000)	(16,000)
	23,000

8.4 **B**

	£
Net assets at 1 January 20X4	150,000
Pro-rated profit	16,000
Ordinary dividend	(5,000)
Interest on irredeemable prefs	(2,000)
	159,000

8.5 *Income statement*: The remaining 60% holding means Najsport Ltd will still be consolidated as a full subsidiary, but minority interests will be calculated in two tranches. They are entitled to 10% of Najsport Ltd's profit after tax for the 9 months upto 30 September and 40% for the remaining three months.

Balance sheet: At 31 December 20X4 Najsport Ltd remains a 60% subsidiary of Soldier Ltd, and will be consolidated using acquisition accounting.

8.6

	£
Proceeds	180,000
Less: Cost (i.e. based on individual company)	(100,000)
	80,000
Taxation at 30%	24,000

8.7 Points to be included:

- For the first six months of the year Beta Ltd is an associate, and hence Alpha plc's 40% share of profit after taxation will be included on the face of the income statement.
- Any profit/(loss) arising on the part disposal will be shown as an item requiring separate disclosure, and thereafter the income statement will disclose only investment income as Beta Ltd will now represent a trade investment.

8.8 Issues arising are:

- Percentage investment will fall below 50% leading to a loss of control . . . Tooms Ltd would be accounted for as an associate.
- A loss will arise on the deemed disposal, and is likely to require separate disclosure.
- Unless a full explanation is given to the capital markets the failure of Honey plc to take up the rights might be perceived as a lack of confidence.

8.9 **B**

8.10 The goodwill originally arising on the acquisition was:

Goodwill = 200,000 − 70%(50,000 + 80,000) = £109,000

Hence the impairment in 2003 = £54,500

Individual books of parent company:

- No direct impact as goodwill not crystallised in individual books.
- However a check will be needed to ensure that the impairment of the goodwill does not represent an indicator that the carrying value of the investment is overstated.

Consolidated financial statements:

- The profit arising on disposal of the investment is £21,500 [160,000 − 70% (50,000 + 70,000) − £54,500].
- If the impairment had not occurred then the profit on disposal would have become a £33,000 loss.

8.11 Goodwill arising on acquisition = 1,000 − 60%(600 + 100) = £580,000

Hence

New carrying value for investment:

	£'000
"New" cost (15% × 850)	127.5
Remaining goodwill (25% × 580)	145
	272.5

Medium answer questions

Question 1 – Deep Ltd

(a) The summarised draft balance sheets of Deep Ltd and Shallow Ltd at 31 December 20X4 are as follows:

	Deep Ltd £'000	*Shallow Ltd* £'000
Non-current assets	1,500	800
Investments – 920,000 shares in Shallow Ltd at cost	1,100	
Current assets	1,000	500
	3,600	1,300

	Deep Ltd £'000	*Shallow Ltd* £'000
Share capital [£1]	1,500	920
Accumulated profits	1,030	300
	2,530	1,220
Proceeds of disposal	550	
Current liabilities	520	80
	3,600	1,300

Additional information:

- The investment in Shallow Ltd was acquired on 1 January 20X1 when the accumulated profits of Shallow Ltd were £100,000.
- On 30 June 20X4 Deep Ltd sold 25% of its holding in Shallow Ltd for £550, but apart from crediting the sale proceeds in the balance sheet no other entries have been made to reflect the disposal.
- The balances on accumulated reserves at 1 January 20X4 were

Deep Ltd	£700,000
Shallow Ltd	£200,000

- Shallow Ltd declared and paid a 5p dividend during the final three months of the accounting period.
- Assume the tax on the gain on disposal to be £75,000.
- There has been no impairments to goodwill since the date of acquisition.

(a) Prepare the consolidated balance sheet of Deep Ltd as at 31 December 20X4, and calculate the profit/(loss) to be recorded for the disposal in the consolidated income statement.

(8 marks)

(b) Briefly comment on the impact of the disposal on the consolidated income statement.

(2 marks)

(Total = 10 marks)

Question 2 – Inca plc

Ralph Singh, the finance director of Inca plc, has just returned from a difficult board meeting at which other board members had gone beyond the scope of the agenda resulting in several questions arising to which he did not have the answer.

In an attempt to diffuse the frustration that pervaded the meeting he has sent you the following email:

To: Jane Soames (XYZ & Co)

From: Ralph Singh

Re: Potential part disposal of Wren Ltd

Sorry to bother you just before you leave for your annual vacation, but I am hoping you might be able to steer me in the right direction regarding some issues that have been raised at today's board meeting.

The company is considering selling half of its stake in Wren Ltd as the market in this sector is currently on a high and the board believes it can "cash in" on this opportunity. However, Jim Dread (Marketing Director) has convinced the other members that I will not need any additional accounting resource to record such a disposal as he believes that the preparation of the group accounts will remain the same as we have several other subsidiary companies. It has been a long time since I completed my CIMA studies, but I am sure there is more to it than this.

Furthermore, Jim has also undertaken a back of an envelope calculation as to the profit on disposal that can be expected. I have expressed concern that this will not be the figure to be shown in the consolidated income statement. The other board members cannot see any reason why we cannot use Jim's figure, and have asked me to prove that there is any significant difference between the profit that I have calculated and Jim's. I know there is a difference, but would not be able to prove this without a push in the right direction from you . . . HELP!

I would be very grateful if you could calculate the figure you believe should be incorporated into the consolidated income statement, and provide me with a brief commentary as to the reason this differs from Jim's calculation; which is shown below.

	£
Proceeds	600,000
Less: Half of cost	(97,500)
	502,500

Additional information:

- Our existing stake in Wren Ltd is 80%.
- Ignore any impact of taxation (we can worry about this later!).
- Goodwill arising on the acquisition of Wren Ltd was £60,000, and this has suffered an impairment of £10,000 since that date.
- At the date of acquisition the accumulated profits of Wren Ltd were £50,000 and its share capital £100,000.
- If Wren Ltd is part disposed at the end of this month then I estimated that its equity and reserves at that date will be £470,000.

(10 marks)

Medium answer questions

Answer 1 – Deep Ltd

(a) Consolidated balance sheet as at 31 December 20X4:

	£'000
Assets	
Non-current assets	2,300
Intangibles [W1]	60
	2,360
Current assets	1,500
Total assets	3,860
Equity and liabilities	
Capital and reserves	
Ordinary share capital	1,500
Accumulated profits [W3]	1,380
	2,880
Minority interests [W2]	305
	3,185
Non-current liabilities (520 + 80 + 75)	675
	3,860

The profit on disposal to be included in the consolidated income statement is:

	£'000
Proceeds	550
Net assets disposed [25% × (1,120 + 50)]	(292.5)
Goodwill disposed	(20)
	237.5

The tax on this disposal would be that calculated on the profit on disposal for the individual books.

W1:

Goodwill

	£'000
Cost of investment	1,100
Net assets acquired [80% × (100 + 150)]	(1,020)
	80

Post-disposal 75% of this goodwill will remain

W2:

Minority interests

25% × (1,220) = £305k

W3:

Accumulated reserves

	£'000
Deep Ltd	1,030
Profit on disposal (550 − 275 − 75)	200
Shallow Ltd (75% × 200)	150
	1,380

(b) Impact on the consolidated income statement

After the disposal Deep Ltd's investment in Shallow Ltd remains in excess of 50% and hence control is retained. This implies that Shallow Ltd will be consolidated as a subsidiary using acquisition accounting throughout the accounting period.

However, for the second 6 months of the year it will be necessary to disclose a minority interest in the profit after tax of Shallow Ltd.

Answer 2 – Inca plc

Guidance notes for Ralph Singh

(1) Impact of part disposal

You are correct about the impact of the disposal being more significant that your other board members initially believe. This is particularly true as a disposal of half the stake held by Inca plc will reduce the effective interest in Wren Ltd from 90 to 45%.

One probable consequence of this reduction is that the control you currently exercise over this company will be lost; although you should retain influence. Consequently the method of incorporating the results of Wren Ltd into the consolidated financial statements will change from acquisition accounting to equity accounting. Wren Ltd will now be viewed as an associate rather than a subsidiary.

In the consolidated balance sheet at the end of financial year, the investment in Wren Ltd will no longer be consolidated on a line-by-line basis, but will be disclosed within non-current assets as a single line. The figure will comprise the group's new 45% holding in the fair value of Wren Ltd's net assets at the balance sheet date plus the remaining unimpaired goodwill (i.e. (£60,000 − £10,000) × 50% = £25,000).

The consolidated income statement will reflect several changes in addition to the disclosure of the consolidated profit on disposal (i.e. not the figure suggested by Jim):

- The results will have to be prorated in the year of disposal as the treatment of a subsidiary and an associate are very different.
- As a subsidiary, the results of Wren Ltd will be added on a line-by-line basis, and the minority interest given their share of the company's profit after tax.
- As an associate, only your 45% stake of Wren's profit after tax will be disclosed (i.e. income and expenses will not be added on a line-by-line basis).
- Investment income from Wren Ltd must be eliminated for the whole year.

(2) Calculation of disposal profits

The profit on disposal figure calculated by Jim is the figure that would be disclosed in the individual income statement of Inca plc, but is not the correct figure for the consolidated financial statements.

The profit to be disclosed in your consolidated income statement would be:

	£'000
Proceeds	600
Net assets disposed [45% × 470]	(211.5)
Goodwill disposed	(25)
	363.5

This can be reconciled to Jim's figure as follows:

	£'000
Profit per individual books	502.5
Less: Post-acquisition profits disposed [320 × 45%]	(144)
Proportion of goodwill impaired (10 × 50%)	5
	363.5

Hopefully this gives you the information you need to go back to the board, but if you need further help, Robert Kielder will be covering for me whilst I am away.

Business Reorganisations 9

Possible scenarios

- To eliminate a debit balance on the profit and loss reserve.
- The breach of debt covenants results in lenders enforcing a reorganisation.
- A predatory group that has made many acquisitions wants to streamline the group structure.
- A new structure to facilitate a flotation.
- A new structure to facilitate the disposal of a company whilst retaining other investments.

A subsidiary becomes a sub-subsidiary

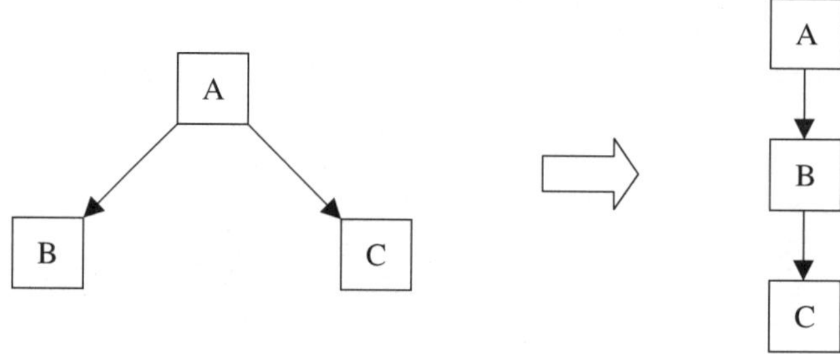

- This strategy might be employed if the directors of A want to create a sub-group.
- The overall effect on the A group is nil.

A sub-subsidiary becomes a subsidiary

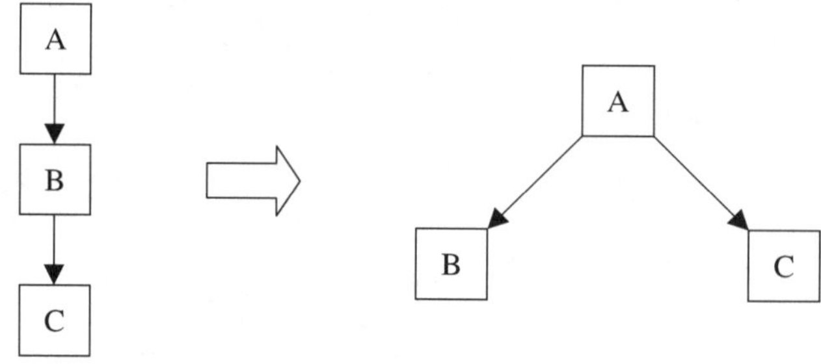

- This strategy might be employed if the directors of A want to dispose of B whilst retaining C.
- It is not possible for this type of reorganisation to be effected by A issuing shares to B in exchange for the shares in C . . . it is illegal for a parent to issue shares to its subsidiary.
- Consequently the transfer is achieved by B making a dividend in specie represented by the shares of C.

The addition of a new parent company

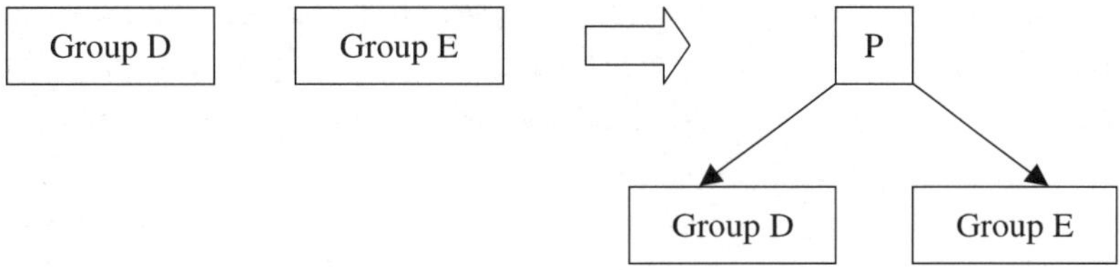

- The shareholders of the parent company of each group conduct a share for share exchange in the new parent bringing all the resources under central control.

A subsidiary moved along

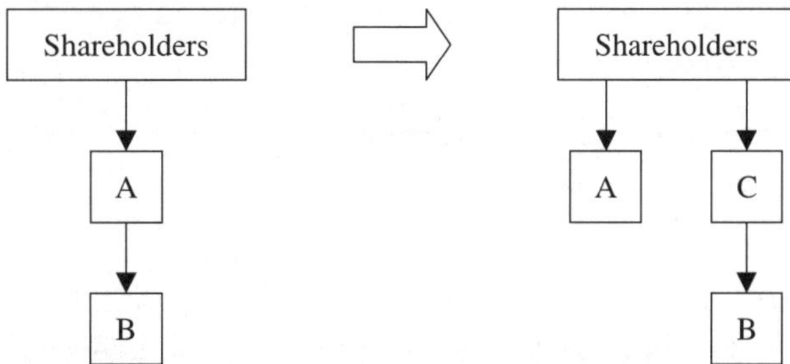

- Company A has effectively made a disposal of the shares in B to the shareholders of A which constitutes a dividend in specie.

Changing the rule book

- The first phase of the IASB's review of business combinations, IFRS 3, does not fully address reorganisations providing only limited direction on the treatment of reverse acquisitions.
- It is anticipated that reorganisations will be more fully addressed in Phase II.

Objective test questions

9.1 Tidal Inc has numerous wholly owned subsidiaries around the world. Two of these, X Ltd and Y Ltd, are based in the United Kingdom.

A decision has been taken to reorganise the group, and this is to be facilitated by X Ltd paying cash to Tidal Inc to purchase the entire share capital of Y Ltd. Given that these changes have no impact on the consolidated financial statements of Tidal Inc give three reasons why the reorganisation might be undertaken.

(3 marks)

9.2 With reference to the group reorganisation shown below, complete the following paragraph.

This result could be achieved by either B transferring its investment in C to A as a _____ [dividend in specie/bonus issue], or by A _____ [paying cash/issuing debt] to B in exchange for C. It _____ [is/is not] possible to effect the transfer by a share for share exchange.

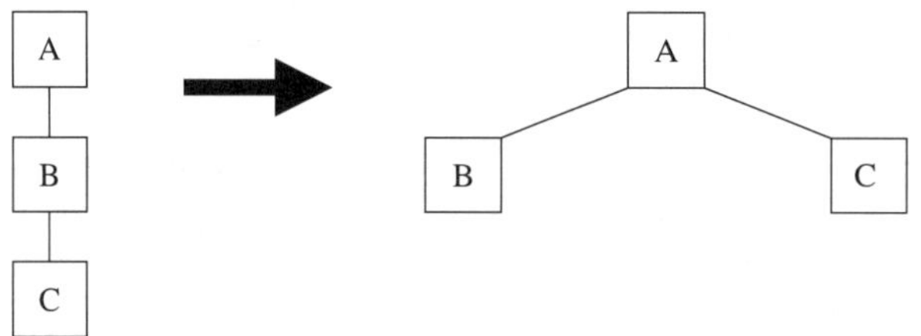

(3 marks)

9.3 Targa Ltd is the parent company for a small manufacturing group. After a very chequered history the company has started to expand rapidly and to help finance continued growth its management team has identified a flotation on a public exchange as a necessity. However, due to its earlier problems Targa Ltd is not perceived positively by some investor groups.

Suggest a possible group reconstruction that might help Targa Ltd achieve its ambition. [Maximum 50 words]

(2 marks)

9.4 B Ltd is a subsidiary of A Ltd. A new company, C Ltd is to be formed which will issue shares to the shareholders of A Ltd in exchange for A Ltd's investment in B Ltd. The balance sheets of the respective entities prior to this transaction were as follows

	A Ltd	*B Ltd*	*"A" Group*
	£'000	£'000	£'000
Investment in B Ltd	250	–	–
Other assets	600	400	1,000
	850	400	1,000
Share capital	500	250	500
Accumulated profits	250	150	400
	750	400	900
Liabilities	100		100
	850	400	1,000

If C Ltd issues 500 £1 ordinary shares to the shareholders of A Ltd in exchange for the shares in B Ltd held by A Ltd what is the value of the dividend in specie in the group financial statements and the individual books of A Ltd?

(2 marks)

9.5

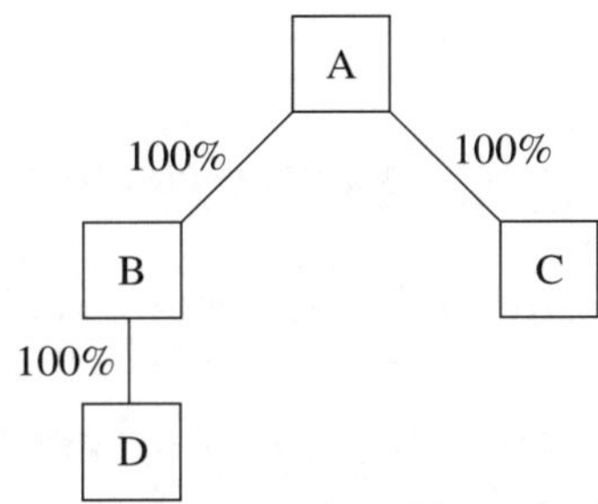

As part of a group reconstruction company D is to be 'sold' to company C. Using a maximum of 60 words outline a commercial reason for such a change, and state why the consideration will be in the form of cash/assets and not shares in company C.

(3 marks)

✓ Objective test answers

9.1

(i) The directors of Tidal Inc may want to create a sub-group that can be sold off as a separate economic entity.
(ii) X Ltd and Y Ltd will form a UK sub-group, which more readily takes advantage of local tax laws and so on.
(iii) A more hierarchical structure may be consistent with vertical operating relationships between group members.

9.2 This result could be achieved by either B transferring its investment in C to A as a dividend in specie, or by A paying cash to B in exchange for C. It is not possible to effect the transfer by a share for share exchange.

9.3 Targa Ltd could incorporate a new public limited company to act as the ultimate parent to the group, and hence as a vehicle for flotation. This would mean that Targa was no longer perceived as the lead company, and thereby this would reduce any negative market perceptions.

9.4 Dividend in specie

A Ltd = £500,000

Group = £400,000 (i.e. net assets).

9.5 A restructuring of this type is often a prelude to company B leaving the group (e.g. a streamlining of group activities). If the consideration was in shares there is a danger that Company C might become an associate or subsidiary of Company B; this would defeat the purpose of the reorganisation.

Medium answer questions

Question 1 – The ABC group

A Ltd acts as the ultimate parent company for a group that specialises in the production, assembly and sale of kitchen furniture. The original company was only involved in resale of furniture, but as it diversified into manufacture and assembly it incorporated new subsidiaries to have bespoke responsibility for each stage.

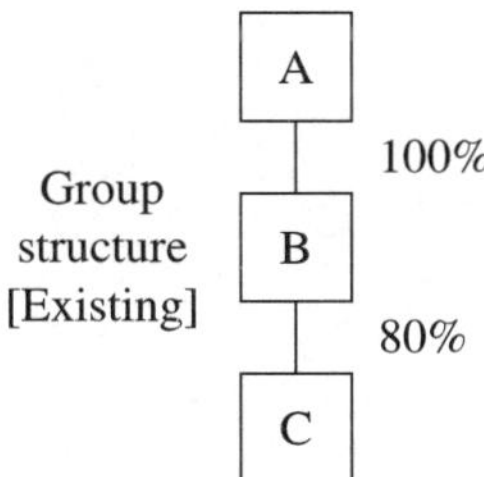

In recent years it has become less economic to manufacture the furniture components, and the senior management has decided they will attempt to sell C Ltd, and buy components from the Far East where the cost base is lower. To facilitate this process the group is to be restructured.

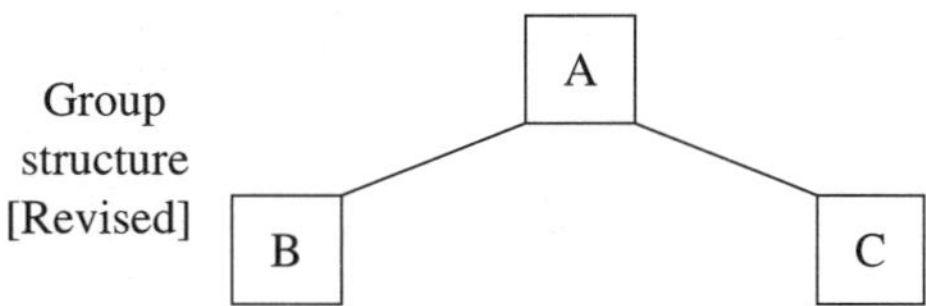

The balance sheet of each company immediately prior to the restructuring was as shown below

	A Ltd	*B Ltd*	*C Ltd*	*Group*
	£'000	£'000	£'000	£'000
Assets				
Non-current assets				
Property, plant and equipment	340	150	80	570
Investment in A [100,000 shares]	100	–	–	–
Investment in B [40,000 shares]	–	40	–	–
Current assets	50	40	30	120
Total assets	490	230	110	690
Equity and liabilities				
Capital and reserves				
Ordinary share capital [£1 shares]	100	100	50	100
Accumulated profits	330	110	50	480
	430	210	100	580
Minority interests				20
Current liabilities	60	20	10	90
	490	230	110	690

To facilitate the reconstruction, B Ltd is to make a dividend in specie, which will result in the shares of C Ltd being transferred to A Ltd.

Requirements

(a) Prepare the revised individual and group balance sheets immediately after the reconstruction and comment on the revised consolidated figures.

(8 marks)

(b) What action, if any, would need to have been taken prior to the reconstruction if the accumulated profits of B Ltd had been £30,000?

(2 marks)
(Total = 10 marks)

✓ Medium answer questions

Answer 1 – The ABC group

(a) Revised balance sheets

	A Ltd £'000	*B Ltd* £'000	*C Ltd* £'000	*Group* £'000
Assets				
Non-current assets				
Property, plant and equipment	340	150	80	570
Investment in A	100	–	–	–
Investment in B	40	–	–	–
Current assets	50	40	30	120
Total assets	530	190	110	690
Equity and liabilities				
Capital and reserves				
Ordinary share capital [£1 shares]	100	100	50	100
Accumulated profits	370	70	50	480
	470	170	100	580
Minority interests				20
Current liabilities	60	20	10	90
	530	190	110	690

The "new" consolidated balance sheet is identical to that prior to the reconstruction. This would be expected as the interests of parties external to the group have not been effected by changes internal to the single entity.

(b) The reduction in the reserves of B Ltd would present a difficulty as the dividend in specie exceeds the value on the reserves. This would imply a distribution being made out of funds that did not exist!

To overcome this problem B Ltd would have to undertake its own reconstruction prior to the dividend to "create" additional accumulated profits. This would normally require legal approval as it often involves reducing share capital which would normally act as the creditor's buffer.

However, such a reconstruction would be facilitated by A Ltd being the only shareholder, and the driving force behind the main reconstruction.

Foreign Currency Transactions 10

Functional and presentational currencies

- Functional currency – the currency of the primary economic environment in which the entity operates.
- To determine the functional currency consider factors such as
  - which currency principally influences selling prices of goods and services;
  - in which currency are the funds for financing activities generated; and
  - in which currency are receipts from operations generally kept.
- Presentational currency – the currency in which the financial statements are presented.
- The presentational currency is a currency of choice, and the management may elect for this to differ from the functional currency when the latter is relatively obscure or is different to that used by the principal investors.

An individual company's own foreign currency transactions

- Transactions should be translated using the spot rate.
- An average rate maybe used as an approximation.
- At the balance sheet date, monetary items should be retranslated to the closing rate.
- Non-monetary items should remain at their historic rate or the rate at the date on which they were revalued to fair value.

Translating foreign operations

- The basic rules are
  1. Assets and liabilities should be translated using the closing rate at the balance sheet date.
  2. Income and expenses should be translated at the exchange rate in force at the date of the transactions [or average for the period as an approximation].
  3. All resulting exchange differences are recognised as part of equity, until such time as the investment in the foreign operation is realised.
- Goodwill arising on consolidation should be treated as any other asset acquired and translated at the closing rate.
- Fair value adjustments should be translated at the closing rate.

Hedging

- The mitigation of foreign exchange exposure on a net investment in a foreign operation by use of a hedging instrument.
- The rules on the use of hedging are now covered by IAS 39 Financial Instruments: Recognition and Measurement.

? Objective test questions

10.1 The functional currency of an entity is the currency of the primary economic environment in which it operates.

Which of the following factors could be used as an indicator of the functional currency?

(i) The currency that mainly influences sales prices of goods and services.
(ii) The currency that mainly influences labour, material and other costs of providing goods and services.
(iii) The currency in which funds from financing activities are generated.

A (i) only
B (i) and (ii)
C (i) and (iii)
D All

(2 marks)

10.2 The concept of hedging is often differentiated from hedge accounting. Briefly explain what you understand to be the difference. [Maximum 100 words]

(3 marks)

10.3 Trent Ltd purchased goods on credit terms from a Spanish company on 1 August 20X4 for €2,000,000. On 31 December 20X4, Trent Ltd's financial year end, the liability payable had not yet been settled. The rates of exchange on the two dates were

1 August 20X4	£1 = €1.70
31 December 20X4	£1 = €1.60

How will the purchases and amount payable be shown in the 31 December 20X4 financial statements?

	Purchases	*Payables*
	€	€
A	1,176,471	1,176,471
B	1,176,471	1,250,000
C	1,250,000	1,176,471
D	1,250,000	1,250,000

(2 marks)

10.4 The finance department of Hercules Ltd is preparing the consolidated financial statements for the year ended 30 June 20X4. The group's principal subsidiary, Mellor Inc, was purchased on 1 April 20X2 and prepares its accounts in US dollars.

Mellor Inc has a strong management team who run the day-to-day operations of the business independently from the parent to whom they remit an annual dividend. Its functional currency is different to that of the parent.

Uncertainty exists as to the most appropriate rates of exchange to use in the translation of Mellor Inc'c accounts into sterling; particularly with reference to

- Property, plant and equipment
- Loans [loan agreement signed at 16 February 20X4]
- Goodwill.

The finance team has identified several possibilities

1 April 20X2	£1 = $1.45
16 February 20X4	£1 = $1.70
Average for year ended 30 June 20X4	£1 = $1.68
30 June 20X4	£1 = $1.8

State the rate to be used for each of the items specified, and a brief explanation for the choice made.

(3 marks)

10.5 Complete the following statement

When an entity initially records a foreign currency transaction in its own books it should apply the _____ [exchange rate at the date of the transaction/closing rate]; although it is common for the _____ [mid-point rate/average rate] to be used as an approximation.

At the subsequent balance sheet date the non-monetary items should _____ [be retranslated to the closing rate/remain at their historic rate], whereas monetary items will _____ [be retranslated at the closing rate/remain at their historic rate].

If a non-monetary asset is revalued to fair value the exchange rate applied should be that at _____ [the original purchase date/the date of the revaluation].

(3 marks)

10.6 Briefly describe how the nature of the relationship between a foreign operation and the reporting entity differs, dependent on the functional currencies used by each. [Maximum 80 words]

(3 marks)

10.7 Raphael DeCruz has been the finance director of a small manufacturing company for many years. Historically the company sourced its raw materials from suppliers local to its business, and also sold its finished product exclusively in the home market.

However, in the most recent accounting period, the company has tried to broaden its horizons to make a modest number of purchases from and sales to entities in neighbouring countries. To refamiliarise himself with the rules on translating foreign currency transactions for inclusion within the financial statements, Raphael has been reading the study texts of a new CIMA recruit, the company has recently employed.

Raphael is confused by a statement he has read that indicates there are two different occasions when a foreign exchange movement could arise on an individual credit trade sale or purchase could arise in the accounting period.

Explain to Raphael the two circumstances referred to in the study text, and why they give rise to exchange movements.

(4 marks)

10.8 When using a net investment hedge to mitigate exposure to foreign currency movements arising from a net investment in a foreign operation which of the following statements is true?

A The effective portion of the gain/loss on the hedging instrument is taken directly to the income statement.

B The effective portion of the gain/loss on the hedging instrument is taken directly to equity and has no impact on the income statement.

C The effective portion of the gain/loss on the hedging instrument is allocated against exchange movements in the individual assets/liabilities of the overseas entity.

D The effective portion of the gain/loss on the hedging instrument is taken to equity, and then recycled to the income statement when the net investment impacts profit or loss.

(2 marks)

Objective test answers

10.1 **D**

10.2 Hedging describes the commercial mitigation of risk by management. It covers a multitude of possibilities including the reduction of exposure to movements in foreign exchange rates, interest rate risk and credit risk.

Hedge accounting is the specific mechanics by which a hedge is reflected within the financial statements to the stakeholders. In the case of foreign exchange this includes the translation of a foreign investment at the period end to "crystallise" its exposure to exchange rate fluctuations, and allow them to be matched against corresponding fluctuations on the hedge instrument.

10.3 **C**

Monetary items must be retranslated to the rate at the balance sheet date.

10.4 All the items identified will be translated at the closing balance sheet rate. Mellor Inc. represents an investment to the holding company rather than an extension of its own operations, and hence both monetary (e.g. loan) and non-monetary items (e.g. property) will be translated at the closing rate.

IAS 21 requires the goodwill arising on consolidation to be treated as an asset like any other.

10.5 When an entity initially records a foreign currency transaction in its own books, it should apply the exchange rate at the date of the transaction; although it is common for the average rate to be used as an approximation.

At the subsequent balance sheet date, the non-monetary items should remain at their historic rate, whereas monetary items will be retranslated at the closing rate.

If a non-monetary asset is revalued to fair value the exchange rate applied should be that at the date of the revaluation.

10.6 If the reporting entity and the overseas operation have the same functional currency then the latter should be perceived as an extension of the reporting entity's operations.

By contrast when the functional currencies differ, the foreign operation will be perceived as semi-autonomous and viewed in its entirety as an investment. Typically such operations accumulate cash and other monetary items and arrange borrowings in their own local currency.

10.7 Individual entity exchange movements

Situation 1 – If a credit sale or purchase is both originated and settled within the same accounting period it is probable that the exchange rates at the two dates will be different; thereby giving an exchange gain/loss on settlement.

Situation 2 – Some credit transactions will remain unsettled at the balance sheet date. The payable or receivable outstanding in the balance sheet represents a monetary item, and the best reflection of its current value is given by the exchange rate applicable at the balance sheet date. Consequently, monetary items are retransalated to the closing rate at the balance sheet date creating an exchange movement.

10.8 **D**

Medium answer questions

Question 1 – Sizewell Ltd

Sizewell Ltd trades in the UK, and on 1 January 20X4 it acquired a subsidiary, Trent GmbH, in Germany. The balance sheets of the two companies as at 31 December 20X4 were as follows

	Sizewell Ltd		*Trent GmbH*	
	£'000	£'000	€'000	€'000
Assets				
Non-current assets				
Property, plant and equipment		150		25
Investment in Trent Gmbh		70		–
		220		25
Current assets				
Inventory	80		17	
Receivables	24		10	
Cash	36		2	
		140		29
Total assets		360		54
Equity and liabilities				
Capital and reserves				
Ordinary share capital		100		20
Accumulated profits		210		20
		310		40
Non-current liabilities				
Loan		30		5
Current liabilities				
Trade payables		20		9
		360		54

Further information:

- At the date of acquisition the accumulated profits of Trent GbmH were €10,000.
- Sizewell Ltd acquired 80% of the share capital of Trent GbmH.
- Trent GbmH has retained control over its day-to-day operations with Sizewell Ltd deliberately adopting a hands-off approach.
- A range of exchange rates are available:

1 January 20X4	£1 = €1.8
Average for 20X4	£1 = €1.64
31 December 20X4	£1 = €1.6

Requirements

(a) Prepare the consolidated balance sheet of Sizewell Ltd for the year ended 31 December 20X4.

(9 marks)

(b) Briefly explain the selection of the rate of exchange used for the translation of goodwill.

(1 mark)

(Total = 10 marks)

✓ Medium answer questions

Answer 1 – Sizewell Ltd

(a) Consolidated balance sheet as at 31 December 20X4

	£'000	£'000
Assets		
Non-current assets		
Property, plant and equipment		165.625
Intangibles [W1]		63.75
		229.375
Current assets		
Inventory	90.625	
Receivables	30.25	
Cash	37.25	
		158.125
Total assets		387.5
Equity and liabilities		
Capital and reserves		
Ordinary share capital		100
Accumulated profits [W4]		223.75
		323.75
Minority interests [W2 and W3]		5
		328.75
Non-current liabilities		
Loan		33.125
Current liabilities		
Trade payables		25.625
		387.5

W1:

Goodwill

	'000	'000
Cost of investment [70 × €1.8]		126
Share capital at acquisition	20	
Reserves at acquisition	10	
	30	
80% stake		(24)
		102
Translated at the closing rate [£1 = €1.6]		€63.75

W2:

Translation of Trent GbmH balance sheet

	Trent GmbH			
	€'000	Rate [£1 =]	£'000	£'000
Assets				
Non-current assets				
Property, plant and equipment	25	1.6		15.625
				15.625
Current assets				
Inventory	17	1.6	10.625	
Receivables	10	1.6	6.25	
Cash	2	1.6	1.25	
				18.125
Total assets	54			33.75
Equity and liabilities				
Capital and reserves				
Ordinary share capital	20	1.8		11.111
Accumulated profits: Pre-acq.	10	1.8		5.555
Accumulated profits: Post-acq.	10	Bal fig		8.334
				25
Non-current liabilities				
Loan	5	1.6		3.125
Current liabilities				
Trade payables	9	1.6		5.625
	54			33.75

W3:

Minority interest

20% × €25,000 = €5,000

W4:

Consolidated accumulated profits

	£'000
Sizewell Ltd	210
Trent GbmH [80% × 8.334]	6.667
Goodwill exchange gain [W5]	7.083
	223.75

There was no indication of a goodwill impairment since acquisition.

W5:

Gain for the year on the retranslation of goodwill

	£'000
Goodwill at start of period [€102,000/1.8]	(56.667)
Goodwill at end of period [€102,000/1.6]	63.75
	7.083

(b) Selection of exchange rate for the translation of goodwill

Goodwill arising on the acquisition of a subsidiary undertaking should be treated as an investment by the reporting entity in an asset. Consequently it should be translated at the closing rate to be consistent with this designation.

Cash Flow Statements

11

The big picture

- Cash generation is the key to corporate survival, and hence cash flows are often seen as a benchmark for the quality of profit.
- Cash-rich profits help ensure the going concern status of an entity does not come under threat.

The basics

- The standard headings under which cash flows are reported are
  - operating activities
  - investing activities
  - financing activities
  - net change in cash and cash equivalents for the period.
- Cash comprises cash in hand and demand deposits.
- Cash equivalents are short term, highly liquid investments that are readily convertible into known amounts of cash and which are subject to an insignificant risk of changes in value.
- Calculating operating cash flows:

DIRECT METHOD	INDIRECT METHOD
Records major classes of gross operating cash receipts and payments	Adjusts net profit or loss to remove effect of non-cash items

Group issues

- Consistent with the consolidated income statement and balance sheet, the consolidated cash flow must reflect only those cash flows that are external to the group.
- Dividends paid to minority interests should be disclosed within cash flows from operating activities.

- Dividends received from associates should be shown within investing activities.
- When an investment is acquired during the financial period only post-acquisition cash flows should be shown in the cash-flow statement.
- Cash expensed in the purchase of an investment should be netted against cash and overdrafts in the books of the investment at the acquisition date and the net figure shown within investing activities.
- When a new investment is acquired do not double count the cash flows relating to items already reflected in the books of the subsidiary at the purchase date (this is not an issue for associates and trade investments as they are not consolidated on a line-by-line basis).
- When the financial data of the investment has to be translated from a foreign currency, the exchange differences arising do not constitute cash flows and will need to be taken into consideration when identifying the "pure" cash flows to be included in the cash-flow statement.

? Objective test questions

11.1 The following information is available from Flame Ltd's consolidated balance sheets at the start and end of the accounting period

	At 1 January 20X1 £'000	*At 31 December 20X1* £'000
Inventory	300	280
Trade receivables	120	130
Trade payables	(170)	(130)

During the accounting period the company purchased a 100% stake in Match Ltd. Included in the balance sheet of this new subsidiary at the date of acquisition were the following

	At acquisition £'000
Inventory	25
Trade receivables	5
Trade payables	(30)

What is the overall working capital adjustment to operating profit to identify operating cash flows?

A £30,000 decrease
B £30,000 increase
C £70,000 decrease
D £80,000 decrease

(3 marks)

11.2 If an entity is financed by a five-year bank loan repayable in annual instalments, what is the most appropriate treatment of each payment in the cash-flow statement? [Maximum 40 words]

(2 marks)

11.3 Your client, Radar plc, is in the process of completing its year-end financial statements. During this process they have encountered problems with the classification of items within the cash-flow statement. In particular they have asked you to identify which of the following would normally be considered as financing cash flows.

(i) Cash proceeds from the issue of shares.
(ii) Cash receipts from the sale of property, plant and equipment.
(iii) Cash proceeds from issuing debentures.
(iv) Cash receipts from the sale of goods.
(v) Cash receipts from the repayment of loans made to other parties.
(vi) Cash receipts from royalties.

A (i) and (iii)
B (i) and (v)
C (i), (ii), (iii) and (v)
D (i), (ii), (iii), (iv), (v) and (vi)

(2 marks)

11.4 Nail plc has two subsidiary undertakings

- Cube Ltd – purchased in 20X2
- Paral Ltd – purchased on 30 September 20X4

The trade receivable figures of the three companies were

	31 December 20X3	*30 September 20X4*	*31 December 20X4*
	£'000	£'000	£'000
Nail plc	3,000	2,800	2,450
Cube Ltd	800	820	890
Paral Ltd	200	190	210

The consolidated financial statements are prepared using acquisition accounting.

The consolidated cash-flow statement for the year ended 31 December 20X4 would show the decrease in receivables as

A £60,000
B £250,000
C £440,000
D £640,000

(2 marks)

11.5 Outline the way in which the direct method of reporting net cash flows from operating activities differs from the indirect method. [80 words maximum]

(2 marks)

11.6 The finance manager of GHJ plc is close to completing the year end financial statements for the group but is uncertain about the treatment of the group's associate, Athlone Ltd, in the consolidated cash-flow statement. He has emailed you asking for assistance.

Extracts of the email are shown below

I have completed this year's consolidated balance sheet for the year ended 30 June 20X4 and relevant extracts (including comparatives) are

	20X3	*20X4*
	£m	£m
Investment in Athlone Ltd	950	965
Dividends receivable from Athlone Ltd	25	30

Athlone Ltd has a profit before taxation of £70m as per its financial statements and taxation of £10m.

As you are aware we have held a 40% investment in the ordinary shares of this company for many years.

What is the amount to be shown in the consolidated cash-flow statement for the associate?

(3 marks)

11.7 The following information is available for TYU Group with reference to the year ended 31 December 20X4

- During the period, a provision for a specific receivable balance was increased by £10,000.
- Depreciation on non-current assets for the period was £55,000.
- Several pieces of plant and equipment were disposed during the year at a loss of £1,000. The loss had been included in cost of sales and no adjustment to classification was being considered due to the low value.
- Working capital movements

	20X4	*20X3*
	£'000	£'000
Inventory	120	130
Trade receivables	105	100
Trade payables	80	95
Cash	19	23

Based on the above details, what is the operating cash flow to be shown in the consolidated cash-flow statement if the operating profit for the year ended 31 December 20X4 was £250,000?

(3 marks)

11.8 During the year ended 30 September 20X4 the Sherpa Group disposed of its 70% investment in Peak Ltd, but retained several other subsidiary investments.

In the closing balance sheet there was property, plant and equipment with a net book value of £500,000 (2003: £470,000), and reference to the asset register revealed that disposals of assets from the parent company costing £70,000 had been made in the period. The accounting policy for depreciation is to charge a full year in the year of acquisition and nothing in the year of disposal. The assets disposed had a ten-year life and were eight years old at the start of the current accounting period.

Extracts from the books of Peak Ltd also revealed the net book value of its non-current assets at various dates throughout the period.

	1 October 20X3	*Disposal date*	*30 September 20X4*
	£'000	£'000	£'000
Net book value	70	75	68

If the Sherpa Group's annual depreciation charge had been calculated at £40,000, what was the value of cash purchases of non-current assets in the period (you may assume that no credit purchases were made).

A £159,000
B £103,000
C £219,000
D £163,000

(2 marks)

✓ Objective test answers

11.1 **A**

For example Inventory – The fall in inventory over the accounting period represents a cash increase of £20,000, but the subsidiary has already paid for the £25,000 inventory in its balance sheet at the date of acquisition, and hence the total adjustment for inventory is an increase of £45,000.

A similar process is adopted for trade receivables and trade payables; these decrease by £5,000 and £70,000, respectively.

11.2 Loan repayments

Although each payment is a single transaction it contains both an interest and a capital element. The former would usually be classified as an operating cash flow whereas the latter would be shown as a financing activity.

11.3 **A**

11.4 **C**

	£'000
Consolidated receivables at 31 December 20X4 [2,450 + 890 + 210]	3,550
Consolidated receivables at 1 January 20X4 [3,000 + 800]	3,800
	(250)
Adjustment for receivables of Paral Ltd at 30 September 20X4	(190)
	(440)

11.5 Direct method – This discloses operating cash receipts and payments including

- cash receipts from customers
- cash payments to suppliers
- cash payments to and on behalf of employees.

These amounts are then aggregated to give the net cash flow.

Indirect method – This starts with the profit before taxation and adjusts for non-cash charges, such as depreciation.

11.6 Dividends received from the associate during the accounting period are £4m.

	£m		£m
Balance b/f	950		
	25	Cash received	4
Share of PBT [40% × 70]	28	Share of tax [40% × 10]	4
		Balances c/f	965
			30
	1,003		1,003

11.7 Operating cash flow

	£'000
Operating profit	250
Increase in provision	10
Depreciation	55
Loss on disposal	1
Decrease in inventory	10
Increase in receivables	(5)
Decrease in payables	(15)
	306

11.8 **A**

	£'000		£'000
Balance b/f	470	Parent disposals (NBV)	14
Additions (bal.)	159	Depreciation charge	40
		Disposal of Peak Ltd	75
		Balances c/f	500
	629		629

? Medium answer questions

Question 1 – Understanding cash flows

(a) IAS 7 *cash-flow statements* requires that this statement gives the users of financial statements a clear understanding of the movements in cash and cash equivalents over the accounting period. Cash includes not only cash but demand deposits and overdrafts.

What are the features of a cash equivalent?

(2 marks)

(b) The inclusion of a cash-flow statement within published financial statements is often said to give the user a clearer picture as to the quality of profits.

Outline your understanding of this statement.

(4 marks)

(c) WER plc acquired Loren Ltd for $21,500,000 during 20X4. The consideration comprised 3 million 25c shares with a market value of $4 each with the balance in cash.

The net assets of Loren Ltd on acquisition were as follows.

	$'000
Tangible non-current assets	14,500
Current asset investments (>3 months to maturity)	27
Inventories	7,222
Receivables	9,999
Cash at bank and in hand	458
Payables	(16,343)
Bank overdrafts	(4,234)
Loans	(1,000)
Deferred taxation	(333)
Minority shareholders' interests	(16)
	10,280

Describe the impact the acquisition will have on the consolidated cash-flow statement of WER plc for the year ended 31 December 20X4; illustrating your answer with figures where appropriate.

(4 marks)
(Total = 10 marks)

Question 2 – Grime Ltd

Cash-flow statement for the year ended 31 December 20X4

	€m	€m
Cash flows from operating activities		
Profit before taxation	150	
Adjustments for:		
Investment income	(6)	
Interest expense	9	
Depreciation of PPE	45	
Loss on sale of PPE	10	
Amortisation of intangible non-current assets	39	
Operating profit before working capital changes	97	
(Increase) decrease in inventories	(58)	
(Increase) decrease in receivables	(101)	
Increase (decrease) in payables	49	
Cash generated from operations	(110)	
Interest paid	(9)	
Income taxes paid	(132)	
	(141)	
Net cash from operating activities		(4)
Cash flows from investing activities		
Purchase of PPE	(89)	
Purchase of non-current investments	(4)	
Proceeds from sale of PPE	111	
Dividends received	21	
Interest received	5	
Receipt of government grants	1	
Net cash (used in)/from investing activities		45
Cash flows from financing activities		
Proceeds from issue of share capital	100	
Proceeds from issue of long-term borrowings	50	
Payment of finance lease liabilities	(17)	
Dividends paid	(100)	
Net cash (used in)/from financing activities		33
Net increase in cash and cash equivalents		74
Cash and cash equivalents at beginning of period		369
Cash and cash equivalents at end of period		443

Grime Ltd is an established manufacturing company operating within a mature market, and has been struggling to increase its market share. After much deliberation and protracted discussions with a local venture capital company it has been decided that the acquisition of a competitor is the only way to effect change.

The preparations for a bid have been extensive and as part of this the finance director, Shazeed Zaman, has been refreshing his memory on group accounting issues as this would be the first occasion on which Grime Ltd would need to produce consolidated figures.

Requirements

(a) The venture capital company have been very cautious about the level of funding they are prepared to inject into Grime Ltd. They have just received the latest cash-flow statement for the year ended 31 December 20X4 (as shown above), and have immediately requested a meeting with the Board. This has surprised the Grime Ltd management team as they had assumed that an overall positive cash flow would be favourably received.

From a review of the cash-flow statement identify potential issues that the venture capitalist might want to discuss before proceeding with their investment.

(4 marks)

(b) Shazeed has delegated several tasks relating to the bid to his accounts team asking them to leave him a list of any issues requiring his personal attention so that he can address them between meetings. Two items on the list read:

1 If the bid is not successful and Grime Ltd continues to trade as normal my projections show that trade payables will decline by €25,000 over the next accounting period. However, following your guidance to assume that the target company has trade payables of €30,000 at acquisition and for the foreseeable future I have estimated the group payables (ignoring any intra-group transactions) would show a net increase of €5,000. This is consistent with your projected balance sheet figures, but the projected cash flow still shows a decline?

2 My understanding of the bid deal is that we will acquire an 80% stake. How should this be tackled in the projected cash-flow figures?

(4 marks)

(c) You have just received an email from the Managing Director of Grime Ltd extracts of which are shown below:

> As you know this is a frantic time for all of the management team and Shazeed is understandably looking stressed. I do not want to add to his burden, but have spotted something strange in the latest published financial statements of our target company; hopefully you could provide some clarification.
>
> Their cash-flow statement shows that interest paid was €34,000 and yet only €7,000 is shown as an expense in the income statement. What is going on, and should I be worried about this?

Briefly respond to the query raised.

(2 marks)
(Total = 10 marks)

✓ Medium answer questions

Answer 1 – Understanding cash flows

(a) Cash equivalents

A cash equivalent is a short term, highly liquid investment that is readily convertible into known amounts of cash, and which is subject to an insignificant risk of changes in value.

Normally cash equivalents have a short maturity of three months or less from the date of their acquisition. If the maturity period was longer it would be hard to state that the investment was exposed to an insignificant risk of changes in value.

Various investments can potentially meet the definition of a cash equivalent including short-term gilts and short-term corporate bonds.

(b) The quality of profits

It is rare for an entity that generates positive cash flows to be threatened with going concern risks even if it is making accounting losses, whereas a profitable entity that does not have strong controls over cash management could face disaster. The ideal for a successful business is that it makes cash rich profits, and for this reason cash flows are often seen as a measure of the quality of profits.

Let us consider the example of an entity that is overtrading:

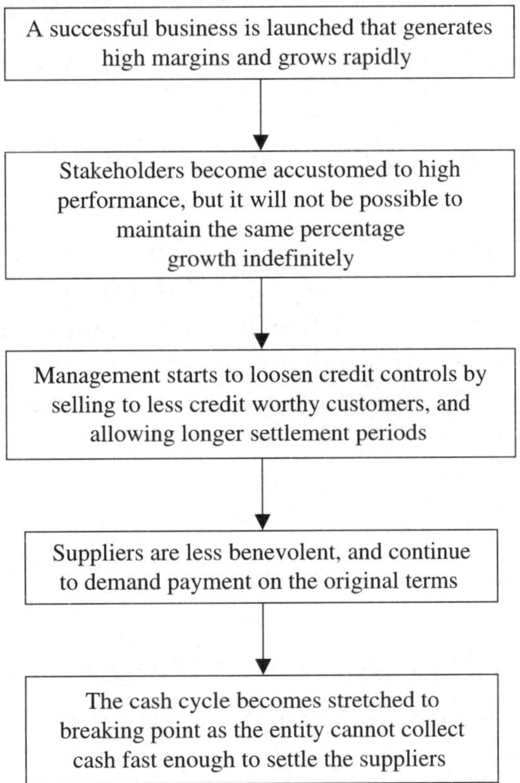

The cash-flow statement discloses the cash movements of the business attributable to operating, investing and financing activities. It is operating cash flows that are most typically associated with the quality of profit as they reflect the efficiency of the working capital cycle.

Good cash management is also a reflection of corporate governance, and hence the quality of the management team, and not just the profits their company produces.

(c) WER plc

The consideration given for the acquisition of Loren Ltd comprises $12,000,000 in equity with the balance ($9,500,000) in cash. However, part of the net assets acquired comprises cash balances comprising $458,000 cash at bank and $4,234,000 overdrafts, and these need to be netted against the cash consideration given, and the resultant figure shown within the investing activities section of the cash-flow statement.

	$'000
Cash consideration	(9,500)
Cash at bank and in hand	458
Overdrafts	(4,234)
	(13,276)

Based on the information available the current asset investments would not be included as cash equivalents as they have more than three months to maturity.

IAS 7 requires further information to be disclosed relating to the acquisition; primarily

- the total acquisition consideration ($21,500,000)
- the amount of the acquisition consideration that comprises cash ($9,500,000) or cash equivalents
- the amount of cash and cash equivalents in the subsidiary transferred as a result of the acquisition
- the assets and liabilities of the subsidiary, other than cash and cash equivalents, acquired.

As a result of the acquisition it is also important that cash flows are not double counted.

For example, it is Loren Ltd that had purchased the inventory of $7,222,000 in its books at the date of acquisition. As a consequence of this the cash balances of the subsidiary are already reduced, and these have then been incorporated into the consolidated cash-flow statement as detailed above. Hence, if the inventory of the WER plc group has increased by $10,000,000 (say) the movement shown in the cash-flow statement would be a $2,778,000 outflow as $7,222,000 is already reflected in the cash flows of Loren Ltd at the date of its acquisition.

Answer 2 – Grime Ltd

(a) Issues arising from a review of the cash-flow statement

Operating activities show a net cash outflow: Working capital management would be of particular concern

- Grime Ltd has been struggling to grow and operates within a mature market. Unless it has cut selling prices to encourage a greater volume of sales there would appear no reason to substantially increase inventories.
- A dramatic increase in receivables suggests poor credit control procedures and may call into question the governance capabilities of the management team.

- Rising trade payables suggests these are being used for short-term funding. This might improve cash flow now but cannot be used indefinitely and conceals poor operating cash-flow management.

One off cash flows: Extensive sales of non-current assets and issues of both debt and equity have given the business positive cash flows. However, the assets are being sold at a loss, and to some extent being replaced suggesting obsolete or outdated equipment rather than excess.

The issue of both shares and debt lessens the scope for future finance injections and would make the venture capitalists nervous about the security of their own return.

Dividend levels: It is unclear as to who are the shareholders of the company, but it is not possible to support high revenue returns on investments and capital expansion at the same time.

Taxation: The tax cash burden seems very high compared to the profits being generated. This would need further investigation.

(b) Matters for the finance director's attention

1 Impact of the acquisition on trade payables

If the projections are correct then the trade payables in the consolidated balance sheet will increase by €5,000 compared to the current position. However, the €30,000 of trade payables in the books of the target company at acquisition form part of its working capital at that date, and hence will already be reflected in its cash balances. The latter will be "acquired" by Grime Ltd as part of the net assets for which it has given consideration. It is important that double counting of cash flows is avoided and hence this €30,000 must be stripped out of the trade payables when calculating the cash flows.

Consequently the consolidated cash-flow statement will show a cash outflow of €25,000 relating to trade payables.

2 80% stake

The 80% stake would give Grime Ltd control over its target company, and hence consolidated financial statements would be prepared using acquisition accounting. To reflect this control the total cash flows of the two companies will be combined.

The dividends paid to minority interest during the period will be shown within operating cash flows.

(c) Query from the Managing Director

The cash-flow statement is often said to be a measure of the quality of profits. The discrepancy noticed by the Managing Director indicates that the company in question is capitalising nearly 80% of the interest cost it incurs, and holding it within the balance sheet. However, the cash flow shows the reality of the amounts being paid.

The capitalisation of interest is allowed under some circumstances such as the finance costs of a construction project, but this would need further investigation to ensure that the concept of prudence was being applied.

Financial Instruments: Disclosure and Presentation

12

Core definitions

- Financial instrument – any contract that gives rise to both a financial asset of one entity and a financial liability or equity instrument of another entity.

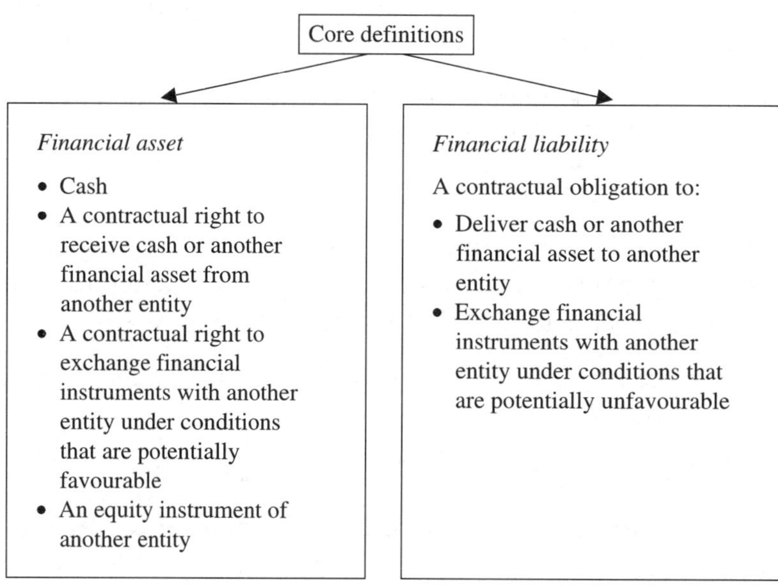

- Equity instrument – any contract that evidences a residual interest in the assets of an entity after deducting all of its liabilities.
- Financial instruments not captured under the remit of IAS 32 are:
  - interests in subsidiaries
  - interests in associates and joint ventures
  - employee benefit plans
  - obligations arising under insurance contracts.

Manipulation of gearing

$$\text{Manipulation of gearing} = \frac{\text{Total long-term debt}}{\text{Shareholders' funds plus long-term debt}}$$

- Gearing is a key indicator of the risk levels within a business.
- Many complex financial instruments have features of both debt and equity and hence can be used for creative accounting.
- There are many potentially dubious strategies available to the management of a business to reduce debt or increase equity, for example,
  - Special purpose entities
  - Revaluation of assets
  - Inclusion of intangibles within non-current assets
  - Sale and leaseback.

IAS 32 rules

- When a financial instrument is issued the issuer must designate its classification as either a liability or equity.
- The classification principles are:
  - Substance prevails over legal form.
  - Where there is a contractual obligation, potentially unfavourable to the issue of the instrument, to deliver either cash or another financial asset to the holder of the instrument, the instrument meets the definition of a financial liability.
  - Where a financial instrument does not give rise to a contractual obligation under potentially unfavourable conditions, then the instrument is classified as equity.
  - Where there is a requirement for mandatory redemption of the instrument by the issuer at a fixed or determinable future date, the instrument meets the definition of a financial liability.

Specific examples of financial instruments and their treatment

Warrants and options	equity;
Perpetual debt	debt;
Redeemable preferred shares	debt unless redemption is solely at the option of the issuer when they are closer to equity;
Non-redeemable preferred shares	if distributions are at the discretion of the issuer then these are likely to be classified as equity, but when the distribution is mandatory the instrument is more akin to debt;
Convertible securities with options	these often contain a put option that allows the holders of the debt to require redemption at a premium, and consequently they often carry a low rate of interest to balance the high premium;

Financial instruments with contingent settlement	as redemption is dependent on the occurrence of an uncertain future event the instrument should be classified as debt;
Zero coupon bonds	debt;
Hybrid instruments	separate the debt and equity components.

- The determination of the debt/equity status of a financial instrument has a knock-on effect for the treatment of cash flows arising from it (i.e. interest via the income statement or dividends via the statement of changes in equity).

IAS 32 disclosures

- The standard aims to ensure that users of the financial statements understand the risk exposure created by financial instruments
  - Market risk
  - Credit risk
  - Liquidity risk
  - Cash flow interest rate risk.
- The disclosures given must include:
  - Risk management policies and hedging activities
  - Terms, conditions and accounting policies
  - Interest rate risk
  - Credit risk
  - Fair value.

The Future

- ED7 Financial instrument disclosures
- Will ultimately replace IAS 32 and IAS 30 Disclosures in the financial statements of banks and similar financial institutions.

Objective test questions

12.1 IAS 32 Financial Instruments: Disclosure and Presentation identifies four types of risk; namely market risk, credit risk, liquidity risk and cash flow interest rate risk. The standard requires extensive disclosures of these risks to assist financial users in assessing their impact.

Describe what you understand by the term market risk. [Maximum 100 words]

(3 marks)

12.2 Helviticus plc has recently added to its portfolio of investments by purchasing £72 million of 3% Fixed Rate Eurobonds issued by Berlin City Council. The investment is held at cost, but at the balance sheet date the value of the Euro had strengthened by 10% compared to the Euro:Sterling exchange rate at the date of purchase. Interest rates in the Euro Zone are 1% higher than the rate on the bonds.

What are the financial risks to which Helviticus plc is exposed as a result of this investment?

(3 marks)

12.3 IAS 32 Financial Instruments: Disclosure and Presentation stipulates minimum disclosure requirements. Which of the following are principal areas of disclosure under this Standard?

(i) Risk management
(ii) Fair value
(iii) Hedging activities
(iv) Terms, conditions and accounting policies
(v) Credit risk
(vi) Interest rate risk

A (ii), (v) and (vi)
B (i), (iii), (v) and (vi)
C (i), (iii), (iv), (v) and (vi)
D All

(2 marks)

12.4 When is the offset of financial asset and a financial liability, such that the net amount is presented on the balance sheet, allowed under IAS 32 Financial Instruments: Disclosure and Presentation?

(2 marks)

12.5 John Bergin has just started a new job as financial controller for a company that regularly trades in financial instruments. He is aware that you have studied this area and has asked you to clarify in simple terms why derivatives represent a particular challenge to accountants.

(3 marks)

12.6 Wreak Ltd issues 3,000, 4% convertible bonds on 1 January 20X4. The bonds have a four year term and were issued at a par value of £1,000 to give total proceeds of £3,000,000.

Other relevant information includes:

- At any point during the four year period each bond can be converted into 500 ordinary shares.
- The interest rate for equivalent non-convertible bonds issued on 1 January 20X4 was 8%.
- Interest is paid in arrears.

Applying the concept of split accounting what amount of the £3,000,000 proceeds would be recorded as equity?

(4 marks)

12.7 Rempton plc has extensive bank borrowings which are secured on several of its properties. The bank has also asked for covenants based on the financial statements one of which prohibits the company from allowing its gearing to deteriorate beyond a specified level.

In recent months the company has encountered some difficult trading conditions and is aware that it is in danger of breaching the banks' gearing covenant; although the balance sheet is not fundamentally weak. To address this situation the management team is reviewing the business to ascertain ways in which the gearing could be improved. Which of the following suggestions would not achieve the desired objective?

[*Note*: It is possible that some of the suggestions would be classed as creative accounting, but you are not being asked to question their validity only their effectiveness.]

A Revaluation of non-current assets.
B Switching from finance leases to operating leases.
C Using a special purpose entity (SPE) as a separate vehicle to "hold" the company's debt.
D Excluding intangibles such as patents from the balance sheet.

(2 marks)

12.8 Using the relevant items from the list below complete the table looking at the attributes of equity and debt:

- Repayment of capital
- Dividend
- Residual
- Appropriation
- Preferential
- Interest
- Legal ownership of entity.

	Equity	*Debt*
Return on investment		
Rights conveyed		
Interest on winding up the business		

(2 marks)

Objective test answers

12.1 Market risk comprises:

- *Currency risk* – the risk that the value of a financial instrument will fluctuate because of changes in foreign currency exchange rates.
- *Fair value interest rate risk* – the risk that the value of a financial instrument will fluctuate because of changes in market interest rates.
- *Price risk* – the risk that the value of a financial instrument will fluctuate as a result in market prices, whether those changes are caused by factors specific to the individual instrument or its issuer or factors affecting all instruments traded in the market.

12.2 The bond generates no cash-flow risk as the income is measured in Euros and is fixed irrespective of what happens to the market, but there is exposure to currency risks as the Euro:Sterling exchange rates move.

However, the fixed interest rate does create interest price risk as the price of the bonds will fall as market interest rates rise and vice versa. This will occur as investors strive to maintain their effective return.

Although Berlin city council could technically default on the bonds' the probability of this is very small and hence credit risk will be minor.

12.3 **D**

12.4 Offset of a financial asset and a financial liability is allowed only when two conditions have been met:

(i) There is a legal right of set off.
(ii) The entity intends to settle on a net basis, or to rely on the asset and settle the liability simultaneously.

12.5 A derivative is simply a financial instrument derived from an underlying asset or stock, often referred to as "the underlying". They can generate returns far in excess of that obtained by more conventional means, but also expose the entity to considerable risk. [A more formal definition of a derivative will be found in IAS 39 – see Chapter 13]

Many derivatives (e.g. interest rate swaps) may have no current value and/or conceal substantial unrealised gains and losses. The challenge for accounting has been to create standards that ensure there is sufficient disclosure of the risks, and which provide a mechanism by which derivatives can be measured to facilitate recognition in the financial statements.

12.6 The equity component is £397,457

Derived by:

	£
Present value of the principle (3,000,000) payable at the end of 4 years	2,205,090
Present value of interest (£120,000 per annum) payable annually in arrears for four years	397,453
Total liability component	2,602,543
Equity component (by deduction)	397,457
	3,000,000

12.7 **D**

12.8

	Equity	*Debt*
Return on investment	Dividends	Interest
Rights conveyed	Legal ownership of the entity	Repayment of capital
Interest on winding up the business	Residual	Preferential

Medium answer questions

Question 1 – PQR plc

(a) IAS 32 Financial Instruments: Disclosure and Presentation is often referred to as a specialised accounting standard that has little meaning for the average company. However, the engine room of the standard is centred around the identification and disclosure of financial risks, and this extends to a much wider audience than large financial organisations with large derivative portfolios.

Illustrate the validity of this statement in the context of the outline balance sheet for PQR plc shown below.

PQR plc		
	€m	€m
Assets		
Non-current assets		
Property, plant and equipment		620
Current assets		
Inventory	101	
Receivables	62	
		163
Total assets		783
Equity and liabilities		
Capital and reserves		
Ordinary share capital		100
Accumulated profits		459
		559
Non-current liabilities		
Debentures	60	
7% redeemable preference shares	45	105
Current liabilities		
Overdraft	88	
Trade payables	31	119
		783

(8 marks)

Further information:

- Property, plant and equipment comprises assets used exclusively to maintain the operational capacity of the business.
- The debentures carry a floating rate of interest calculated on the base rate stipulated by the European central bank plus 1%, and are repayable in three years.

(b) Cash is recognised as a traditional asset in the balance sheet of an entity, but does it constitute a financial asset as specified by IAS 32?

Briefly comment.

(2 marks)
(Total = 10 marks)

✓ Medium answer questions

Answer 1 – PQR plc

(a) Applying IAS 32 Financial Instruments: Disclosure and Presentation

IAS 32 has potential repercussions for many of the items recognised with the financial statements of an entity. This can be demonstrated by considering the balance sheet of PQR plc.

Property, plant and equipment – All of these assets are used to maintain operational capacity and hence are not held for resale. Consequently there are no financial risks associated with them. However, financial risk would exist had they included assets such as investment properties.

Inventory – Outside the scope of IAS 32.

Receivables and payables – These represent financial assets and financial liabilities as defined by IAS 32. However, although they carry credit risk and liquidity risk respectively it is rare that any specific risk disclosures are required. Most stakeholders who use financial statements would be fully conversant with these risks in the context of these items.

Ordinary share capital – Equity does not bear financial risk as there is no obligation for it to be repaid.

Equity reserves – As for ordinary share capital. The payment of dividends does not represent a cash flow risk as there is no obligation on the issuer to pay them.

Debentures – The obligation to repay the debenture in three years creates a liquidity risk, but there is also a cash flow risk arising from the payment of interest. The latter creates a risk as these are floating rate debentures and hence the amount to be paid out in future years is not known.

Redeemable preference shares – Unlike the debentures these do not carry a cash flow risk as the rate of return is fixed, but this feature does generate market risk as fluctuations in market rates of return cause the price of the financial instrument to rise or fall.

Overdraft – Most overdrafts are subject to variable rates of interest, and are repayable on demand. Consequently both cash flow risk and liquidity risk disclosures are likely to be appropriate.

(b) Cash

Cash is a financial asset as defined by IAS 32 because it represents the medium of exchange and is therefore the basis on which all transactions are measured and recognised in financial statements.

A deposit of cash with a bank is a financial asset because it represents the contractual right of the depositor to obtain cash from the institution or to draw a cheque or similar instrument against the balance in favour of a creditor in payment of a financial liability.

Financial Instruments: Recognition and Measurement

13

Core definitions

- Financial instruments and equity instruments have the same definition as given by IAS 32.
- Examples of financial instruments include
  - Cash
  - Deposits available on demand
  - Commercial debt
  - Loans receivable and payable
  - Debt and equity securities that are financial instruments from the viewpoint of both the issuer and the holder
  - Asset backed securities
  - Derivatives.

Initial recognition of a financial instrument

- Recognise when the party becomes party to the contractual provisions of the instrument.
- Financial assets and liabilities must be recognised on the balance sheet including derivatives.
- Upon recognition the instrument must be classified within one of the following categories:

Financial assets held for trading	Held with a view to selling them on in the short term
Loans and receivables	Non-derivative assets with fixed or determinable payments that are not quoted on an active market
Held-to-maturity investments	Non-derivative financial assets with fixed or determinable payments that an entity intends to hold until they mature
Available-for-sale financial assets	Financial assets that do not fall into the other three classes

Measurement of financial instruments

- At fair value.
- Take transaction costs into consideration.
- Quoted market price should always be used as a measure of fair value when it is available.
- If no active market is available use a valuation technique that refers to market conditions (e.g. option pricing models).
- When there is no active market and no other reliable estimate of fair value then use cost less any impairment.

Subsequent measurement

- This is a contentious issue dependent upon the categorisation of the instrument
- Financial assets:

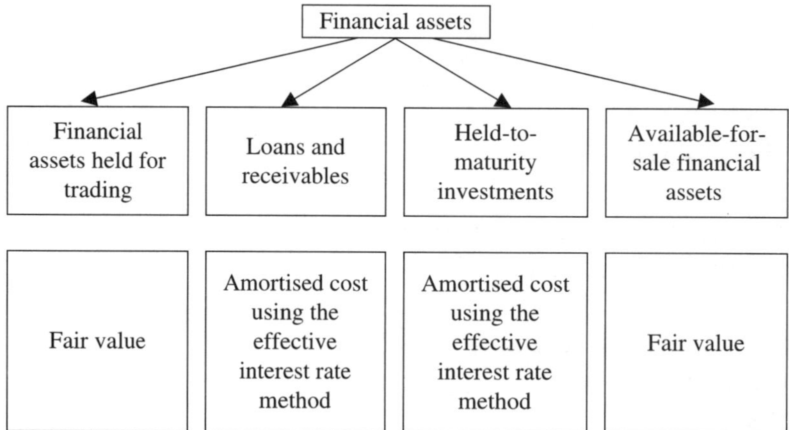

- Financial liabilities:

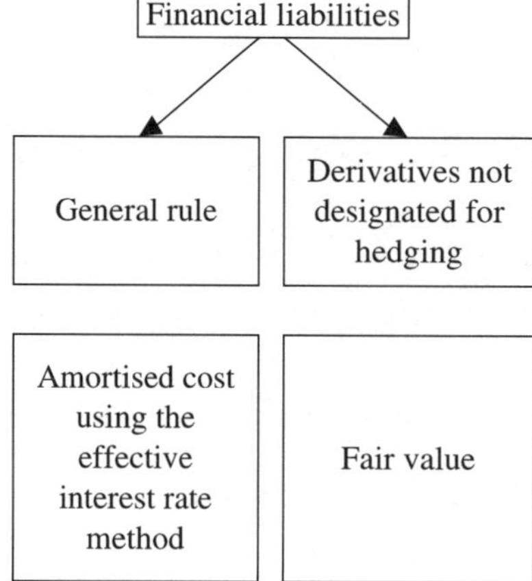

Impairment

- Reassess carrying value at each balance sheet date.
- If indicators of impairment exist then a full review must be undertaken.
- Impairment losses recognised in the income statement.

Derivatives

- A derivative demonstrates all of the following characteristics:
  1 its value changes in response to the change in a specified interest rate, security price, commodity price, foreign exchange rate, index of prices or rates, a credit rating or credit index or other variable
  2 it requires no initial net investment
  3 it is settled at a future date.

Hedging

- A management strategy to reduce risk.

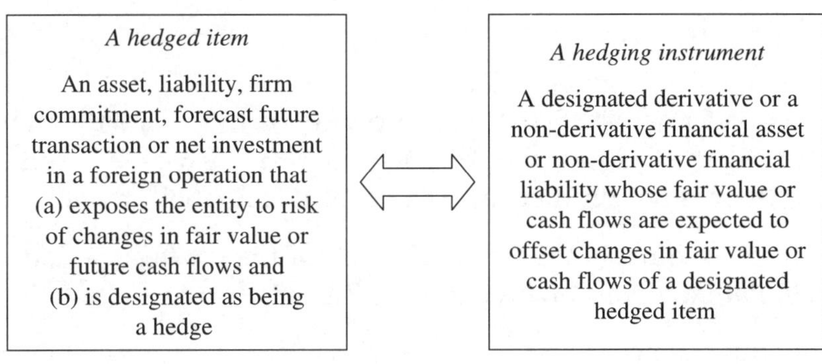

- A hedge must be formally designated and documented.
- There must be an expectation that it will be effective.
- Examples include:

Fair value hedge	The value of the item being hedged changes as market price changes
Cash flow hedge	The cash flows of the item being hedged change as market price changes

- A retrospective measure of hedge effectiveness is that an effective hedge falls within the 80–125% window from the bench mark value.

The Future

- IAS 39 has not met universal approval, and will ultimately be replaced
- A good example of the problems associated with the current standard is the "carve outs" implemented by the Eu on portfolio hedging and the use of the full fair value option.

? Objective test questions

13.1 IAS 39 tackles the issue of financial instrument recognition and measurement, but there are some financial instruments that fall outside its remit under normal circumstances.

Which of the following fall outside the scope of the standard?

(i) Obligations arising under insurance contracts
(ii) Commercial debt
(iii) Employee benefit plans
(iv) Cash
(v) Options and warrants.

A (ii) only
B (i), (iii) and (iv)
C (ii), (iv) and (v)
D (ii), (iii) and (v)

(2 marks)

13.2 Rymist plc lends Dune plc £500,000 for a period of 10 years with annual repayments scheduled under the terms of the contract. Interest is variable based on market rates plus 1%, but there is no commercial market for this financial asset.

Rymist plc intends to retain the financial asset for the ten year period, and has always honoured similar intentions involving other financial assets.

Identify how this financial asset would be classified per IAS 39 Financial Instruments: Recognition and Measurement, and explain the basis for your decision.

(2 marks)

13.3 A financial instrument is defined as:

> Any contract that gives rise to both a financial asset of one entity and a financial liability or equity instrument of another.

For each of the items listed below outline when they would first meet the definition and be recognised in the financial statements.

- A forward contract
- Unconditional receivable/payable

(2 marks)

13.4 Talbot plc issued a £120,000 bond on 1 January 2002 at £20,000 below its face value. The bond carries a 4% coupon, and is redeemable at a premium in 10 years.

Issue costs of £8,000 were incurred.

However, after three years 30% of the bond holders decided to exercise a redemption clause within the contract, which allows them to redeem their interest at a 10% premium on the carrying value at that date.

If the effective rate associated with the bond is 9% what is the value of the redemption to those exercising this right?

(4 marks)

13.5 Ralph Soammes has recently been seconded to the financing department of his employer, and his first task is to assist in the review of the financial instrument portfolio to check for evidence of impairment. He has approached you for guidance as to what to look for as indicators of impairment, and has also queried whether it is appropriate to complete such a review for all the assets in the portfolio.

Provide Ralph with three typical indicators of impairment, and give clarification regarding the extent of the impairment review.

(3 marks)

13.6 Which of the following attributes does not describe a characteristic of a derivative?

(i) It is settled at a future date
(ii) It will always be settled in cash
(iii) It requires no initial investment
(iv) Its value changes in response to variables such as foreign exchange rates, credit rating and commodity prices
(v) It will always be secured.

A (ii) and (v)
B (ii) and (iii)
C (i), (ii) and (iv)
D (i), (ii), (iv) and (v)

(2 marks)

13.7 The management team of Retro plc has been actively involved in the hedging of financial risk for several years. They are aware that IAS 39 Financial Instruments: Recognition and Measurement specifies various criteria that must be met if hedge accounting is to be adopted, and that two of these criteria are:

- The hedge is expected to be highly effective.
- The effectiveness of the hedge can be reliably measured.

With reference to their largest hedge arrangement it has been identified that the hedging instrument has made a gain of $150,000, whilst the cash instrument associated with it has made a loss of $125,000.

Comment on the effectiveness of this hedge in the context of the IAS 39 rules.

(3 marks)

13.8 Cash flow hedges and fair value hedges as defined by IAS 39 Financial Instruments: Recognition and Measurement are not accounted for in the same way. Briefly outline how they differ.

(3 marks)

✓ Objective test answers

13.1 C

13.2 Classification – Held-to-maturity investment

A held-to-maturity investment is a non-derivative financial asset with fixed or determinable payments and fixed maturity, and there must be a demonstrable intent to hold to maturity.

13.3 Forward contract: Although the exchange detailed in such a contract is for some future date it should initially be recognised when the commitment is signed.

Unconditional receivable/payable: At the moment the contract is signed the legal right to receive or pay cash has been established as there are no further conditions to fulfill. Consequently the contract date will be the date of recognition.

13.4 To calculate the carrying value of the bond at 31 December 20X4:

Year ended	*b/f*	*Interest*	*Cash*	*c/f*
	£	£	£	£
31 December 20X2	92,000	8,280	(4,800)	95,480
31 December 20X3	95,480	8,593	(4,800)	99,273
31 December 20X4	99,273	8,935	(4,800)	103,408

The bond holders redeeming early will receive a 10% premium on the carrying value at 31 December 20X4.

Redemption value = 30% [103,408 × 110%] = £34,125

13.5 Indicators of impairment to a financial asset include:

- A breach of contract such as default in interest payments.
- It is becoming probable that the borrower will enter bankruptcy.
- Observable data indicate that there is a measurable decrease in the estimated future cash flows.

Impairment reviews are only required for those financial assets that are measured at amortised cost, and not those that are regularly remeasured at fair value.

13.6 A

13.7 The hedging arrangement used by Retro plc would be deemed an effective hedge on the basis of the information provided by the management team.

- The movements have been measured reliably (i.e. assume good management practice in deriving the figures given).
- If the movements on the hedge components are compared:

  125/150 = 83%

  150/125 = 120%

  These fall within the 80%–125% band set by IAS 39 to establish effectiveness.

13.8 Fair value hedges require the hedging instrument to be remeasured to fair value and all gains/losses taken to the income statement. A similar approach is adopted for the hedged item.

Cash flow hedges also require the hedging instrument to be remeasured to fair value, but the gain/loss is taken to equity (i.e. statement of changes in equity). If the related transaction gives rise to an asset or liability then the gains/losses previously taken to equity will adjust this carrying value. Whereas if the related transaction has been charged to the income statement then the gain/loss taken to equity must be redirected to the income statement.

? Medium answer questions

Question 1 – Investior plc

Investior plc already holds several financial instrument investments, and is in the process of adding to its portfolio. Details of the additions are:

Item 1 – A financial asset specifically purchased to be traded on. Investior plc intends to receive pricing details via an on-line pricing service.

Item 2 – Perceived as a long-term investment this instrument has seven years remaining to maturity, and there is no active market on which it could be readily traded.

At the board meeting to approve the purchase of both items the main subject of discussion has been the value at which the instruments will initially be recorded, and their subsequent valuation. Comments heard at the meeting include:

> With the exception of financial instruments that are traded on an exchange the only sensible option available is cost
>
> Surely we can use discounted cash flows?

Investior plc also intends to issue £12m of 0% bonds on the first day of the next accounting period at a discount of £1.8m, but one director has queried the effectiveness of this strategy. He has argued that the lack of a coupon over the four year term of the bonds and the substantial premium due at the date of their redemption will confuse stakeholders.

> Everyone will believe we are doing well for three years and then our results will be decimated in the year of redemption . . . this is ludicrous!
>
> The two things we all seem to agree on is that the effective return based on a premium above par of £3.180m is 11%, and the issue costs will be £200,000.

Requirements

(a) Draft a letter to the board of Investior plc based at the London head office explaining how the proposed financial assets should be valued initially and the approach for their subsequent treatment.

(5 marks)

(b) Explain why the issue of zero coupon bonds might be a good financial decision, and how the bonds detailed above should be accounted for over their four year term.

(5 marks)
(Total = 10 marks)

✓ Medium answer questions

Answer 1 – Investior plc

(a)

The Board,
Investior plc,
London.

Date:

Dear Sirs,
Re: Measurement of financial instruments

Thank you for approaching us for clarification of issues arising from your proposed purchase of two financial assets in the near future. The comments raised by some of the board members capture some of the issues relevant to this complex subject, but care is needed to ensure the correct application.

IAS 39 Rules

The basic rule for initial measurement of financial instruments to be recognised in the financial statements is that they should be recognised at fair value. However, this is not always practical, and IAS 39 Financial Instruments: Recognition and Measurement identifies three possibilities.

1. Quoted market price – this is the ideal measure of fair value.
2. If there is no active market it may be possible to ascertain fair value by using a valuation technique such as discounted cash flows or option pricing models.
3. If neither of the above are feasible then fair value cannot be ascertained and the only alternative is to record the financial instrument at cost as adjusted for impairment.

Item 1

A financial instrument is regarded as quoted in an active market if quoted prices are readily available. These prices could be available from an exchange, broker or as in the case of item 1 from a pricing service. However, you will need to demonstrate that the prices available from this pricing service represent actual and regularly occurring market transactions conducted on an arms-length basis.

It also appears that Item 1 will be categorised as a financial asset held for trading, and hence will need to be subsequently remeasured to fair value on a regular basis (e.g. balance sheet date) with movements being taken to the income statement.

Item 2

Without the provision of additional information as to the nature of the financial asset Item 2 we cannot be certain as to the basis of its initial valuation, although it is clear that fair value cannot be ascertained from the use of quoted market prices. However, unless fair value can be derived from other means such as discounted cash flows then this asset will be recorded at cost less any impairments of which you are aware.

Your intention to retain Item 2 to maturity implies that its subsequent measurement will be at amortised cost using the effective interest rate method.

We hope that this synopsis provides you with the information required, but we would be happy to discuss any remaining matters of concern at your convenience.

Yours faithfully,

(b) Zero coupon bonds

Zero coupon bonds potentially offer cash-flow advantages to an entity that wants to maximise short-term liquidity as with the exception of any direct issue costs incurred there are no cash outgoings until maturity. The bonds are often redeemed at their par value, but premiums above this are allowed.

The deeper the discount the greater the return to the investor, and for investors that do not require an immediate cash flow the ultimate return can be attractive.

Accounting treatment

	b/f £'000	*Interest* £'000	*Cash* £'000	*c/f* £'000
Year 1	10,000	1,100	0	11,100
Year 2	11,100	1,221	0	12,321
Year 3	12,321	1,355	0	13,676
Year 4	13,676	1,504	0	15,180

The bond must initially be recorded at its net proceeds, and hence the direct issue costs are not separately recorded.

Dr	Cash	£10m
Cr	Bond	£10m

Over the duration of the bond the income statement is charged with the effective rate of interest. This means that the directors' fears about the distortion of performance are unfounded as the total finance cost of £5.18m will be spread over the duration of the bond and not recognised in one lump sum upon maturity. As none of the finance cost is physically being paid in cash the interest is "rolled up" into the carrying value of the bond on the balance sheet.

When the bond matures in 4 years the cash settlement of £15.18m will eliminate the outstanding balance.

Financial Reporting in an Environment of Price Changes

14

The historic cost problem

- Historic cost is very objective and reliable, but may not be relevant to those trying to base decisions on the financial statements
  - Changing prices means that the income statement compares current revenues with historic costs.
  - The carrying value of assets in the balance does not reflect their current value.
  - The comparison of key financial indicators over time is undermined.
  - Holding gains are not differentiated from true performance figures.
- Two IASs have been issued to tackle this problem (IAS 6 and IAS 15), but both were subsequently withdrawn.
- Current guidance derives from the IASC Framework.

Capital

- There are two concepts of capital maintenance:

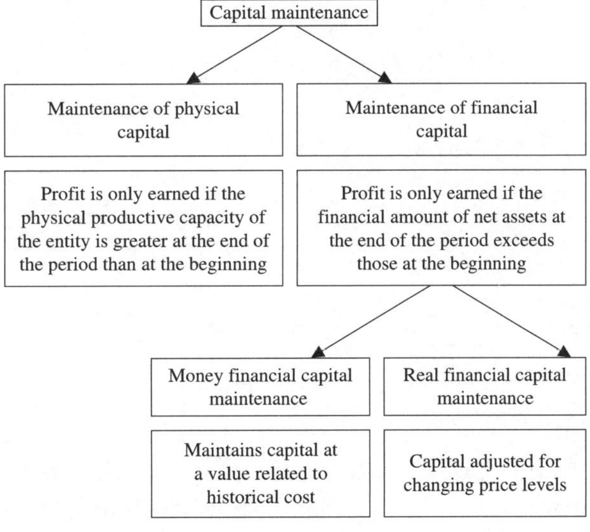

Replacement cost accounting

- Replacement cost – the price at which identical goods or capital equipment could be purchased at the date of valuation.
- In times of rising prices leads to higher balance sheet values and hence revaluation surpluses.
- Net current replacement cost is more appropriate for non-current assets as it reflects their existing state of consumption.
- Pros and cons include:

For	*Against*
Separates holding and operating gains	Some values subjective
Balance sheet more relevant	Focus on operating capital rather than financial capital and hence less relevant to investors

Exit values

- Value in the balance sheet on the basis of the selling values of the assets.

Current cost accounting (CCA)

- Based on the principle of value to the business.
- Value to business is the lower of replacement cost and recoverable amount.
- Recoverable amount is the higher of realisable value and value in use.
- The CCA income statement effectively represents the historic cost equivalent adjusted for the following:
  - The cost of sales adjustment (COSA)
  - The depreciation adjustment (DA)
  - The monetary working capital adjustment (MWCA)
  - The gearing adjustment (GA).

  Hence at times of inflation:

	£'000
Historic cost profit	X
COSA	(X)
DA	(X)
MWCA	(X)
GA	X
Current cost profit	X

- Pros and cons include:

For	*Against*
Assists decision-making	It is not widely understood
Gives a prudent estimate of profit at times of rising prices	It is not appropriate for service industries that do not have large quantities of physical capital

Current purchasing power accounting

- Based upon the concept of real capital maintenance.
- Non-monetary items are adjusted for a general price index.
- Pros and cons include:

For	*Against*
Uses an index that is widely available It is more widely understood than CCA	The index may bear little relationship to the assets of the business, and hence it is a weak measure of asset valuation

The real terms system

- A hybrid system that takes the best aspects of CPP and CCA.
- To ensure that asset values are realistic it retains the CCA approach to asset valuation.

  However, shareholders are interested in the valuation of their investment as a whole rather than that of individual assets, and hence the real terms system also discloses the amounts needed to maintain the purchasing power of shareholders' funds.

Hyperinflationary economies

- IAS 29 specifies that indicators of a hyperinflationary economy include
  - Inhabitants keep their wealth in non-monetary assets or in a relatively stable foreign currency.
  - Prices are often quoted in a stable foreign currency.
  - Credit sales and purchases occur at prices that compensate for the expected loss in purchasing power over the settlement period.
  - Interest rates, wages and prices are linked to a price index.
  - Cumulative inflation over a three year period exceeds 100%.
- Recommended accounting practice is to restate the financial statements of entities subject to hyperinflation by applying a general price index.

? Objective test questions

14.1 Filips Ltd purchased two new processing machines on 1 January 20X1 for £40,000 each. The machines are estimated to have a useful economic life of eight years, and at the end of this period will have a nil residual value.

On 31 December 20X4 the company had investigated the possible cost of buying an equivalent third machine, and had been informed by the supplier that this would cost £56,000.

Based on the information available what is the net current replacement cost of the two existing machines?

(2 marks)

14.2 Peter Drogba, the financial director for a national power supply installation, has been undertaking an exercise to convert the historic cost accounts of the business to current cost accounting. The information has been input to a spreadsheet, but Peter unfortunately pressed the wrong key whilst making a correction, and has lost the sign (i.e. positive or negative) for all of the adjustments to the income statement. Consequently he is now presented with the following list.

	£m
Cost of sales adjustment	12
Monetary working capital adjustment	7
Depreciation adjustment	19
Gearing adjustment	14

He knows that the historic cost profit was £132m, and there has been a low rate of positive inflation in the country for several years.

Calculate the revised profit under current cost accounting rules. **(2 marks)**

14.3 Racing Ltd reported a profit of £240,000. Net assets at the beginning of the year were £1.6m.

The retail price index had risen by 7% over the year whereas the company faced specific price changes of 9%.

What would the reported profit of Racing Ltd be using real financial capital maintenance and using operating financial capital maintenance?

(2 marks)

14.4 Selecting from the options given below complete the grid detailing the appropriate combinations for different methods of reflecting price changes.

- Historic cost
- Indexed historic cost
- Current cost
- Real financial capital maintenance
- Money financial capital maintenance
- Operating financial capital maintenance.

	Concept of value used	*Concept of capital maintenance used*
Current purchasing power		
Current cost accounting		
Real terms accounting		

(4 marks)

14.5 Mercury Ltd is a retail company with stores in many of the new out of town shopping developments. In the last two years it has decided to consolidate its position in the market, and is not intending to open any new stores in the foreseeable future. At the latest AGM a shareholder asked the following question:

> I see from this years' income statement that the company has had an excellent year. Given the recent policy decision to keep the same number of stores the business needs minimal capital investment. Hence it would seem appropriate that the shareholders reap a healthy return in terms of a high dividend. However, the dividend is surprisingly modest, and I see from the director's report that this is attributed to something called a holding gain.
>
> Surely if this is some extra gain to the company the dividend should be bigger not smaller?

Briefly explain to the shareholder why a holding gain might affect their dividend in the manner described. [Maximum 90 words]

(3 marks)

14.6 Which of the following statements about CCA is not correct?

A CCA is a true inflation accounting system, as it looks at changes specific to the business and not to the economy as a whole.
B In times of inflation CCA profits will be lower than their historic cost accounting equivalents.
C If it costs £16 at the date of sale (on credit terms), to replace an item of inventory purchased for £10 the money working capital adjustment is £6.
D CCA allows users of financial statements to make more informed decisions.

(2 marks)

14.7 Describe two of the perceived advantages and disadvantages of using the CPP to reflect changing prices.

(2 marks)

14.8 When using CCA, an asset should be valued at net realisable value when its:

A net realisable value $<$ replacement cost $<$ economic value (i.e. value in use)
B replacement cost $<$ net realisable value $<$ economic value
C economic value $<$ replacement cost $<$ net realisable value
D economic value $<$ net realisable value $<$ replacement cost

(2 marks)

14.9 Every income measure has a particular capital maintenance concept associated with it. The concept associated with CCA is best described as maintaining the:

A Current value of the entity's assets
B Capacity of the entity to continue its operations
C Capacity of the entity to replace its original assets
D Current value of the original shareholders' investment

(2 marks)

14.10 Trill plc prepares financial statements for 31 December.

The following information is available about the company:

- The company was formed on 1 January 20X1 with 100,000 £1 ordinary shares being issued on that day at par.
- Two delivery vans were purchased for £20,000 each on 1 January 20X2. They are considered to have a ten year useful economic life and a nil residual value.

The company intends to prepare its 20X4 financial statements using the current purchasing power system, and wants you to assist in calculating the value of vans and share capital to be shown in the balance sheet.

The value of the retail price index at various dates was as follows:

	Index
1 January 20X1	140
31 December 20X1	152
31 December 20X2	159
31 December 20X3	178
31 December 20X4	192

(3 marks)

14.11 Under the real terms system of income measurement, total real gains are calculated by adjusting historical profit for:

(i) Unrealised holding gains
(ii) An inflation adjustment to shareholders funds

Which of the following pairs of adjustments is correct?

	Unrealised holding gains	*Inflation adjustment to shareholders' funds*
A	Minus	Plus
B	Minus	Minus
C	Plus	Plus
D	Plus	Minus

(2 marks)

14.12 An item of equipment was purchased for £100,000 and now has a net book value of £40,000. It could currently be sold on the open market for £32,000, whilst it would cost £140,000 to buy a new equivalent.

The discounted value of the expected future benefits arising from continued use of the asset is £48,000.

Calculate the value to the business of this item of equipment.

A £48,000
B £56,000
C £32,000
D £40,000

(2 marks)

Objective test answers

14.1

	£
Gross current replacement cost	56,000
Less: Accumulated depreciation [3/8]	(21,000)
Net current replacement cost	35,000

Hence the net current replacement cost of the two machines is £70,000

14.2 Current cost accounting profit:

	£m
Historic cost profit	132
Cost of sales adjustment	(12)
Monetary working capital adjustment	(7)
Depreciation adjustment	(19)
Gearing adjustment	14
Current cost profit	108

14.3

	Real FCM £'000	*OCM* £'000
Profit as reported	240	240
Adj (1.6m × 7%)	(112)	
Adj (1.6m × 9%)		(144)
	128	96

14.4

	Concept of value used	*Concept of capital maintenance used*
Current purchasing power	Indexed historic cost	Real financial capital maintenance
Current cost accounting	Current cost	Operating capital maintenance
Real terms accounting	Current cost	Real financial capital maintenance

14.5 During times of inflation the cost of buying an item of replacement inventory will be higher than the original price. Hence, if an item purchased for £10, and sold for £15, would now cost £12 to replace the true profit is only £3 if the business is to have the capacity to buy replacement inventory and continue to trade. The £2 retained is referred to as a holding gain, and represents funds the business would want to retain and not distribute.

14.6 C

14.7 Advantages of CPP

- The use of a widely used price index eliminates subjectivity, and hence provides a sound basis for the comparison of results on a year by year basis.
- It is easy to calculate and readily understood by non-technical users of the financial statements.

Disadvantages of CPP

- The retail price index used may bear little resemblance to the specific price changes faced by the business. Hence the carrying value of assets in the balance sheet may be unrealistic.
- Some argue that it is less prudent with regard to tax provisions which are based on inflation adjusted accounts and hence lower profits.

14.8 **D**

Take the lower of replacement cost and recoverable amount, where the latter is the higher of net realisable value and economic value.

14.9 **B**

14.10

		£
Vans – HC (£40,000)	192/152	50,526
Vans – Depreciation (£12,000)	192/152	15,158
Vans – NBV		35,368
Share capital – (100,000)	192/140	137,142

14.11 **D**

14.12 **A**

Net realisable value = 32,000

Value in use = £48,000

Net current replacement cost = (40/100) × £140,000 = £56,000

Remember the recoverable amount is the higher of net realisable value and value in use. This is then compared to the net current replacement cost and the lower figure selected.

? Medium answer questions

Question 1 – Wellers Ltd

Wellers Ltd is a corporate research company that collects and interprets information on key industry sectors and then sells this information on to interested parties. They are considering the development of a new analysis tool which takes data prepared under historical cost accounting rules and represents it to show the effects of price changes.

To pilot the scheme they have taken the accounts of an existing client, HRN plc, and have run the figures through the computer program that has been developed. The results look promising, but checks need to be made that the information produced is accurate and this will need to be done manually to allow comparison to be made.

The historic cost income statement of HRN plc is as follows:

	20X3	*20X4*
	£'000	£'000
Revenue	2,000	2,400
Cost of sales		
Opening inventory	300	420
Purchases	1,100	1,200
Closing inventory	(420)	(470)
Gross profit	1,020	1,250
Selling and administration costs	(300)	(370)
Operating profit	720	880

Additional information collected was as follows:

- It has been assumed that inventory held at the year end has been in the warehouse for 1 month.
- Some balance sheet data was also available:

	20X3	*20X4*
	£'000	£'000
Receivables	600	800
Cash	70	100
Payables	(490)	(500)

- Current cost accounting adjustments were estimated to be:

	£'000
Cost of sales adjustment	96
Monetary working capital adjustment	84
Depreciation adjustment	9

- At the end of the year ended 31 December 20X4 the company had purchased non-current assets with a cash cost of £20,000.

- The company trades evenly over the accounting period.
- Price index statistics:

	RPI
30 November 20X3	155
31 December 20X3	162
Average 20X3	156
30 November 20X4	189
31 December 20X4	195
Average 20X4	184

Requirements

(a) Prepare revised profit figures for the year ended 31 December 20X4 applying the principles of current purchasing power and current cost accounting.

(6 marks)

(b) On the basis that HRN plc is a niche market chemicals company comment briefly on which of the two methods performed in part (a) would be the most appropriate?

(2 marks)

(c) HRN plc is considering opening an operation in a developing country, but has received warnings that the economy therein was on the brink of becoming hyper inflationary. What indicators should the company watch for as evidence that these concerns are justified?

(2 marks)

(Total = 10 marks)

Medium answer questions

Answer 1 – Wellers Ltd

(a) Calculation of revised profits

Current cost accounting

	£'000
Historic cost operating profit	880
Less: Cost of sales adjustment	(96)
Monetary working capital adjustment	(84)
Depreciation adjustment	(9)
Current cost profit	691

Current purchasing power

	20X4 £'000		*CPP* £'000
Revenue	2,400	195/184	2,543
Cost of sales			
Opening inventory	420	195/155	528
Purchases	1,200	195/184	1,272
Closing inventory	(470)	195/189	(485)
Gross profit	1,250		1,228
Selling and administration costs	(370)	195/184	(392)
Operating profit	880		836
Loss on monetary items [W]			(676)
			160

Working: CPP loss on holding monetary items

	HC £'000		*CPP* £'000
Opening monetary items (i.e. receivables + cash − payables) = 600 + 70 − 490	180	195/162	217
Revenue	2,400	195/184	2,543
Purchases	(1,200)	195/184	(1,272)
Purchases of non-current assets	(20)	195/195	(20)
Overheads	(370)	195/184	(392)
	990		1,076
Closing monetary items [800 + 100 − 500]			(400)
			676

(b) Selection of method

The specialist nature of HRN plc's business implies that CCA is likely to be more appropriate than CPP. The latter adjusts for general changes in inflation as measured by a price index, whereas CCA makes specific adjustments.

The price fluctuations associated with the supply and demand for specialist goods are unlikely to track a general index.

(c) Indicators of a hyper-inflationary economy

- Cumulative inflation over three years is approaching or exceeds 100%.
- The general population prefer to keep their wealth in non-monetary assets.
- Alternatively investments are made in a stable currency rather than the local currency.
- Interest rates, wages and prices are linked to a price index.

The Measurement of Income and Capital: Selected Topics 15

IAS 19 – Accounting for employee benefits

The basics

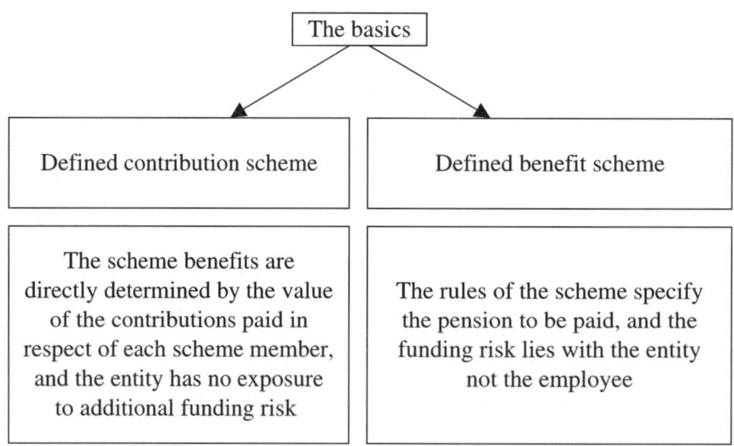

- The valuation of pension funds is a complex process as it requires anticipation of numerous future events (e.g. inflation, interest rates, life expectancy), and this work will be undertaken by actuaries who specialise in this field.
- A funded pension plan is one in which the assets are held externally to the employer company's business.

Accounting for pensions

- Defined contribution scheme – the pension costs are expensed against operating profits for the period similarly to other overheads.
- Defined benefit scheme:

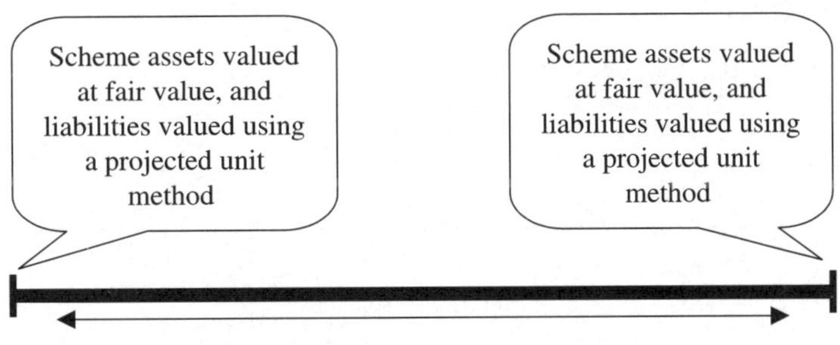

- Current service cost, interest expense and expected return taken to income statement
- Actuarial gains and losses not recognised in income statement immediately unless 10% corridor exceeded

- Cumulative unrecognised actuarial gains and losses are only recognised in the income statement if they exceed 10% of the greater of:
  - the present value of the pension obligation before deducting plan assets
  - the fair value of any plan assets.
- Excesses above the 10% corridor are not recognised in one accounting period, but spread over the average remaining service lives of employees in the plan.
- Under the accounting rules for a defined benefit scheme the balance sheet shows the net of the following figures:
  - the present value of the defined benefit obligation
  - plus the unrecognised actuarial gains less any unrecognised actuarial losses
  - less the fair value of plan assets.

Amendments to IAS 19

- An option has been introduced that allows actuarial gains/losses to be recognised immediately rather than spread over several periods
- To mitigate profit volatility the movement goes to a statement of recognised income and expense; not to the income statement
- The new disclosure is not the same as the statement of changes in equity.

The concept of substance over form and off-balance sheet financing

- There is no stand alone IAS on substance over form, but useful sources of reference include:
  - IAS 1 Presentation of financial statements
  - IAS 18 Revenue
  - IAS 39 Financial Instruments: Recognition and Measurement.

- Incentives for taking liabilities off the balance sheet include:
  - lowering gearing
  - increasing the apparent scope for further borrowing
  - cost maybe lower thereby increasing profit and triggering management incentives.

IAS 18 – Revenue

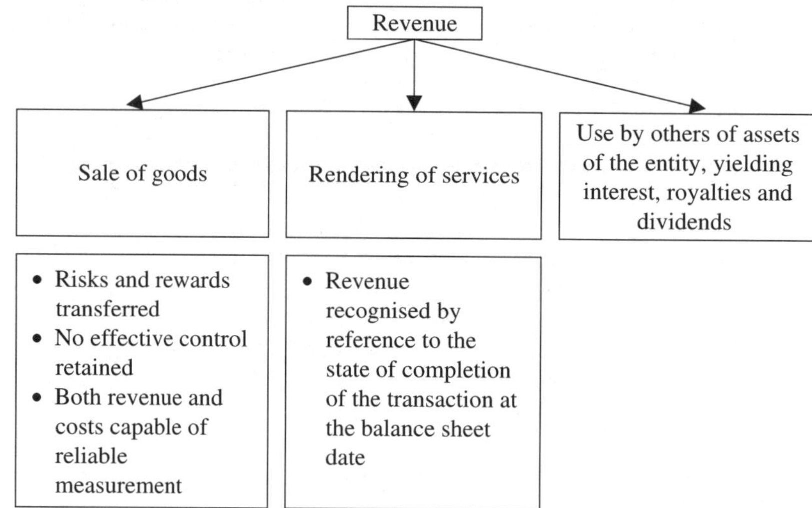

Special purpose entities (SPE)

- Consider the true substance of the relationship of the SPE with the group.
- If the SPE is controlled by the other entity then it should be consolidated.

Recognition and derecognition of assets and liabilities

- The *Framework for the Preparation and Presentation of Financial Statements* indicates that an asset or liability should be recognised if:
  - there is sufficient evidence of existence of the item
  - the item can be measured at a monetary amount with sufficient reliability.
- IAS 39 specifies that derecognition occurs when an asset or liability is transferred together with the rights and rewards that attach to it.

Specific examples of substance over form

- Consignment stock
- Factoring of receivables.

Objective test questions

15.1 Give a snapshot of the accounting treatment to be adopted for a defined contribution pension scheme. [Maximum 60 words]

(2 marks)

15.2 Jegan Durai is the finance director for a chain of car dealerships, and is in the process of deciding which vehicles should be included in the inventory of the company at the year end.

Each week the company receives a consignment of cars direct from the manufacturer in accordance with a contract that contains the following clauses:

(i) The inventory transfer price charged by the manufacturer is based on their list price at the date of delivery.
(ii) The car chain has responsibility for insuring the vehicles from the time they are offloaded onto the forecourts.
(iii) The dealer has no right to return the cars to the manufacturer.
(iv) The manufacturer can require the dealership to transfer vehicles to competitor dealers without compensation.

Which of the clauses are indicative of the cars at the showrooms belonging to Jegan's company at the year-end date?

A (i), (ii) and (iii)
B (ii), (iii) and (iv)
C (ii), (iii) and (iv)
D All

(2 marks)

15.3 San Martin Ltd is a newly established whisky distillery company. To provide additional finance whilst the initial whisky blends mature the company has approached the bank, and put forward a business plan for the next five year period. They hope to convince the bank to advance £1 million under the following conditions:

- The bank will buy their maturing whisky inventory for £1 million.
- At the end of five years San Martin Ltd will buy back the inventory repaying the £1 million plus a compound return equivalent to the bank's long-term interest rate.
- The bank will never take delivery of the inventory.

Describe how San Martin Ltd should account for this transaction if the bank agrees to their proposal.

(3 marks)

15.4 Angus Ltd has undergone a period of rapid expansion, and is in danger of overtrading. To improve its cash position it has decided to enter into an agreement with a factoring company, which will result in it receiving an upfront cash payment equivalent to 95% of the face value of its receivables. The balancing 5% represents the factoring company's return on the transaction.

Angus Ltd's trading difficulties have resulted in it not checking the credit status of new customers, and there is significant doubt about the collectability of some receivables. This weakness has been recognised by the factoring company who has included a clause requiring Angus Ltd to return cash advanced to the value of receivables that go bad.

If the receivables balance at the date of the factoring arrangement is £50 million what figures will be included in the receivables and liabilities sections of the balance sheet, and is there any impact on the income statement?

	Income statement	*Receivables*	*Liabilities*
	£m	£m	£m
A	–	50	47.5
B	(2.5)	47.5	–
C	–	50	–
D	(2.5)	47.5	47.5

(2 marks)

15.5 Sahota plc have decided to set up a defined benefit pension scheme for their employees believing that this will help staff retention and attracted high caliber recruits. As part of this process they are employing the services of a well-known firm of actuaries at the cost of a substantial fee.

Some of the board members have questioned the necessity for the actuaries believing that it would be cheaper for them to dedicate some of their own time to the actuarial work. However, the financial controller has intimated that the directors will not have the requisite skills, and he has been asked to draft a list of the typical issues considered by actuaries to vindicate his comments.

List six subjects on which the specialist skills of an actuary would be required.

(3 marks)

15.6 "IAS 19 Accounting for Employee Benefits safeguards the income statement from the natural fluctuations of the capital markets"

Briefly discuss the validity of this statement.

(4 marks)

15.7 Raptor plc has two wholly owned subsidiaries, and is now looking to expand its operations into Europe. To fund this growth it has obtained a loan from Friend Ltd at an interest rate 2% below that available from the bank, and with flexible repayment terms dictated by Raptor plc.

Friend plc does not trade, and consequently has a simple balance sheet principally comprising of a substantial loan from a high street bank, and an equivalent asset in the form of funds receivable from Raptor plc.

What is the nature of the relationship between Raptor plc and Friend Ltd, and what are the accounting consequences?

(3 marks)

15.8 In December 2004 IAS 19 was amended to allow actuarial gains and losses to be recognised immediately within a statement of recognised income and expense.
List three potential criticisms of this change.

(3 marks)

✓ Objective test answers

15.1 The rules of the scheme specify a percentage of current employee payroll costs that need to be paid into the pension scheme. These are charged as an operating expense in the income statement. There is no balance sheet impact unless payment has not been made at the period end date when an accrual will be recognised.

15.2 **A**

15.3 San Martin Ltd

The substance of the agreement is that the inventory has never been sold to the bank, and should remain in the inventory of San Martin Ltd. The £1 million effectively represents a loan upon which a commercial rate of interest is being accrued.

The loan should be recognised as a non-current liability, and the interest charged as a finance cost to the income statement.

15.4 **D**

Angus Ltd still has full exposure to the risks associated with the receivables, and can never receive more than the 95% value given by the factor.

15.5

- Average remaining service lives of employees in the scheme
- Post retirement life expectancy
- Future inflation rates
- Estimation of long-term interest rates
- Investment strategy for pension fund portfolio
- Estimation of employee numbers joining and leaving the scheme.

15.6 Pension fund investment portfolios normally contain a mix of financial instruments plus cash and property. As the capital markets fluctuate this has a direct impact on the valuation of the fund and this is a matter of fact. However, unless there is a dramatic one off event the market will tend to fluctuate both up and down, and IAS 19 adopts the philosophy that it is generally inappropriate to recognise these short-term variations in the financial statements.

Consequently, it is not necessary to recognise such actuarial gains and losses providing they do not exceed a 10% corridor. The 10% parameter is measured in relation to:

- The present value of the pension obligations before deducting plan assets.
- The fair value of plan assets.

Which ever is the larger figure is the corridor selected.

If the corridor is exceeded the surplus or deficit is spread over the average remaining service lives of the employees in the scheme. This is recognised in the income statement.

15.7 Raptor plc

Raptor plc benefits from its relationship with Friend Ltd by receiving flexible finance on preferential terms. The substance of the transaction appears to be that Raptor plc controls Friend Ltd, and consequently should treat the latter as a SPE.

Although there is no suggestion of any shareholding in Friend Ltd this SPE should be consolidated as a subsidiary in the consolidated accounts of Raptor plc. The current arrangement is a form of off-balance sheet finance, and substance requires that the true position is shown to the stakeholders.

15.8

1. There is a general drive in accountancy to reduce the number of accounting policy options; this amendment to IAS 19 does the opposite.
2. The addition of an additional disclosure statement risks confusing users of financial statements.
3. The approach is inconsistent with that in the US and hence acts against convergence.

? Medium answer questions

Question 1 – Jennens plc

Jennens plc heads a diversified group of companies that provide a range of goods and services to more than fifty countries. The year-end audit has been completed, and a clean audit report issued, but the auditors have submitted a long management letter highlighting some serious concerns about the recognition of revenues. There is a clear suggestion in the letter that as the group continues to grow the issues raised could ultimately prove sufficient to lead to a qualified opinion in future years unless resolved.

An extract from the letter is shown below:

> Areas of particular concern brought to our attention during our audit of your systems and year-end position are:
>
> (i) When new industrial gas cookers are delivered to customers from your French manufacturing plant the sale is recognised upon delivery at the clients' premises.
>
> (ii) To improve group cash flows you have wisely convinced two of your largest customers in the USA to make a 30% advance payment when they place orders irrespective of whether or not the inventory is currently held in the warehouse. This cash is recognised within your balance sheet and revenues on the payment date.
>
> (iii) As part of the contract to deliver and install new textiles processing equipment in Malaysia you undertake a six month training programming for the employees of your customers in the use of the equipment. This involves a trainer visiting the clients' premises for one day a month over the training period. You currently recognise the full value of the sale on the date the plant is brought into operation.

Requirements

(a) Briefly comment on the rules under IAS18 for the recognition of revenues on the sale of goods and services.

(4 marks)

(b) Comment on the appropriateness of revenue recognition procedures adopted by Jennens plc in each of the cases raised by the auditor's management letter.

(6 marks)
(Total = 10 marks)

Question 2 – Loach plc

Chris Daryanani, the financial controller of Loach plc, is struggling to prepare the necessary pension disclosures for the year-end financial statements. He has already collected the following information:

- The company operates a defined benefit scheme for senior executives
- The fair value of the schemes assets and liabilities are:

	As at 31 December 20X3	*As at 31 December 20X4*
	£m	£m
Assets	5,656	5,966
Liabilities	6,101	6,221

- Discount rate on "AA" corporate bonds is 8%.
- Estimated long-term rate of return on plan assets is 10%.
- Estimated current service cost is £270m.
- Total contribution by Loach plc during the accounting period was £290m.
- At 1 January 20X4 there are net cumulative unrecognised actuarial gains of £50m.
- None of the original directors have yet retired and hence no benefits are being paid to scheme members.

The rules of the pension scheme dictate that employees will be entitled to a lump sum payment on termination of service equal to 1.5% of final salary for each year of service. This payment is capped at 60% of final salary.

Chris has just received a letter from an employee who joined the company on 1 January 20X1 at a salary of £10,000 per annum. They are enquiring what lump sum they are currently eligible for if they leave the company prior to emigrating on 31 December 20X7.

Requirements

(a) Calculate the amounts to be disclosed in the respect of the pension scheme in the balance sheet at 31 December 20X4 and in the income statement for the accounting period ended on that date. [Assume that the average service life of employees within the scheme is 10 years]

(6 marks)

(b) Calculate the payment due to the employee when they leave (Assume that the employee's salary grows at 5% per annum throughout their period of employment, and that the applicable discount rate is 10%). [All calculations to the nearest £100,000]

(4 marks)

(Total = 10 marks)

✓ Medium answer questions

Answer 1 – Jennens plc

(a) IAS 18 Revenue recognition criteria

Revenue is the gross inflow of economic benefits during the period arising in the ordinary course of business, when those inflows result in increases in equity, other than increase relating to contributions from equity participants. Revenue should be measured at the fair value of the consideration received.

Sale of goods: The recognition of revenue from the sale of goods should only occur when the following conditions have been met:

- The entity has transferred the significant risks and rewards of ownership of the goods.
- The entity retains neither managerial involvement to the degree usually associated with ownership nor effective control over the goods sold.
- The amount of revenue can be measured reliably.
- It is probable that the economic benefits associated with the transaction will flow to the entity.
- The cost incurred or to be incurred in respect of the transaction can be measured reliably.

Although the most usual point of recognition will be the transfer of possession or the transfer of legal title. It is important to look at the substance of the transaction in each case.

Sale of services: Revenue should only be recognised when the outcome of the transaction can be estimated reliably. This will be indicated by the following criteria:

- The amount of revenue must be measured reliably.
- It is probable that the economic benefits associated with the transaction will flow to the entity.
- The stage of completion of the transaction at the balance sheet date can be measured reliably.
- The costs incurred for the transaction and the costs to complete the transaction can be measured reliably.

(b) Specific scenarios

Gas cookers

It is normal for revenue to be recognised when a buyer accepts delivery, and both installation and inspection are complete. It is unlikely that the customers in France will install the new gas cookers delivered by Jennens plc, and hence the revenue should not be recognised when the goods are delivered to the premises.

Recognition on delivery would only be appropriate if:

- the installation process is simple and requires minimal resource . . . this seems unlikely in this case
- another supplier will complete the installation and Jennens plc only has responsibility to manufacture the cookers and get them to the premises of the customer.

Advance payments

The payment of a cash advance will have to be recognised in the balance sheet of Jennens plc on the date of receipt, but it is inappropriate to recognise revenues in the income statement as the inventory has not yet been delivered to the buyer.

Consequently when the cash arrives it should be shown as a liability in the balance sheet. It is reasonable to assume that if the goods are not delivered by Jennens plc they will be liable to repay the cash advance.

Customer training

To be certain of the most appropriate pattern of revenue recognition in this case it would be necessary to know more about the contract. If the training is a separately identified component with a known cost then this element should not be recognised upon the delivery of the machines. It would be more appropriate to recognise it over the period of instruction. Effectively this is matching the cost and benefit.

However if the contract shows a single price and it is estimated that the tuition element is minor in comparison to the overall price it would be appropriate to recognise the full fee on delivery. If Jennens adopts this approach it must do so consistently.

Answer 2 – Loach plc

(a) Balance sheet and income statement disclosures

Balance sheet

	£m
Present value of defined benefit obligation	6,221
Fair value of plan assets	(5,966)
Unrecognised actuarial gain [W2]	142.6
	397.6

Income statement [W1]

	£m
Operating costs – Current service cost	(270)
Interest income	565.5
Interest payable	(488.1)

[W1] Movements on the scheme

	£m
Opening net liabilities (5,656 – 6,101)	(445)
Current service cost	(270)
Expected return on assets (10% × 5,656)	565.6
Interest on unwinding of liabilities (8% × 6,101)	(488.1)
Contributions to the scheme	290
Actuarial gain on scheme net assets [Balance]	92.7
Closing net liabilities (5,966 – 6,221)	(255)

[W2] The 10% Corridor

At start of year:

The larger of:

- 10% × Assets at start of period = 10% × 5,656m = £565.6m
- 10% × Obligations at start of period = 10% × 6,101 = £610.1m

The actuarial gain (50) falls within the corridor and hence has no impact on the income statement.

At the end of the year the corridor as adjusted for the movements in working 1 is clearly in excess of the actuarial gain (50 + 92.7). Hence the entire unrecognised gain will be held in the balance sheet.

(b) Payment due to employee

When the employee leaves on 31 December 20X7 their salary at that date will be:

$£10,000(1.05)^7 = £14,071$

Each years' service earns an extra lump sum of 1.5% of final salary, and so the lump sum entitlement increases by £211 per annum (i.e. 1.5% × 14,071).

The employee's current entitlement is 4 × £211 = £844, which in current money terms is worth $£844/(1.10)^3 = £634.1$.

Analysis of Financial Statements: Techniques of Ratio Analysis

16

The stakeholders

- Different user groups refer to financial statements to achieve different objectives
  - Present and potential investors
  - Lenders and potential lenders
  - Suppliers and creditors
  - Employees
  - Customers
  - Government
  - The general public.

The basis of effective analysis

- Calculating financial ratios alone will not give a complete picture and must be complemented with other attributes
  - History of the business
  - Knowledge of the risks to which the business is exposed
  - Capabilities of the management team
  - Awareness of broader economic factors.
- Sources of data should not be restricted to the balance sheet, income statement, etc., but should have regard to the range of voluntary disclosures made by many companies (e.g. environmental review) plus external sources such as specialist business research agencies.

Ratios

Performance ratios

$$\text{Gross profit margin} = \frac{(\text{Sales} - \text{Cost of sales})}{\text{Sales of the period}} \times 100$$

$$\text{Operating profit margin} = \frac{\text{Operating profit}}{\text{Revenue}} \times 100$$

$$\text{Net profit margin} = \frac{\text{Net profit}}{\text{Revenue}} \times 100$$

- EBITDA – earnings before interest, taxation, depreciation and amortisation.

Activity ratios

$$\text{Asset turnover} = \frac{\text{Revenue}}{\text{Total assets}}$$

$$\text{Inventory turnover} = \frac{\text{Cost of sales}}{\text{Average inventory}}$$

or

$$= \frac{\text{Average inventory}}{\text{Cost of sales}} \times 365$$

Return on capital ratios

$$\text{Return on capital employed} = \frac{\text{Profit}}{\text{Capital employed}} \times 100$$

$$\text{Return on assets} = \frac{\text{Operating profit}}{\text{Total assets}} \times 100$$

$$\text{Return on shareholders funds} = \frac{\text{Profits attributable to shareholders}}{\text{Shareholders funds}} \times 100$$

- Within the ROCE calculation the capital employed includes issued share capital, reserves, preferred shares, minority interests, loan capital, provisions and bank overdrafts.

Liquidity ratios

$$\text{Current ratio} = \frac{\text{Current assets}}{\text{Current liabilities}}$$

$$\text{Quick ratio} = \frac{\text{Current assets less inventory}}{\text{Current liabilities}}$$

$$\text{Receivable days} = \frac{\text{Average receivables}}{\text{Credit sales}} \times 365$$

$$\text{Payables days} = \frac{\text{Average payables}}{\text{Credit purchases}} \times 365$$

- The working capital cycle – The length of the cycle is calculated by adding the inventory turnover days and receivable days and deducting the payables days.

Valuation and investor ratios

$$\text{Price/Earning ratio} = \frac{\text{Current market price per share}}{\text{Earnings per share}}$$

$$\text{Profit retention ratio} = \frac{\text{Profit after dividends}}{\text{Profit before dividends}} \times 100$$

$$\text{Dividend payout rate} = \frac{\text{Dividend per share}}{\text{Earnings per share}} \times 100$$

$$\text{Dividend yield} = \frac{\text{Dividend per share}}{\text{Market price per share}} \times 100$$

$$\text{Dividend cover} = \frac{\text{Earnings per share}}{\text{Dividends per share}}$$

Cash flow ratios

$$\text{Return on capital employed to cash} = \frac{\text{Cash generated from operations}}{\text{Capital employed}} \times 100$$

$$\text{Cash generated from operations to total debt} = \frac{\text{Cash generated from operations}}{\text{Total long-term borrowings}}$$

$$\text{Net cash from operating activities to capital expenditure} = \frac{\text{Net cash from operating activities}}{\text{Net capital expenditure}} \times 100$$

Objective test questions

16.1 There are many stakeholders who have an interest in the financial statements of an entity other than the existing shareholders. Give three examples of other interested parties and specify their interest in 20 words or less.

(3 marks)

16.2 It is often said that ratio analysis is merely a start point to understanding financial statements as the technique has limitations that restrict its use on a stand-alone basis. Which of the following would be classed as such a limitation?

(i) The commercial requirements of businesses in different commercial sectors means that comparison of ratios between sectors can often be misleading.
(ii) Ratios may give an insight to the future, but tell little about what has happened in the past.
(iii) Financial statements include estimation and judgement based on management experience.
(iv) International Accounting Standards still allow more than one accounting policy for the treatment of certain items.

A (i) and (iii)
B (i), (ii) and (iii)
C (i), (iii) and (iv)
D (i), (ii), (iii) and (iv)

(2 marks)

16.3 As part of a larger financial analysis exercise you have been provided with the following information on Murphy Ltd.

	Year ended 30 June 20X4 £'000	*Year ended 30 June* 20X3 £'000
Inventory	640	570
Trade receivables	400	430
Trade payables	380	380
Sales	4,100	3,900
Purchases	2,800	2,300

All sales and purchases are made on credit terms.

Calculate the working capital cycle for 20X4.

(4 marks)

16.4 The quick ratio should include which of the following:

(i) Raw materials
(ii) Cash balances
(iii) Trade receivables

(iv) Non-current liabilities
(v) Trade payables
(vi) Non-current tangible assets.

A (i), (ii), (iii) and (v)
B (i), (iii), and (v)
C (ii), (iii) and (v)
D (i), (ii), (iii), (iv), (v) and (vi)

(2 marks)

16.5 The management team of Street plc is about to settle, in cash, a dividend they proposed earlier in the financial year. They are concerned as to the impact this payment will have on some of the key financial indicators of the business.

Prior to this payment the quick ratio was 1.5:1 and working capital positive.

Complete the following statement:

As a result of paying the cash dividend the quick ratio will [increase/decrease/remain unchanged] __________ whilst working capital will [increase/decrease/remain unchanged]. __________

(2 marks)

16.6 Based on the information provided below calculate the return on shareholders funds.

	£'000
Revenue	850
Cost of sales	(350)
Gross profit	500
Selling and administration costs	(210)
Operating profit	290
Dividend income	10
Interest receivable	40
Interest payable	(60)
Profit before taxation	280
Taxation	(160)
Profit after taxation	120

Equity and liabilities

	£'000
Capital and reserves	
Ordinary share capital [50p shares]	100
10% Irredeemable preference shares [£1]	120
Accumulated profits	810
Non-current liabilities	
Loan	320
Current liabilities	
Trade payables	70
	1,420

(2 marks)

16.7 Grape Ltd has a current ratio of 3:1.

Which of the following would result in a decrease to this ratio?

A A trade receivable, previously provided for, is written off
B A trade payable balance is settled in cash
C The purchase of a three month bond for cash
D Receiving cash on a current loan

(2 marks)

16.8 Both interest cover and dividend cover are seen as important measures of the risk associated with these elements of the financial statements. However, when an analyst first reviews the numbers they will usually calculate the interest cover in preference to the dividend cover. Briefly explain why this preference would be shown. [Maximum 50 words]

(2 marks)

16.9 Tern Ltd has average trade receivables of £30,000, and the trade receivables collection period is 50 days.

If the mark up on goods sold is 20%, and inventory levels are held constant what is the cost of credit sales for the period?

(2 marks)

16.10 Tring plc has a current ratio of 2.5 and a quick ratio of 0.7. These figures reflect a dividend declared earlier in the year.

If the dividend is now paid in cash what is the impact on the two ratios?

	Current ratio	*Quick ratio*
A	Increases	Increases
B	Increases	Decreases
C	Decreases	Increases
D	Decreases	Decreases

(2 marks)

Objective test answers

16.1

(i) *Lenders* – To ascertain ability to repay and the existence of adequate security.
(ii) *Employees* – Provides an indication of job security and acts as a basis for future wage claims.
(iii) *Government* – Acts as one indicator of good governance and also represents basis for specialist reports such as tax returns.

16.2 **C**

Ratios are often used as a technique to estimate the future performance of a business, but they are based on historic information and hence it is not true to say they tell us little about the past.

16.3

Inventory

$[(640 + 570)/2] \times 365/2{,}730$	81 days

Receivables

$[(400 + 430)/2] \times 365/4{,}100$	37 days

Payables

$[(380 + 380)/2] \times 365/2{,}800$	50 days

Working capital cycle $= 81 + 37 - 50 = 68$ Days

Note: Cost of sales $= 570 + 2{,}800 - 640 = 2{,}730$.

16.4 **C**

Current assets excluding inventory divided by current liabilities

16.5 "As a result of paying the cash dividend the quick ratio will increase whilst working capital will remain unchanged".

Remember that the payment of the dividend not only lowers cash but also eliminates a current liability and hence working capital will not alter in absolute terms. However, the proportion of assets to liabilities will change.

16.6 Return on shareholders funds comprises profits after tax (i.e. £120k) and after non-equity appropriations such as preference dividends (i.e. £12k) divided by equity shareholders funds.

$(120 - 12)/(100 + 810) = 0.119$

16.7 **D**

A trade receivable, previously provided for, is written off – Has no net affect on net assets as both receivables and the provision are reduced.

A trade payable balance is settled in cash – This increases the current ratio.

The purchase of a three month bond for cash – As one current asset increases so cash is reduced . . . there is no net effect.

Receiving cash on a current loan – As there are net current assets this will result in a decrease to the ratio.

16.8 Interest is a direct cost against profit and must be paid, as failure to pay could threaten the continuity of funding and hence going concern. Equity dividends represent a discretional appropriation of profits, and hence need not be paid in difficult times.

16.9 If trade receivables of £30,000 equates to 50 days credit sales this implies that trade receivables for a full year would be [(365/50) × 30,000] £219,000. As the mark up on cost is 20% this means the credit cost of sales is [219,000 × (5/6)] £182,500.

16.10 **B**

The easiest way to prove this is with some hypothetical numbers. If current assets are £2,500 and current liabilities £1,000 then after a dividend of £500 (say) the current ratio becomes 2,000:500 (i.e. it has increased to 4:1).

By contrast if current assets excluding inventory were £800 prior to the payment of the dividend the quick ratio becomes 300:500 (i.e. it has decreased to 0.6).

? Medium answer questions

Question 1 – Clanmur plc

Seamus Murphy, the Head of Internal Audit at Clanmur plc has always been responsible for undertaking regular reviews of the financial data produced by the accounts department. He then reports back to the main board at their planning meetings where decisions are made about the future strategy of the company.

Seamus is always looking for ways to improve his analysis, and has approached the partner, Pauline Faststep, of the company's external auditors for assistance. Pauline has recommended that she prepares a short presentation for Seamus and his team on two key areas:

1 Understanding the significance of cash over profit in determining the future viability of a business.
2 The exclusion of discretional amounts from the income statement with particular emphasis on the concept of EBITDA.

Requirements

(a) To assist the attendees at the presentation Pauline has prepared a handout based on the financial statements of Clanmur plc for 20X4 and 20X3.

Extracts of this handout are shown below:

	Notes	*20X4*	*20X3*
Comparison of cash generated from operations to capital employed in the business	Capital employed includes equity shares, accumulated reserves and overdrafts	19%	31%
Comparison of net cash generated from operations to the level of capital expenditure in the business		72%	117%

During the equivalent period the profitability of the company has remained stable.

Comment on the significance of the figures in the handout, and what they might mean for Clanmur plc.

(5 marks)

(b) Prepare the lead slide for the section of Pauline's presentation on EBITDA, and the explanatory notes that she will use to give an overview of this subject.

(5 marks)
(Total = 10 marks)

Question 2 – DMA Ltd

DMA Ltd has been established for seven years. It manufactures and sells a variety of plastic kitchen utensils to the wholesalers who supply the large retail chains, and is now the fourth largest operator in this sector measured by turnover.

The management team is proud of the company's performance, and believes the business is on track to meet the objectives set in the original operating plan.

- Obtain a public listing within ten years.
- Outperform the sector averages for both return on investment and capital growth.

The growth achieved to date has not involved any acquisitions, but has been founded on an aggressive marketing and sales strategy; although the management have always drawn the line at getting involved in any activities that could be viewed as "sharp practice".

Consequently the DMA brand has good consumer recognition, although as is typical for this sector customer loyalty is low.

In the knowledge that a successful public listing requires good internal control systems and a good financial track record the company has approached a firm of financial analysts, and commissioned a review of their current status. The latter have calculated some key financial indicators for the business and these are given below together with the equivalents for the business sector.

	DMA Ltd	*Industry sector*
Gross profit margin	47%	52%
Net profit margin	22%	25%
Return on capital employed	24%	21%
Trade receivables days	57	33
Trade payables days	60	60
Inventory turnover (days)	20	23
Gearing	43%	42%

All companies within this market source the raw materials for their plastics from one supplier. The latter has created such a dominant position that it can now establish high barriers to entry, and there is no short-term prospect of alternative suppliers becoming available.

Requirement

Based on the information provided comment on the financial position of DMA Ltd, and produce a brief list of additional information that would be needed from management before a final evaluation could be made.

(10 marks)

✓ Medium answer questions

Answer 1 – Clanmur plc

(a) Cash ratios

The fact that the profits of the company have remained stable in the last two years could create a false sense of security within the management team. Whilst it is true that all successful businesses and their stakeholders want profitability in the long term it is cash that is the key determinant of short-term viability. A trade creditor or provider of finance may not be prepared to wait until tomorrow when they want repayment today.

Cash rich profits will usually be seen as higher quality than those of a business where the profits are built on finance, but as always it is important not to rely on a single indicator.

Without access to further information both of the cash ratios calculated by Pauline appear to have deteriorated. The fall in net cash from operating activities compared to capital expenditure is particularly significant as it have fallen below the 100% threshold. This suggests that the business can no longer fund capital investment solely from operations and will need to search for other forms of financing.

If such expansion is planned and the funding in place then it is possible that the new investment has yet to generate improved cash flows, but will do so in later years. However, if no such planned expansion is being undertaken the fall in the generation of cash from operations compared to capital employed would raise further concerns. This may indicate that the business has gone overdrawn thereby increasing the capital employed.

Overdrafts represent a short-term stop gap rather than a long-term solution, and carry a high finance cost that must be serviced; thereby increasing the strain on the business.

(b) EBITDA

Lead slide:

EBITDA
• Elimination of management bias. • Does not equate to cash. • Can give a rose tinted view.

EBITDA is an acronym for earnings before interest, tax, depreciation and amortisation, and has become a well-established measure of company performance.

Those who advocate its use highlight that by removing depreciation and amortisation two of the most subjective figures within the income statement are being removed. It is management who decide useful economic life, residual value and revaluation policy.

The removal of taxation also eliminates a figure over which management have little influence as the taxation calculation is determined by tax legislation.

Finally the removal of interest, although determined by the capital funding policy of management, is not directly linked to the operational activities of the business.

However, although EBITDA is a useful performance measure it does have limitations. First the removal of non-cash costs such as depreciation and amortisation does not result in a true cash measure due to factors such as:

- Movements on provisions
- Accruals and prepayments.

Secondly, EBITDA can give a rose-tinted view of company performance as the costs excluded have not ceased to exist; interest and tax must still be paid, and ultimately capital assets will be consumed and require replacement.

Answer 2 – DMA Ltd

Financial review

The financial data available for DMA Ltd appears to give conflicting messages with its return on capital employed outstripping that of the market sector, but with profit margins being lower and receivables taking longer to collect. However, based on the other indicators the return on capital is misleading, and there is a strong suggestion that the company's aggressive approach to gaining market share has resulted in overtrading.

It is to be hoped that the high receivable days cannot be attributed to poor credit control procedures as indicators of poor systems and corporate governance will not enhance the prospects of a future flotation.

The significantly higher trade receivable days suggests that DMA Ltd is either giving its customers longer to pay or is prepared to trade with less reputable customers. The fact that they supply the wholesale market may indicate that the former is the most likely as there are presumably a relatively small number of wholesale operators. The lower-than average inventory days is consistent with DMA Ltd's objectives as they will be looking to move stock items as quickly as possible.

Payable days would be expected to be similar across the market due to the dominant nature of the plastics supplier; although the allowance of two months appears quite generous.

The working capital cycle of DMA Ltd would give particular concern compared to their competitors as represented by the sector averages. The total of inventory and receivable days exceeds creditor days indicating that additional funding will be required by the business. This appears to be a recent phenomenon as the gearing levels of the business are not excessive, and it cannot obtain short-term credit by withholding payment to its major supplier.

This also serves to indicate that the higher return on capital employed is misleading as the profits generated are likely to be "low quality" as they will not be represented by an equally strong cash flow. More information is also required on the capital base of the company as low capital investment would also drive this ratio upwards, but would not create a sound platform for the continued growth required by the company for a flotation.

It seems unlikely that the asset base is low due to the age of property, plant and equipment as DMA Ltd has been operating for only seven years.

Although DMA Ltd's net profit margin is also below the sector this is by a proportionally smaller amount than the gross profit margin. This suggests that DMA Ltd may have greater control over its expenses.

Additional information that would assist the financial analysis includes:

- Current sources of funding
- Cash flow analysis
- Level of proposed dividend to meet the operating plan objective of above average returns on investment
- Analysis of fixed and variable overheads.

Analysis of Financial Statements: Interpretation

17

Basic ground rules

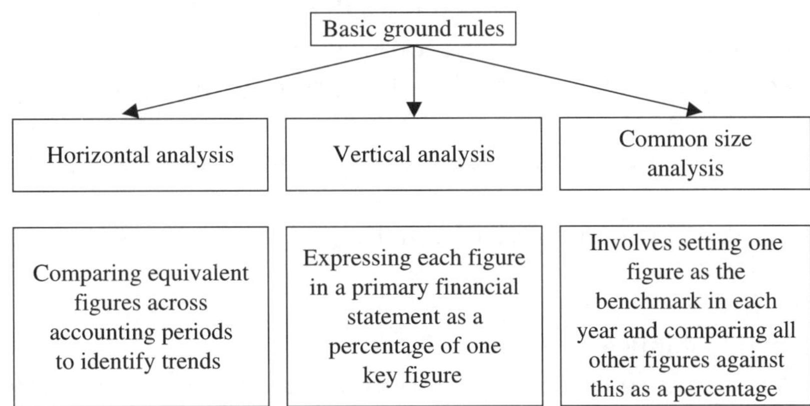

Exam technique – writing a client response

- Whatever the format request by the requirement of the question (e.g. report, memorandum, letter, etc.) make sure that the layout of your answer fully reflects this layout style.
- Detailed ratio calculations are best separated in an appendix.
- Make sure you have identified the user and the key issues which are of concern to them . . . in a time pressured exam these must be given priority as they will be the main focus of the marking guide.
- It is always good practice to have a conclusion.
- Remember you are acting as a business adviser and the recipient of your report is expecting to be given added value over the basic data they have provided you with in the question.

Exam technique – question styles

- Analysis and interpretation questions can have many varied styles and include:
  - reviewing extracts from published financial statements
  - reporting on ratios that have already been calculated and given in the question
  - comparing key financial indicators before and after you have adjusted the information provided
  - reviewing the performance of different segments.

Segmental analysis [IAS 14]

- This standard applies to entities whose debt or equities are publicly traded.
- To determine a reportable segment the following materiality criteria must be applied:
  - A segment is reportable if >50% of its revenue is earned from sales to external customers, and
  - It represents >10% of any of the following:
    (a) Total revenue arising from internal and external transactions
    (b) Combined result of all segments in profit or the combined result of all segments in loss, whichever is the greater
    (c) Total assets of all segments.
- If the reportable segments do not account for at least 75% of total external revenues then additional segments must be added until this threshold is reached.
- The entity must select a primary and secondary reporting format (i.e. the geographical or business analysis could be elected as the primary format depending on the risk profile of the entity).
- The disclosures for the primary segment format must be more extensive and include:
  - segment revenue (internal and external)
  - segment result
  - the total carrying amount of segment assets
  - the segment liabilities
  - the total cost incurred during the period to acquire non-current assets
  - the total amount of expense for depreciation and amortisation of non-current assets
  - the total amount of significant non-cash expenses other than depreciation and amortisation.

Objective test questions

17.1 When provided with a five-year summary of the income statement and balance sheet for a company this enables greater identification of trends, and can highlight unusual fluctuations in performance. However, why might it be risky to place too much reliance on these figures alone? [Maximum 70 words]

(3 marks)

17.2 Which of the following statements about common size analysis are true?

(i) It requires changes in key figures to be immaterial
(ii) It can be applied to any key figure within the financial statements
(iii) When used on the income statement the profit retained pre-appropriations must be used as the benchmark

A (i) only
B (ii) only
C (i) and (ii)
D (ii) and (iii)

(2 marks)

17.3 Mayo Ltd has increased its revenues from £5m to £8.3m over the three year period ended 31 December 20X4.

Based on the information provided below which of the observations about Mayo Ltd provides the most credible explanation for the changes?

	20X4	*20X3*	*20X2*
	%	%	%
Revenue	100	100	100
Cost of sales	(61)	(62)	(65)
Gross profit	39	38	35
Selling and administration costs	(15)	(17)	(18)
Operating profit	24	21	17
Interest payable	(2)	(2)	(2)
Profit before taxation	22	19	15

	Fixed overheads are negligible	*Mayo Ltd is demonstrating signs of overtrading*	*The company is funded via a fixed rate long-term loan*
A	Yes	Yes	Yes
B	No	Yes	No
C	Yes	No	Yes
D	No	No	No

(2 marks)

17.4 Which of the following statements about the selection of the primary segment reporting format is false as prescribed by IAS 14 *Segment Reporting*?

A The internal organisation and management structure determine the primary format.

B The primary segment represents the dominant risks to which the business is exposed.

C The manner in which information is presented internally within the business is a key factor in determining the primary segment format.

D When measured in fair value terms the primary segment will represent the majority of the net asset value.

(2 marks)

17.5 Complete the following statement:

IAS 14 *Segment Reporting* requires companies that have publicly traded______ [equity/debt/debt or equity] to provide a segmental analysis in their financial statements.

The primary segment format requires the disclosure of:

Segment revenue – internal	[yes/no]
Segment revenue – external	[yes/no]
Segment result	[yes/no]
Segment assets	[yes/no]
Segment liabilities	[yes/no]

(3 marks)

17.6 Karen Street-Murphy, the managing director of Slishwood plc, has received a memo from the financial controller relating to the preparation of the year-end financial statements. He expresses the view that the implementation of IAS 14 *Segment Reporting* is totally prescriptive, and as such there is no scope for him to exercise judgement in the preparation of the figures.

Comment on whether or not you agree with the financial controller's assertion.

(4 marks)

17.7 Rebrov plc has grown by acquisition and consequently now has divisions involved in seven distinct types of business activity. These divisions trade with each other in addition to selling to third parties.

Sales figures for the year ended 30 September 20X4 are shown below for each division as a percentage of total sales.

Division	*Internal* (%)	*External* (%)	*Total* (%)
1	0	32	32
2	2	22	24
3	8	7	15
4	0	9	9
5	0	8	8
6	3	4	7
7	0	5	5
	13	87	100

Which of the above are reportable segments per IAS 14 *Segment Reporting*?

A Divisions 1, 2 and 3
B Divisions 1, 2 and 4
C Divisions 1, 3 and 4
D Divisions 1, 2, 4 and 5

(3 marks)

17.8 Which of the following statements regarding IAS 14 *Segment Reporting* is false?

A A segment is reportable if its gross assets represent 10% or more of the gross assets of the entity.
B Secondary segment formats do not require the disclosure of segment liabilities.
C If management believe that publication of a segmental analysis is prejudicial to the business it can be excluded.
D Segments are usually differentiated by having different risks and returns.

(2 marks)

✓ Objective test answers

17.1

- Historic data is not a guarantee of future performance.
- Changes in accounting policy over the five-year period could distort trends.
- Different segments of the business will be exposed to different risks, growth rates, etc.
- The figures do not reflect future management intentions for the business.

17.2 **B**

Ratios are often used as a technique to estimate the future performance of a business, but they are based on historic information and hence it is not true to say they tell us little about the past.

17.3 **D**

Mayo Ltd has grown in absolute terms and yet the finance cost has remained a constant percentage; hence it cannot be fixed.

Overheads are falling as a percentage as the company grows, suggesting that some are fixed.

17.4 **D**

17.5 IAS 14 *Segment Reporting* requires companies that have publicly traded debt or equity to provide a segmental analysis in their financial statements.

The primary segment format requires the disclosure of:

Segment revenue – internal	Yes
Segment revenue – external	Yes
Segment result	Yes
Segment assets	Yes
Segment liabilities	Yes

17.6 It is true that IAS 14 *Segment Reporting* sets quantifiable measures for the identification of reportable segments and specifies a minimum level of disclosure that is required for primary and secondary segment formats. However, there is still considerable scope for the exercise of management judgement particularly in the allocations of expenses across the segments.

Furthermore it is management who select the accounting policies of the business, within the constraints of accepted practice, and these can change both the recognition and measurement of figures to be included within the segments. These policy selections can be technical (e.g. benchmark and allowed alternative treatments within a standard) or commercial such as setting the price levels at which goods are transferred internally.

17.7 **D**

Segment 3 is excluded as the majority of its sales are internal.

Segments 4 and 5 are included as they are needed to get coverage of external sales above 75%.

17.8 **C**

? Medium answer question

Question 1 – Segmental reporting

"Segmental reporting is essential for stakeholders to understand modern financial statements, and represents additional disclosure that management can provide with minimum effort."

Discuss.

(10 marks)

✓ Medium answer question

Answer 1 – The arguments for and against segmental reporting

In recent years many business sectors have seen a consolidation of the participants leading to larger trans-national groups that fall beyond the jurisdiction of a single country. These changes have been seen as the prompt to give increased segmental disclosure within published financial statements to facilitate the core concepts of comparability and understanding.

Risks

The risks and returns associated with operating in different regions of the World or different business sectors will bear little similarity to each other. If the financial results are blended into a single figure the user of the financial statements will have no understanding of the true performance.

It is also easier to spot trends, and hence make more accurate predictions about the future when information is broken down. Key ratios such as return on capital employed can be calculated for each segment, and compared against equivalents for that specific business type. This facilitates decisions regarding which parts of the business to keep or sell as it is now possible to compare like with like.

Legal shortfall

The additional rules/guidance given on segmental reporting by IAS 14, and equivalent standards released under local GAAP can also compensate for lack of disclosure required by legislation. For example, the UK Companies Act 1985 only requires turnover to be analysed segmentally.

The head office problem

It is not true to say that the provision of segmental information comes at no cost to the entity. As a minimum the accounting systems must be set up to allow the extraction of data on this basis.

Greater problems come from shared costs such as a head office which provides administration and marketing services to all the segments. It is usually a judgmental decision. Similarly what about the finance costs of a loan which has been raised to fund the activities of the entity as a whole?

Window dressing

Comparability between different entities can be undermined by the scope for management judgement in defining segments. Additionally the performance of different segments can be legitimately altered by inter-segment pricing policies used as an incentive to management or to minimise the entity's tax burden on a worldwide basis.

Conclusion

It is true to say that for large companies segmental information is essential to help give a clearer understanding on issues such as performance and governance. However, this information is neither without cost nor an element of judgement.

Analysis of Financial Statements: Earnings per Share

18

Basic EPS

$$EPS = \frac{\text{Net profit attributable to ordinary shareholders}}{\text{Weighted average number of ordinary shares}}$$

Consolidated profit after tax, minority interests, preference dividends

Weighted on a time basis this reflects the issues and repurchases of ordinary shares in the year

- Special attention needs to be given to:

Issues at full market price in the period	These generate new earning potential from their issue date, and hence are factored into the weighted average from this date
Bonus issues	These generate no new earnings and are assumed to be in issue throughout the accounting period irrespective of their issue date It is also necessary to adjust the corresponding EPS to reflect these issues
Rights issues	These effectively constitute an issue of shares at full market price and an additional bonus issue To identify the bonus element the theoretical ex-rights price (TERPs) must be calculated and compared to the fair value of the shares prior to the issue

Diluted EPS

- This reflects that an entity has financial instruments in issue that carry rights to become ordinary shares in the future
  - Convertible debt or equity instruments
  - Share warrants and options
  - Rights granted under employee share schemes.
- Convertible financial instruments

Earnings	Will increase by the saving in interest or preference dividends Remember that interest is a tax deductible expense, and hence part of the interest saving will be lost in the form of a higher tax charge
Number of shares	Assume conversion on the most advantageous terms to the holder of the financial instrument thereby recording the maximum dilution

- Share warrants and options

Earnings	No effect on basic earnings
Number of shares	The holder of an option or warrant will only exercise their conversion rights if the price is favourable compared to that of the market Hence increase the number of shares by the difference between the number of shares that would have been issued at fair value, for the proceeds obtained from the options, and the actual number of new shares

- When there are several potentially diluting factors each must be considered individually (starting with the most dilutive), and only those that have a genuinely dilutive effect should be included in the diluted EPS calculation.

EPS disclosure

- The basic and diluted EPS should be shown on the face of the income statement.

Objective test questions

18.1 When calculating basic earnings per share which of the following statements is true regarding the constitution of the earnings figure used?

A Profit before taxation and minority interests and inclusive of share of profit from associates and joint ventures.
B Profit after taxation, minority interests and preference dividends and inclusive of profit from associates and joint ventures.
C Profit after taxation and preference dividends but before minority interests are deducted, and exclusive of profit from associates and joint ventures.
D Profit after taxation, minority interests and preference dividends and exclusive of profit from associates and joint ventures.

(2 marks)

18.2 On 1 January 20X4 Romeo plc had in issue 20 million £1 ordinary shares. On 1 April of that year it made a bonus issue on a 1 for 2 basis. On 1 October it issued a further 10 million shares at their full market price of £2.40.

Romeo plc's earnings for the year ended 31 December 20X4 were £7,900,000.

What was Romeo plc's basic earnings per share?

A 13.7p
B 19.8p
C 24.3p
D 26.3p

(2 marks)

18.3 Earnings per share can be calculated for any company, but IAS 33 *requires* EPS disclosures under specific circumstances.

Briefly describe for which companies disclosure is mandatory, and the reason for this selection. [Maximum 80 words]

(3 marks)

18.4 On 1 January 20X4 Deel plc had in issue 5 million 50p ordinary shares. On 1 June of that year it made a bonus issue on a 1 for 4 basis. On 1 November it issued a further 2 million shares at their full market price of £7.10.

The company's basic EPS for the year ended 31 December 20X3 was 10p.

What is the EPS comparative to be shown in the 20X4 accounts?

(2 marks)

18.5 The management team of Inspiration plc have a reputation for their innovative approach, and this extends to the methods by which the company is funded and the approach to rewarding shareholders.

Four months into the accounting period started 1 April they doubled the issued share capital to 15 million shares. This was to take advantage of an upsurge in the equity markets, which resulted in a full take up of the shares even at what was an all time market high of £3.45 per share.

Two months prior to the year end they declared a special dividend of 40p per share in issue, which represented a significant proportion of the £7.5 million reported earnings for the year. On the same date it was announced that the shares would be consolidated with one new share being issued for every three shares held.

The basic earnings per share for the preceding year had been 57p.

Calculate the EPS for the current year and the comparative.

(3 marks)

18.6 XYX plc, whose issued share capital consists of 2 million £1 ordinary shares makes a 1 for 4 rights issue when the mid-market price of the shares is £4. The rights price is £3.

If all other factors remain unchanged at what price should the shares be quoted after the rights issue?

(2 marks)

18.7 Rhone plc had one million £1 shares in issue at 1 January 20X4. On 30 June the company made a rights issue on a 1 for 3 basis at a price of £2.80 per share. The cum rights price of the shares at that date was £3.60 each.

Earnings for the year ended 31 December 20X4 were £400,000.

What was Rhone plc's earnings per share for the year?

A 30.0p
B 33.4p
C 34.2p
D 35.1p

(3 marks)

18.8 The financial controller of Cairo plc has recently seen the following quote in a technical journal:

"When calculating earnings per share a rights issue can be viewed as having two separate components. It is partially a bonus issue and part issue at full market price". The controller knows that the company is planning a rights issue in the near future, and has requested that you provide a brief explanation of the extract so that they are prepared.

Your explanation should not exceed 80 words.

(3 marks)

18.9 IAS 33 requires a company with publicly traded ordinary shares to disclose both basic and fully diluted EPS. Which of the following are factors that might dilute the basic EPS?

(i) Share options
(ii) Shares to be issued at the current mid-market price
(iii) Convertible debt
(iv) Convertible preference shares
(v) Contingently issuable shares.

A (i), (ii) and (iii)
B (i), (ii), (iii) and (iv)
C (i), (iii), (iv) and (v)
D All

(2 marks)

18.10 The financial statements of Shannon plc show profits attributable to ordinary shareholders of £150,000.

The company currently has £1 million of 5% convertible loan stock in issue. The terms of conversion are such that 20 new ordinary shares will be issued for every £100 of loan stock if the conversion rights are exercised.

Shannon plc currently has 500,000 ordinary shares in issue, and the rate of corporation tax is 30%.

Based on the above information what is the fully diluted EPS for the company?

(2 marks)

18.11 Retro plc has £2 million of 4% convertible loan stock in issue. The terms of the stock specify that it can be converted at any time over a three year period starting next year. However, the terms of conversion depend on when the conversion rights are exercised.

Year 1 12 new ordinary shares for ever £100 of loan stock
Year 2 14 new ordinary shares for ever £100 of loan stock
Year 3 17 new ordinary shares for ever £100 of loan stock

Briefly comment on the significance of the difference in the conversion terms to the calculation of the fully diluted EPS. [Maximum 60 words]

(2 marks)

18.12 When calculating the fully diluted EPS of a company which of the following statements is false?

A Warrants and options will only impact on the weighted average number of shares and not the earnings.
B The earnings adjustment attributable to convertible preference shares must be increased by the preference dividend saved net of tax.
C Diluted EPS must be disclosed on the face of the income statement.
D To determine if a potentially diluting factor should be included in the fully diluted EPS calculation its impact on the net profit from continuing activities must be considered.

(2 marks)

18.13 Rendeen plc has profits attributable to ordinary shareholders of £2 million. In addition to the 5 million ordinary shares currently in issue, its management team hold 1 million options exercisable at £3.

If the average price of an ordinary share during the accounting period has been £5 what is the fully diluted EPS?

A 33.3p
B 35.7p
C 37.0p
D 92.6p

(2 marks)

✓ Objective test answers

18.1 **B**

18.2 **C**

	Actual no. £m	*Time*	*Bonus*	*Weighted average* £m
1 January	20	3/12	3/2	7.5
Bonus issue	10			
	30	6/12		15
Issue at full price	10			
	40	3/12		10
				32.5

EPS = 7.9/32.5 = 24.3p.

18.3 IAS 33 requires EPS disclosures for enterprises whose ordinary shares or potential ordinary shares are publically traded. Although private companies are not prohibited from giving this disclosure their limited shareholder base and the fact that the shares are not traded on a public exchange means that the costs of providing the disclosure often outweigh any benefit.

18.4 Restated comparative = 10p × 4/5 = 8p.

18.5 EPS = 69.2p

Comparative = 57p

	Actual no. £m	*Time*	*Weighted average* £m
b/f	7.5	4/12	2.5
Issue at full price	7.5		
	15	6/12	7.5
Consolidation	(10)		
	5	2/12	0.83
			10.83

EPS = 7.5/10.83 = 69.2p.

Neither the issue at full market price nor the special dividend have an impact on the prior year comparative.

18.6 In a perfect market the revised share price is £3.8

[(4 × £4) + (1 × £3)]/(4 + 1)].

18.7 **B**

TERPs = [(3 × £3.6) + (1 × £2.8)]/(3 + 1)] = £3.4

	Actual no. £m	*Time*	*Bonus*	*Weighted average* £m
1 January	1,000	6/12	3.6/3.4	529
Rights issue	333			
	1,333	6/12		667
				1,196

EPS = 400,000/1,196,000 = 33.4p.

18.8 An issue of shares at full market price creates new funding that can be invested to generate a return from that date, and in a perfect market does not impact the share price. By contrast a bonus issue generates no new earnings, but does dilute the share price.

A rights issue has attributes of both as new funds are created, but shares are issued below the market price.

18.9 C

18.10 Fully diluted EPS = 26.4p

Earnings = £150,000 + (1,000,000 × 5%) × 70% = £185,000

No. of shares = 500,000 + 200,000 = 700,000.

18.11 When calculating the fully diluted EPS the conversion terms which are most advantageous to the loan stock holder will always be selected (i.e. the terms that maximise conversion). Hence, the year 3 terms will be used even though it is possible the loan stock could be converted at an earlier date.

18.12 **B**

Unlike interest on loan stock dividends are paid after taxation and hence there is no tax impact.

18.13 C

The £3 million received from the exercise of the option would purchase 600,000 shares on the open market. This effectively means that 400,000 shares have been issued free.

Hence: Fully diluted EPS = £2 million/(£5 million + £0.4 million).

? Medium answer questions

Question 1 – The P/E ratio

(a) EPS is often compared to the market price of a share in the form of the P/E ratio. Discuss why this is seen as an important indicator for listed companies, and why its interpretation must be treated with caution.

(5 marks)

(b) Based on the information provided below calculate the basic and diluted EPS:

- Profits attributable to ordinary shareholders is £3 million of which £400,000 relates to discontinuing activities.
- 10,000,000 ordinary shares were in issue throughout the year.
- Average mid-market price of ordinary shares during the year was £5.
- Corporate profits to be taxed at 30%.

In addition to the ordinary shares the company has the following in issue:

1 £5 million of 3% convertible loan stock exercisable in two years at the rate of 90 shares for each £1,000 of stock.
2 1 million options with an exercise price of £5.
3 1 million 4% convertible preference shares. The terms of conversion are one ordinary share for every four preference shares.

(5 marks)
(Total = 10 marks)

Question 2 – BDB plc

(a) The finance team of BDB plc is in the final phase of preparing the financial statements for the year ended 31 December 20X4. This includes the completion of a published accounts checklist and the calculation of the EPS figures to be shown below the income statement.

20X4 has been an interesting year for the company which has more than doubled in size primarily through acquisition. This expansion has been funded by the issue of both loan stock and equity as follows:

- 1 April 20X4 issued £2 million ordinary shares at their full market value.
- 1 June 20X4 issued £5 million of 3% loan stock.
- 1 October 20X4 made a rights issue of 1 new share for every 3 held. The issue was fully subscribed at a rights price of £2 per share. The last cum rights price had been listed at £2.40.

The earnings attributable to ordinary shareholders for 20X4 were £1,600,000 (20X3: £700,000).

The EPS for the year ended 20X3 was 10p based on 10 million £1 ordinary shares in issue.

Calculate the basic EPS for 20X4 and the 20X3 comparative.

(4 marks)

(b) Briefly comment on any changes that might arise to the calculation of EPS if the loan stock had been convertible

(2 marks)

(c) The high profile given to EPS in the published financial statements of listed companies shows the significance attached to this benchmark. However, all financial indicators have flaws if considered in isolation and EPS is no exception.

Comment on weaknesses that might undermine the validity of using EPS as an analytical tool.

(4 marks)
(Total = 10 marks)

✓ Medium answer questions

Answer 1 – The P/E ratio

(a) This ratio is calculated by dividing the market price of ordinary shares by the EPS. Consequently it includes a component that reflects the expectations of the market regarding the future earnings of the company. As such this ratio is often seen as a measure of market confidence . . . the greater the confidence the higher the multiple of earnings, an investor is prepared to pay.

It is common for the P/E of a company to be compared to that of the market as a whole (the price/earnings relative). If the P/E of the company being reviewed is greater than that of the market this indicates that it is a market leader or that the share is currently overpriced.

Difficulties with the P/E ratio:

The World equity markets are notoriously volatile responding to a wide variety of stimuli. Some of these are very specific and relate to circumstances unique to the corporation being reviewed. Other factors are much broader and subjective such as the markets trying to anticipate movements in the World economy.

Such variations make the interpretation of the P/E ratio very challenging particularly if this is done as a snapshot in time. As with many ratios it is better to interpret trends over time to get a true impression of performance.

(b) Basic EPS = 3,000/10,000 = 30p.

To calculate the fully diluted EPS, the EPS for each potentially diluting factor needs to be considered.

Options: 0/167 = 0p.

Convertible loan stock: 105/450 = 23.3p.

Convertible preference shares: 40/250 = 16p.

These determine the order in which each diluting factor is considered. With reference to the net profit attributable to continuing operations.

	Net profit attributable to continuing operations £'000	*Ordinary shares* £'000	*Per share*
Basic	2,600	10,000	26p
Options	–	167	
	2,600	10,167	25.6p
Convertible preference shares	40	250	
	2,640	10,417	25.3p
Convertible loan stock	105	250	
	2,745	10,667	25.7p

Hence, the convertible loan stock is not a diluting factor, and will be excluded.

Hence the figures used to calculate the diluted EPS are:

Earnings = £3,000,000 + £40,000 = £3,040,000

No. of shares = 10,417,000

Diluted EPS = 3,040,000/10,417,000 = 29.2p.

Answer 2 – BDB plc

(a) 20X4 EPS = 1.6/12.869 = 12.4p

20X3 Comparative = 10p × 2.3/2.4 = 9.6p

Calculation of weighted average number of shares for 20X4

	Actual no. £m	*Time*	*Rights*	*Weighted average* £m
1 January	10	3/12	2.4/2.3	2.608
Issue at full market price	2			
	12	6/12	2.4/2.3	6.261
Rights issue	4			
	16	3/12		4
				12.869

Calculation of the theoretical ex-rights price:

TERPs = [(3 × £2.4) + (1 × £2)]/(3 + 1)] = £2.3.

(b) Impact of loan stock

The loan stock has no impact on the calculation of the basic EPS, and this does not change if the stock could be converted into ordinary shares at some future date.

However, convertible loan stock would have an impact on the calculation of fully diluted EPS. The basic earnings figure will be increased by the saving of interest net of the additional tax that would be payable as a consequence. The weighted average number of shares would increase by the maximum number of shares that could be issued under the conversion.

(c) EPS – weaknesses

In spite of its widespread use EPS does have several limitations.

First it is possible that two companies could be identical in every respect except for the number of ordinary shares in issue. This will lead to widely differing EPS. It is also important for the user to understand the impact of bonus issues which increase the number of shares, but do not provide any additional capital for the company.

Secondly the balance between retained earnings and distribution policy can also have a distorting effect. If a company maintains the same percentage return on capital year on year, but only distributes a proportion of the post tax earnings then the capital base expands and the earnings of subsequent periods will increase in absolute terms. This will lead to an increase in the EPS, but the underlying performance of the business has not changed.

However, these limitations do not undermine the use of EPS. As with all ratio analysis it should be viewed as part of an interpretation package rather than a standalone indicator.

Analysis of Financial Statements: Issues and Problems 19

Limitations of financial reporting information

- The IASB's own Framework for the preparation and presentation of financial statements concedes that financial information cannot be "all things to all men".
- Timeliness – the historic information in financial statements is not guaranteed to be an indicator of future performance.
- Comparability can be undermined by a variety of factors:
  - Businesses evolve over time moving into or withdrawing from markets
  - The effects of inflation make chronological comparison difficult
  - Changes in accounting policy
  - Some businesses have unique attributes that make them different from apparently similar entities
  - Different entities have different year ends which can impact significantly on their closing balance sheet position particularly if they have seasonal products
  - Large and small companies in the same sector are subject to different constraints and advantages such as economies of scale
  - Overseas entities will be subject to different regulatory and tax regimes.

Limitations of ratio analysis

- With the exception of EPS there is no mandatory guidance as to the basis of calculation leading to variability between entities; particularly with ratios such as ROCE and gearing.
- Several ratios, such as payables days, use averaged figures based on the position at the beginning and end of the financial period but this may not be representative of the true position.
- For some ratios a "norm" is often quoted, such as the current ratio should not fall below 2, but these may bear no relationship to the figures seen in specific industries.

Creative accounting

- Creative accounting covers a wide range of practices some of which are totally legitimate whilst others are designed to deliberately mislead the user.
- One financial analyst described the graduation of outcomes as follows:
  - Conservative accounting
  - Less conservative accounting
  - Low quality profits
  - Wishful thinking
  - Creative or misleading accounting
  - Fraud.
- The motivation for creative accounting includes:
  - Tax avoidance
  - Personal gain
  - Meeting covenants and retaining funding.
- Methods of creative accounting.

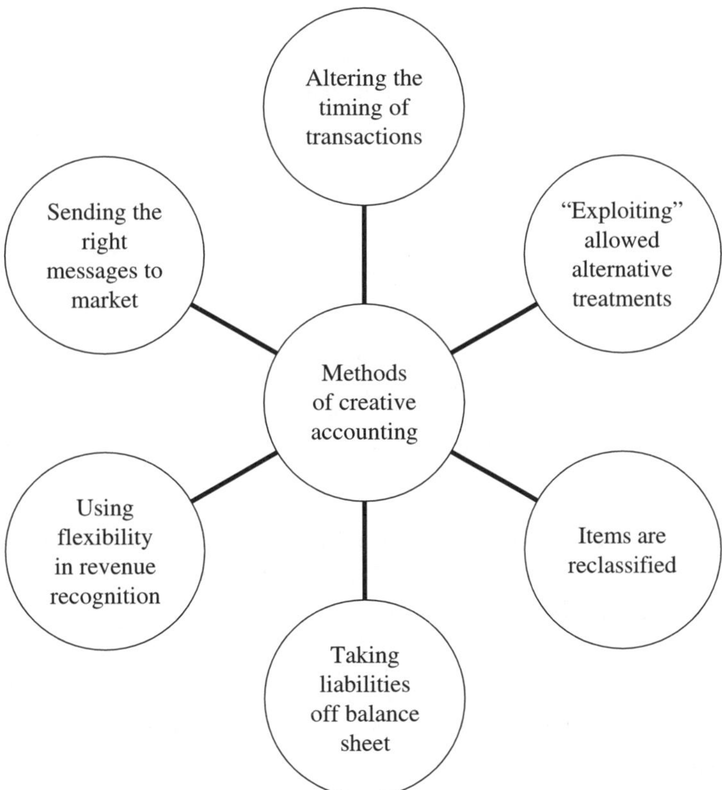

- The treatment of contingencies will remain prominent due to the judgement required in evaluating the probability attached to their final resolution.

Objective test questions

19.1 The Chairman of Lintner plc, a chemicals manufacturer, has recently observed that some of the company's competitors have been disclosing social and environmental information within their financial statements. However, the disclosures appear quite varied, and make comparison of the policies adopted difficult to compare with those of Lintner plc.

Comment on the disparity in the treatment of such disclosures, and the possible reasons why some companies can give no disclosure at all.

(4 marks)

19.2 BQB plc manufactures and sells industrial air extractors which have a retail value of £200,000. The company has strong internal control systems and regularly commissions financial reviews of its major customers to assess their performance, and hence their ability to honour outstanding creditor balances.

Extracts from the most recent review for two of BQB plc's largest customers are given below:

	Leclerk [*Is known to adopt a policy of regular revaluation of non-current assets*]	*Bokree* [*Holds non-current assets at their historic cost*]
ROCE (%)	21	29
Gearing (%)	47	77
Operating profit margin (%)	23	28

Both companies buy approximately six extractors per annum. They also have similar levels or borrowing and working capital.

Briefly explain why the figures given could be misleading. [80 words maximum]

(3 marks)

19.3 Sam Shah, a financial analyst, is comparing the financial statements of Bob Ltd and Tel Ltd for the six months ended 31 March 20X4 and 30 September 20X4. An extract from his report is given below:

	Bob Ltd		**Tel Ltd**	
	6m to 30/3/X4	**6m to 31/9/X4**	**6m to 30/3/X4**	**6m to 31/9/X4**
Gross profit (%)	28	26	23	26
Net profit (%)	15	19	14	14

Further information:

- *Bob Ltd* – Sells meat products specialising in poultry.
- *Tel Ltd* – Sells bottled water.

Based exclusively on the information provided which is the most likely explanation of the figures?

A Bob Ltd is a seasonal business with higher volumes at Christmas which is the only period when the processing plants operate at full capacity. During this period product shortages often lead to premium prices.

B Falling demand for its product has resulted in Tel Ltd cutting prices from June 20X4 to retain existing volumes from its three bottling plants.

C Bob Ltd is a seasonal business with higher volumes at Christmas. Although production levels are lower between April and September it has enough capacity to keep all of its production plants operating at partial capacity with the production line employees working fewer shifts prorata to the reduction in sales.

D Tel Ltd commenced giving settlement discounts from 1 April 20X4 to retain customers.

(2 marks)

19.4 Rimo Ltd has been operating close to its bank overdraft facility for most of the current year, but as the year-end approaches there is a genuine risk that the limit will be transgressed.

The finance director has approached the bank for a long-term loan to place the company on a more stable financial footing. However, the bank is cautious and requests a copy of the year-end financial statements. They have indicated that if the funds are to be given then covenants will be put in place to safeguard their investment.

- The current ratio cannot fall below 2:1.
- The ROCE must exceed 25%.

The finance director has decided to "enhance" the prospects of meeting these criteria by writing cheques to all accounts payable outstanding for more than 45 days, but conveniently forgetting to post them until after the year end.

What is the impact of this creative accounting on the covenants benchmarks?

(4 marks)

19.5 Roberto plc has a reputation for implementing aggressive accounting policies which maximise its short-term profitability within the confines of accepted accounting practice.

Which of the following would be policies you would expect Roberto plc to implement?

(i) Lengthening the estimated useful economic life of a non-current asset
(ii) Expensing of initial start up costs for a new asset
(iii) Use of off-balance sheet finance when the company's balance sheet reflects net assets
(iv) Use of straight line depreciation methods instead of reducing balance

A (i), (ii) and (iv)
B (i), (iii) and (iv)
C (i), (ii) and (iv)
D All

(2 marks)

19.6 The finance manager of Stickle Ltd is trying to understand the impact of different depreciation policies on key numbers within the company's published financial statements. Complete the following grid by indicating the effect of changing from an accelerated depreciation methodology to straight line depreciation for the current year.

Tick the correct impact on each item.

	Increase	Decrease	Unchanged
Profit before taxation			
Gearing			
Asset turnover			
Cash flow			

(4 marks)

19.7 Complete the following statement:

If the carrying value of a non-current asset is impaired the gearing will _____ [increase/decrease] and future returns on equity will _____ [increase/decrease].

Some assets will be held off-balance sheet via the use of operating leases. If the assets and any corresponding lease liability were moved back onto the balance sheet the current ratio would be _____ [higher/lower] and asset turnover would be _____ [higher/lower].

(2 marks)

19.8 Geraldine Barnes is a substantial shareholder in XYZ plc, and always reviews the annual financial statements in detail prior to attending the annual general meeting of the company.

The financial statements for the most recent accounting period have arrived, and Geraldine was reasonably happy with the performance reported by the company until she read an article in the financial section of the daily newspaper. The article was headed "Profits Reported at the Expense of the Balance Sheet", and she is now worried that she has been focusing too much time on the income statement and too little on the other components of the accounts.

Briefly discuss if Geraldine's fears are legitimate.

(4 marks)

✓ Objective test answers

19.1 Environmental and social disclosures

In recent years there has been an increased demand for financial statements of listed companies to give improved qualitative disclosures such as a commentary on their contribution to an improved environment. However, there are few statutory or accounting regulations that stipulate who should give such disclosure and what form it should take.

Consequently many companies give little disclosure either due to the added costs or because they believe that it is only in their interests to do so when it paints the enterprise in a favourable light!

19.2 As the working capital and long-term debt are approximately equal the most likely cause for the differences in the indicators is the differing accounting treatments for property, plant and equipment. If Leclerk revalues its non-current assets then assuming that the useful economic lives are equal the carrying values will be higher in the balance sheet, and depreciation expense in the income statement will also increase. Both of these movements lower the return on capital employed giving the appearance of deteriorating performance.

The increased carrying value in the balance sheet will also improve gearing as equity rises but debt remains unchanged.

Unfortunately, with higher carrying values comes increased depreciation leading to a fall in profitability.

19.3 **A**

19.4 *Current ratio*: If Rimo Ltd has net current assets then the current ratio will improve (the reverse would apply if there were net current liabilities).

ROCE: The strategy has no impact on the profitability of the entity. However, assuming that the bank is using a version of ROCE that incorporates overdrafts as part of the capital employed then this will be increased and ROCE will fall. The finance director might erroneously be assuming that the loan will eliminate the overdraft, but the financial statements being prepared are for the purpose of obtaining the loan which has not yet been granted.

19.5 **B**

19.6

	Increase	Decrease	Unchanged
Profit before taxation	✓		
Gearing		✓	
Asset turnover		✓	
Cash flow			✓

19.7 If the carrying value of a non-current asset is impaired the gearing will increase and future returns on equity will increase.

Some assets will be held off-balance sheet via the use of operating leases. If the assets and any corresponding lease liability were moved back onto the balance sheet the current ratio would be lower and asset turnover would be lower.

19.8 The article read by Geraldine should not cause her undue concern as it refers to a creative accounting practice that has been largely eliminated by improvements to accounting standards. It involved the practice of recognising capital profits in the income statement, whilst directing losses to the reserves. The aim was to improve profitability in the hope that the capital markets would assign a higher price/earnings ratio to the business and thereby enhance its value.

However, Geraldine does need to undertake a less skewed view of the financial statements and look beyond the income statement. Modern accounting practice is driven from the balance sheet with movements between balance sheet dates being accounted for via the income statement or reserves.

Medium answer question

Question 1 – Carmen plc

Carmen plc is a manufacturer and distributor of specialist sports equipment for competition skiing. This market acts as an oligopoly with four dominant players, and the differences in margins can be measured in fractions of one percent as they vie to gain an advantage. Two of its competitors have undergone financial reviews by the regulatory authority in the last three years.

Carmen plc has always delivered on its financial "promises" to its shareholders, and in the most recent financial statements indicated that it intended to diversify into other specialised sporting product lines. This was to be financed by an issue of non-redeemable preference shares in the next accounting period.

This method of funding was seen as the best route by the directors, and there were already £10 million options exercisable in three years in existence. The latter had been issued as part of a management buy-out from the original family members who started the company.

To accelerate the process of diversification it had been decided that the new funds would be used to acquire Hurl Ltd, which supplied shoes for several indoor sports. Discussions with the company had been ongoing for some months, and subject to minor details a purchase price had been agreed. The consideration was to be as follows:

- £2.5 million initial cash payment
- £1.5 million six months after the exchange of contracts
- £1 million after three years if the profit before taxation of Hurl Ltd exceeded £500,000 for each of the years, and key man staff retention exceeded 75%.

Requirements

(a) Based on the information provided identify any pressures on Carmen plc that might incentivise the finance team to become involved in creative accounting.

(6 marks)

(b) Hurl Ltd has always adopted a policy on revaluing its non-current assets. Comment briefly if this will act in its favour under the terms of the acquisition agreement.

(2 marks)

(c) When calculating the amount of goodwill that would arise on the acquisition why do the terms of the agreement make this more difficult to determine, and how should this be accounted for by Carmen plc?

(2 marks)
(Total = 10 marks)

Medium answer question

Answer 1 – Carmen plc

(a) Creative accounting

There are several circumstances unique to Carmen plc which increases the possibility of creative accounting appearing to be an attractive option. However, although creative accounting is not illegal it may affect the fair presentation of the financial statements, and in these circumstances would not be acceptable.

These include:

Oligopoly/Narrow margin differentials

In a market with a small number of key players it is more difficult for one to step away from the policies adopted by the others as a small change in pricing might lead to a large change in market share. Consequently, Carmen plc will find it difficult to use accounting policies that differ from its competitors, and yet there is evidence to suggest that they are using questionable methods as evidenced by the regulatory reviews.

Shareholder expectation

It is commendable that Carmen plc has always delivered on its promises to shareholders, but in periods of financial stress it will be more difficult to meet shareholder expectations on profitability and dividend distributions. A loss of shareholder confidence will lead to a detrimental impact on share price, and P/E ratios will fall.

Although it does not appear to be suffering at the moment any blip when looking for increased market capitalisation would work against the company.

Issue of non-redeemable shares

Successful share issues on the financial capital markets require a company to show a good track record on its key indicators. Hence there will be increased pressures to ensure that profitability, gearing and return on capital all show a positive trend. Creative accounting techniques that contribute to this become more attractive in the lead up to the share issue.

For example a change from reducing balance depreciation to straight line depreciation will improve earnings in the short term.

Share options

The share options arose from a management buy-out, and hence if any of the buy-out team remains with the company they will want the share price to be maximised at the strike date. This will be achieved if the company continues to grow, and the forthcoming share issue and subsequent acquisition are successful.

(b) Revaluation of non-current assets

Hurl Ltd's policy of revaluing non-current assets may work against the company if the acquisition by Carmen plc goes ahead. As asset values increase, and assuming that useful economic lives remain unchanged, the annual depreciation charge will rise. This will impact either the cost of sales or operating expense lines of the income statement, and reduce the profit before tax.

Reduced profits make it less likely that the earn-out consideration due from Carmen plc will be paid, and hence the shareholders of Hurl Ltd will receive a lower ultimate return on the sale.

(c) Contingent consideration

The acquisition consideration due from Carmen plc for the acquisition of Hurl Ltd includes an amount contingent upon the future performance of the latter. At the acquisition date Carmen plc should only include this element of the consideration in the calculation of goodwill if it is probable that the earning targets will be met.

In most earn out transactions the likelihood of payment is high at the initial contract date or there would be little point in incorporating this clause into the deal. However, the performance of Hurl Ltd must be closely monitored.

If the chances of the earn-out being successful reduce to a mere possibility then adjustments will be needed to the carrying value of goodwill.

Non-financial, Environmental and Social Reporting

20

A glimpse of the future

- There is increasing recognition that users of financial statements want more than the figures alone, and this demand is increasing in the light of recent financial scandals.
- The historic view that financial statements were exclusively to provide shareholders with details of how well their business is being run by the management team no longer applies.
  - Some modern corporations are large enough to influence the economic and social environment in which they operate.
  - It is society as a whole that has to bear the consequences of business such as pollution.

The operating and financial review

- Some companies have produced these for many years, but proposed changes to legislation in the UK intends to make them mandatory for all companies over a stipulated size limit.
- The OFR is designed to assist in the assessment of future performance, and is targeted primarily at investors.
- It is to include a range of financial and non-financial measures with the emphasis on description rather than numbers.
- Typical contents will include:
  - description of the business
  - objectives and strategy
  - returns to shareholders in the form of distributions and share repurchases
  - dynamics of the business

  - commentary on issues such as intangible assets, market position and customer/supplier relationships
  - human resource activities
  - research
  - refurbishment programmes
  - a broad financial review including treasury policy
  - cash flows and liquidity.
- Pros and cons include:

For	*Against*
• Use friendly compared to the detail of the financial statements and hence more likely to be read • Added information	• Currently voluntary

Accounting for the impact of an entity on the environment around it

- The pressures for entities to do this are growing as evidenced by the Kyoto Accord on greenhouse gas emissions.
- A direct impact of the interrelationship between an entity and the world around it increasingly seen through the taxation policies adopted by governments
  - Landfill taxes
  - Tax allowances for socially/environmentally friendly expenditure.
- Provisions and contingencies are a key consideration both in the real world and the exam room.
- The level of disclosure given in published financial statements is growing, but is largely voluntary and is most prevalent in the disclosures of those entities who believe they have made a positive contribution.

Accounting for human resource issues

- Current disclosures are voluntary, but there is growing demand for information such as:

Statement of corporate objectives	Would look at issues to all the stakeholder groups originally identified in the *Corporate Report* (1975)
Employment report	Would look beyond remuneration to issues such as training
Value added reports	Would demonstrate the value that is attributable to the interdependency of different stakeholders

- Intellectual capital reporting – this looks at human resources and intellectual assets (e.g. technical drawing), but is a very difficult subject upon which to report due to its largely intangible nature.

- Human asset accounting – this is particularly relevant to service industries and attempts to value the workforce as part of the non-current assets of the business.

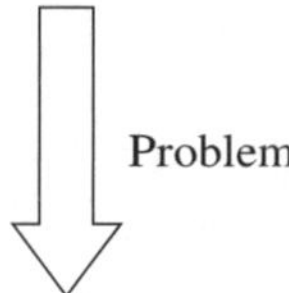

- The IASCs *Framework for the Preparation and Presentation of Financial Statements* defines an asset as:

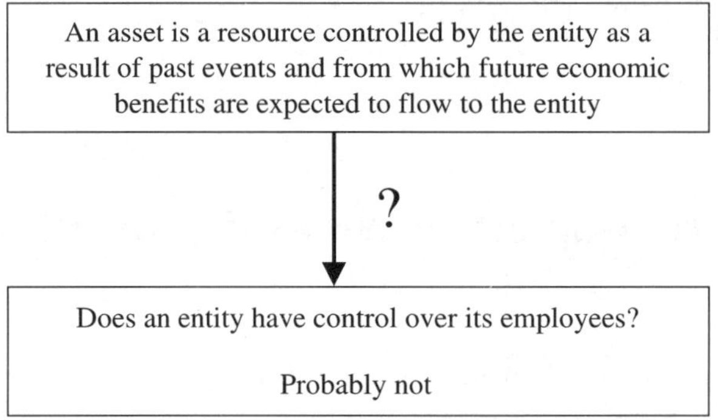

- There is also the not inconsiderable issue of identifying a value for these intangibles.

The global reporting initiative

- A joint initiative of:
  - The Coalition for Environmentally Responsible Economies (CERES)
  - United Nations Environment Programme.
- Launched first guidelines in 2000 and updated then in 2002.
- The guidelines are voluntary and suggest a report with the following headings:

1 Vision and strategy
2 Profile
3 Governance structure and management systems
4 GRI content index
5 Performance indicators
  - Economic
  - Environmental Social

? Objective test questions

20.1 Intellectual capital is one of the most significant assets to any successful business, and yet it does not appear on the balance sheet. Identify two reasons for this apparent omission. [Maximum 80 words]

(2 marks)

20.2 The voluntary guidelines set by the Global Reporting Initiative (GRI) identify a range of performance indicators split into three categories; namely economic, environmental and social.

Many of these indicators cannot be measured in financial terms, but it is informative if they can be quantified. Illustrate how this might be achieved using a specific example.

(2 marks)

20.3 Fossil Ltd specialises in open cast mining, and has recently identified a significant new coal reserve over which it has secured the extraction rights. The reserve is estimated to be viable for 10 years, and at the end of this period the site will have to be environmentally restored as part of the contract terms.

To access the coal seam it is necessary to clear the entire site in the first year so that heavy vehicles can move freely from the diggers to the processing plant. Consequently 80% of the total environmental damage caused to the site will be incurred in the first month, whereas the remaining 20% is attributable to the extraction process.

Insofar as the data allows describe the impact of the accounting treatment of these restoration costs on the restoration provision in the balance sheet of Fossil Ltd for the first and second years of operating the mine.

The restoration cost in ten years is expected to be £20 million.

(4 marks)

20.4 Rebel plc is currently subject to two separate legal actions as described below:

(i) A local farmer is suing for £100,000 damages with reference to soil contamination which he claims has reduced the selling value of crops grown in that location. Rebel plc does not dispute that contamination occurred, but claims that the contaminant has no health consequences, and points to a fall in crop prices generally as the cause of the farmers' losses.

The farmer is supported by leading environmental groups, and during the period when the contamination occurred there was extensive national media coverage.

(ii) At the beginning of the current year a chemical storage tank owned by Rebel Ltd split releasing several thousand litres of caustic waste into a Site of Special Scientific Interest killing several endangered plants. A claim of £175,000 has been raised against the company by the Environmental Agency.

Rebel Ltd has a warranty relating to the tank, and legal advice indicates that they will be able to recoup the full liability.

In its latest income statement Rebel Ltd recorded a retained profit of £438,000.

What action would you recommend to the company in respect of each claim?

	Claim 1	*Claim 2*
A	Disclose	Disclose
B	Disclose	Provide
C	Provide	Disclose
D	Provide	Provide

(2 marks)

20.5 Which of the following matters would you expect to see discussed in an operating and financial review statement?

(i) Development of new products and services
(ii) Returns to shareholders
(iii) Business objectives and a strategy to achieve them
(iv) Liquidity

A (iii) and (iv)
B (i), (iii) and (iv)
C (ii), (iii) and (iv)
D All

(2 marks)

20.6 The GRI (Global Reporting Initiative) aggregates performance indicators into three sustainablity dimensions ; economic, environmental and social. Give four examples of issues to be considered within the social dimension.

(2 marks)

Objective test answers

20.1 Intellectual capital

- Assets such as property, plant and equipment are shown on a balance because they are controlled by the business. Although an employee may have a contract with the entity they always have the right to resign, and hence control is difficult to prove.
- Intellectual property is undoubtedly responsible for generating future cash flows, but the measurement of these, beyond the salary an entity is prepared to pay, is both subjective and difficult to quantify.

20.2 GRI indicator quantification

It is not possible to measure the exact financial impact of the release of pollutants into the atmosphere, but it is possible to quantity the volume released over a specified period. This data can then be compared to other statistics such as disease rates or crop contamination to give a measure of the impact. The financial costs are less easy to ascertain as they may occur many years into the future.

20.3 Fossil Ltd

Year 1: Provision must be made for the 80% damage caused in the first month (i.e. £16 million) as this represents the obligating event. Additionally provision must be made for one-tenth of the total damage caused by coal extraction (i.e. £400,000).

As the restoration is not due until the cessation of mining activities, and on the likely presumption that the amounts are material to Fossil Ltd the provision should be discounted to its present value.

Year 2: The value of the provision established in the previous year will be changed by two events:

1 An additional £400,000 provision, pre-discounting, will be required for the additional damage caused by extraction.
2 The NPV of the provision will increase as the discounting starts to unwind.

20.4 **D**

Claim 1: There is no dispute that an obligating event has occurred and that it can be measured. Although it is possible that Rebel Ltd may be able to claim that the contaminant has no health consequences the media coverage will have reduced the attractiveness of the farmers produce.

Claim 2: The fact that the company can recoup its losses does not negate the need to provide for the legal claim.

In both cases the amounts are material judged against the recent profitability of the company.

20.5 **D**

20.6

1 Human rights
2 Product responsibility (customer health and safety)
3 Labour practices (training and education)
4 Interaction with society (pricing policies)

? Medium answer questions

Question 1

"There is a growing demand for the inclusion of more information within published financial statements on environmental and social issues. Inclusions of this type are to be commended, but have little to do with the detailed application of international accounting standards."

Discuss this statement.

(10 marks)

Question 2

(a) Briefly describe what you understand by the following terms:

- Social reporting
- Operating and financial review
- The global reporting initiative.

(6 marks)

(b) The inclusion of a social report within published financial statements remains an option at the discretion of management for companies in most countries. It is easy to see that omission would be the easy option saving costs and time.

However, many companies have started to include such information on a regular basis.

Highlight why the inclusion of such voluntary information in the financial statements may be seen as a positive inclusion by the management.

(4 marks)
(Total = 10 marks)

Medium answer questions

Answer 1

Environmental and social reporting – The impact of accounting standards

Reporting on the impact that a business has on the environment and the community around it can be very challenging as these issues are often difficult to quantify, and it is then more appropriate to give qualitative information to the stakeholders. Descriptive information can be given via the traditional routes of the directors' or chairman's report or through the medium of bespoke reports.

However, it would be wrong to conclude that there is no overlap with the implementation of international accounting standards as many environmental/social issues have specific quantifiable consequences such as:

- Capital expenditure
- Development expenditure
- Decommissioning costs.

IAS 37 provisions, contingent liabilities and contingent assets

A provision should be recognised in the financial statements if the following conditions are met:

1 an entity has a present obligation, legal or constructive, as a result of a past event
2 it is probable that an outflow of resources embodying economic benefits will be required to settle the obligation
3 a reliable estimate can be made of the amount of the obligation.

In some circumstances this will lead to the earlier recognition of a liability than would have been the case prior to the introduction of this standard. As soon as the obligating event has occurred, then subject to the other conditions being met, a provision must be made immediately; it cannot be built up over the life of the project. This is particularly relevant for decommissioning costs when the damage maybe inflicted on the environment many years before restoration commences.

If conditions (2) or (3) are not met there are still disclosure consequences for the notes to the financial statements in the form of a contingent liability.

IAS 16 property, plant and equipment

To ensure that environmental regulations are complied with it is common for businesses to invest significant amounts into capital equipment (e.g. filtration plants). This capital expenditure must be capitalised and depreciated over its useful economic life, and hence it has a direct impact on both the balance sheet and the income statement.

There may also be an overlap with IAS 20, *Accounting for Government Grants and disclosure of Government Assistance*, when capital grants are recognised and offset against related assets in the balance sheet.

IAS 38 intangible assets

This standard extends to research and development expenditure which is very relevant to environmental issues. If a development project meets specified criteria such as being economically viable then the expenditure must be capitalised as an intangible non-current asset.

Numbers are never enough

It is true that to understand many social and environmental issues the users of financial statements need more than financial disclosure. There needs to be a much wider disclosure that demonstrates an empathy with the issues of the modern world.

However, the best solution is to find a balance between qualitative and quantitative information, and hence the discipline introduced by accounting standards can make a positive contribution when evaluating matters beyond pure financial performance.

Answer 2

(a) (i) Social reporting

Social reporting is the process of communicating the social impact and organisation has on both society as a whole and on specific interest groups. It goes beyond the traditional financial boundaries of stakeholder reporting to cover issues such as:

- Child labour
- Poverty
- Equality.

For some theorists it is seen as a component of a social contract, whereby an entity can only justify its existence in the context of the way in which serves society as a whole.

(ii) Operating and financial review [OFR]

This is a review by senior management of the business that goes beyond the normal remit of a director's report required by the legislation of some countries.

Its target audience is primarily investors, and it aims to allow them to make an assessment of the future performance of the business. The information within the review should be free from bias and highlight both good and bad news.

The OFR usually contains information on trends, which are supported by straight forward analytical narrative.

(iii) The global reporting initiative

This was launched as a joint initiative between United Nations Environment Programme and CERES. It focuses on the issue of sustainability reporting – the social, environmental and economic aspects of performance.

A number of draft guidelines have been issued, and are in the process of being updated. They include:

- a statement by the chief executive describing the key elements of the report
- an overview of the organisation
- a discussion of vision and strategy
- an overview of governance structure and management systems.

(b) Voluntary social reporting

In future years it is likely that aspects of social and environmental reporting will become more prescriptive, but there are good reasons for many companies to provide such information already on a voluntary basis.

Reasons includes:

Brand – Some companies have built their brand on social awareness, and hence have to demonstrate that they are good to their word.

Track record – If a company has contributed positively to social issues it may take the opportunity to paint itself in a good light.

Being first – In some countries such as Sweden and Denmark some aspects of environmental and social reporting is already mandatory for large companies. The spread of such rules is accelerating and many businesses will perceive it is better to implement in advance rather than being seen as only complying when forced to do so.

International Financial Reporting

21

Barriers to harmonisation

- The drive towards international harmonisation has gathered pace in recent years and from 2005 onwards listed companies within the EU will have to produce their consolidated financial statements in compliance with international standards.

  However, those aiming for a single set of global accounting standards still have some significant hurdles to overcome:

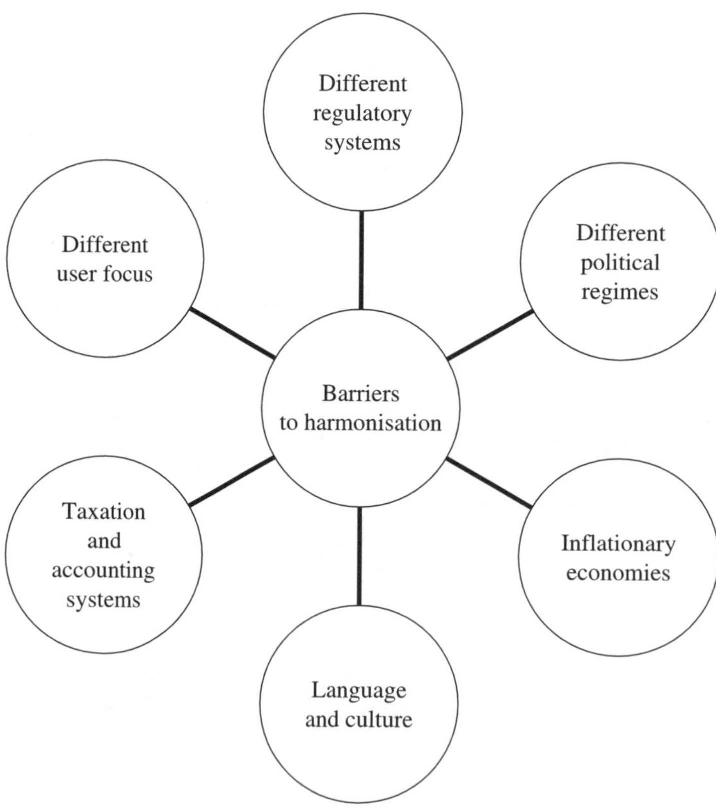

- The rewards of harmonisation will be high for multinational entities who will see cost reductions and easier access to finance.
- Stakeholders will find comparison of financial statements easier.

Interested parties in the harmonisation process

United Nations	Acts as a forum for ideas, and provides assistance to developing countries
Organisation for Economic Co-operation and Development (OECD)	Issued a voluntary guide on disclosures of financial information, and has a committee specifically looking at international standards
European Union	Directives from the EU have influenced the accounting of member states for many years, and it has now decided to insist on the implementation of IAS GAAP

IAS vs US GAAP

- The Securities and Exchange Commission (SEC) plays a key role in the accounting regulatory framework of the USA.
- The SEC has the authority to set accounting standards, but delegates this authority.
- The Financial Accounting Standards Board (FASB) issues accounting standards, and adopts a more prescriptive approach than standards issued under IAS GAAP.
- The Norwalk Agreement – the convergence project currently underway to unify USA and IAS GAAP.

Objective test questions

21.1 In 2000 an agreement was reached between the IASC and IOSCO (International Organisation of Securities Commissions). Briefly describe why was this a significant step towards the wider acceptance of IAS. [Maximum 60 words]

(2 marks)

21.2 Which of the following represent the major objectives of the IASB?

(i) To promote the use and vigorous application of international accounting standards.
(ii) To ensure high ethical standards.
(iii) To facilitate convergence of national and international accounting standards.

A (i) and (ii)
B (i) and (iii)
C (ii) and (iii)
D (i), (ii) and (iii)

(2 marks)

21.3 Complete the following paragraph:

Significant differences remain between US GAAP and IAS as the former adopts a _____ [more prescriptive/less prescriptive] approach. Some differences between the two approaches are very clear cut such as:

- Under US GAAP development expenditure must be expensed whereas under IAS such expenditure _____ [must be/may be] capitalised if certain criteria are met.

(2 marks)

21.4 "It is often said that a strong argument for the introduction of international accounting standards is the cost savings it will allow companies to make after the initial costs of transfer have been incurred. However, these companies will still have to produce financial statements that carry equal, if not more onerous disclosure requirements, and hence the cost saving argument is a false premise."

List three reasons why this statement is incorrect, and the possibility of cost savings under IAS is a real prospect.

(3 marks)

✓ Objective test answers

21.1 IOSCO represents all the major global stock market regulators, and hence their broad acceptance of IAS allowed foreign entities to use IAS for the preparation of their financial statements, and yet still hold a listing on the national exchanges (i.e. without using local GAAP).

21.2 **B**

21.3 Complete the following paragraph:

Significant differences remain between US GAAP and IAS as the former adopts a more prescriptive approach. Some differences between the two approaches are very clear cut such as:

- Under US GAAP development expenditure must be expensed whereas under IAS such expenditure must be capitalised if certain criteria are met.

21.4 Cost savings under IAS:

(i) Large companies that hold a listing on more than one exchange will not incur the costs of preparing their financial statements under more than one GAAP as IAS will be recognised globally.
(ii) Subject to differing statutory requirements a single accounts software package will be needed.
(iii) The workload of group finance directors and external auditors should be reduced for international groups.

? Medium answer questions

Question 1 – Titanium plc

Chas Patel is a senior partner with DHN & Co, a medium sized accountancy practice that has a large portfolio of small and medium sized clients. The firm has always found it difficult to break through into the "blue chip" sector, although they believe they have the expertise to provide high quality advise if requested.

Chas has recently received a letter from the finance director of Titanium plc, and recognises that this could represent the opportunity that the firm requires. Titanium plc is an unusual company in that it has a full public listing, but has never diversified away from its core business, and hence has no subsidiaries or associates.

The finance director is aware that listed companies in the European Union will have to prepare consolidated financial statements that are compliant with IAS for financial periods commencing on or after 1 January 2005. Technically the company is not caught by these regulations as it does not produce consolidated statements, but the finance director is keen to convince the senior management team that it would be better to transfer to the new accounting rules sooner rather than later.

He has invited Chas, who is well known as an expert in this field, to put a presentation to the directors explaining the pros and cons. Although he wants to transfer to IAS he believes that it is better to get the "buy in" of his peers rather than pushing through changes.

Additional factors to be considered are:

- Titanium plc's financial year end is 30 September
- The company trades around the World
- It has always favoured the principles based accounting guidance issued in the UK.

Requirements

Prepare a maximum of four slides on the arguments for and against the transfer to IAS for the presentation, and include brief notes with each to support the points made.

(10 marks)

✓ Medium answer questions

Answer 1 – Titanium plc

Slide 1: Advantages of global harmonisation

- Raising financial capital
- Helping stakeholders
- The Internet.

Notes: A major advantage for listed companies will be better access to foreign investor funds, and a greater variety of markets upon which financial capital can be raised.

The fact that all financial statements will be prepared using a common rule set also makes it easier for different stakeholder groups to make comparisons between entities. A potential investor based in one country will be able to evaluate the relative merits of entities in different geographic locations.

Increasingly large organisations are releasing their financial results on the Internet. This means that users in any location have access to this information.

Slide 2: Further advantages

- Cost savings and efficiency
- Improved analysis.

Notes: Although transfer from national GAAP to IAS will have to be funded (e.g. new accounting systems, etc.), in the longer term there should be significant cost savings. For international companies it will no longer be necessary to prepare financial information using local GAAP for each subsidiary, and this in turn should reduce the costs incurred using professional advisers.

Inter-group and intercompany comparisons will be easier and faster; thereby allowing decisions to be made more efficiently.

Slide 3: Global barriers to harmonisation

- Different cultures and regulatory environments
- Different purposes of financial reporting.

Notes: The regulatory environment under which entities prepare financial information is not restricted to accounting standards. It is unlikely that uniformity will ever be achieved with all legislation and hence this makes the smooth implementation of IAS more difficult. Furthermore there will be resistance to change from local cultures that have evolved over extended periods.

The primary purpose of financial statements also differs in different countries. In the USA and UK the main user of financial statements is perceived to be the shareholders, whereas in other locations the government or creditors take first place. It is impossible for one accounting system to provide complete information to all users without making financial statements too unwieldy.

Slide 4: Specific barriers to harmonisation

- Unique status
- Unproven.

Notes: Some countries are exposed to unique circumstances that influence every stakeholder group. Typical examples would be hyperinflation or government expropriation of assets. These tend to override all other factors, and make it difficult for IAS or any other accounting regime to give parity with users elsewhere across the globe.

Some commentators also argue that the implementation of accounting standards on this scale is an unproven concept. However, the IAS are now recognised as a very resilient accounting regime, and after some initial teething difficulties a successful introduction is expected.

Long Questions and Answers 22

Question 1 – Seed plc

Set out below are the financial statements of Pip plc and its subsidiaries as at 31 December 20X4.

Balance sheets as at 31 December 20X4

	Pip plc		*Seed Ltd*		*Chaf Ltd*	
	£'000	£'000	£'000	£'000	£'000	£'000
Assets						
Non-current assets						
Property, plant and equipment		5,770		4,000		2,800
Investments		6,020		–		–
		11,790		4,000		2,800
Current assets						
Inventory	5,400		2,880		2,520	
Receivables	3,600		1,280		2,380	
Cash	1,710	10,710	320	4,480	560	5,460
Total assets		22,500		8,480		8,260
Equity and liabilities						
Capital and reserves						
Ordinary share capital		7,200		2,000		2,400
Share premium account		1,170		–		–
Accumulated profits		9,900		5,520		3,480
		18,270		7,520		5,880
Non-current liabilities						
Loan		–		–		1,750
Current liabilities						
Trade payables		4,230		960		630
		22,500		8,480		8,260

- Pip plc owns 2,400,000 50p ordinary shares in Seed Ltd which had been purchased on 1 January 20X0 for £3,200,000 cash. On that date, Seed Ltd had accumulated profits of £1,200,000.

- On 30 June 20X2 Pip plc purchased 1,800,000 £1 ordinary shares in Chaf Ltd for £2,820,000 cash. On that date Chaf Ltd had accumulated profits of £560,000, and an expert had estimated that the fair value of land owned on this date exceeded the book value by £160,000.

Income Statements for the Year ending 31 December 20X4

	Pip plc	*Seed Ltd*	*Chaf Ltd*
	£'000	£'000	£'000
Revenue	20,000	21,060	11,480
Cost of sales	(10,400)	(11,520)	(5,880)
Gross profit	9,600	9,540	5,600
Selling and administration costs	(5,600)	(3,960)	(3,220)
Profit before taxation	4,000	5,580	2,380
Taxation	(1,600)	(1,620)	(700)
Profit after taxation	2,400	3,960	1,680
Accumulated profits b/f	7,500	1,560	1,800
Accumulated profits c/f	9,900	5,520	3,480

- Subsequent to the date of acquisition the goodwill arising on Seed Ltd had been fully impaired (this had occurred in 20X2).
- Due to synergy between products there is regular intragroup trading between the three companies. For the year ended 31 December 20X4 this equated to:

Chaf Ltd to Pip plc	£105,000
Pip plc to Seed Ltd	£140,000

The transfer values include a mark up of 25% and at 31 December 20X4, £10,000 remains in the books of both Pip plc and Seed Ltd respectively.

- Prior to the year end of 31 December 20X4 Pip plc and Seed Ltd both declared a dividend of 10p per share, but due to a flaw in the groups' accounting software package no entries have been made to record them. [Pip plc's ordinary share capital comprises of £1 shares.]

Requirement

Prepare the consolidated income statement and statement of changes in equity for the year ended 31 December 20X4 and the consolidated balance sheet on the same date.

(25 marks)

Answer 1 – Seed plc

Consolidated balance sheet as at 31 December 20X4

	£'000	£'000
Assets		
Non-current assets		
Property, plant and equipment [inc FV adj.]		12,730
Intangibles [W4]		480
		13,210
Current assets		
Inventory [after PURP]	10,796	
Receivables	7,260	
Cash	2,590	20,646
Total assets		33,856
Equity and liabilities		
Capital and reserves		
Ordinary share capital		7,200
Share premium account		1,170
Accumulated profits [W6]		12,678.5
		21,048.5
Minority interests [W5]		4,357.5
		25,406
Non-current liabilities		
Loan		1,750
Current liabilities		
Trade payables		5,820
Dividends payable by Pip plc		720
Dividends payable to minority interests		160
		33,856

Consolidated income statement for the year ended 31 December 20X4

	£'000
Revenue [20,000 + 21,060 + 11,480 − 105 − 140]	52,295
Cost of sales [10,400 + 11,520 + 5,880 − 105 − 140 + 4]	(27,559)
Gross profit	24,736
Selling and administration costs [5,600 + 3,960 + 3,220]	(12,780)
Profit before taxation	11,956
Taxation [1,600 + 1,620 + 700]	(3,920)
Profit after taxation	8,036
Minority interest [W7]	(2,003.5)
Profit attributable to the shareholders of Pip plc	6,032.5

Consolidated statement of changes in equity for the year ended 31 December 20X4

	Share capital £'000	*Share premium* £'000	*Accumulated profit* £'000
b/f	7,200	1,170	7,366 [W8]
Profit for year			6,032.5
Pip – Dividend			(720)
c/f	7,200	1,170	12,678.5

[W1] Group structure

Seed Ltd = 60% subsidiary

Chaf Ltd = 75% subsidiary

[W2] Net assets

Seed plc

	At acquisition £'000	*At balance sheet date* £'000	*Post-acquisition* £'000
Share capital	2,000	2,000	–
Accumulated profits	1,200	5,520	
Adjustments			
Declared dividend		(400)	
	3,200	7,120	3,920

Chaf Ltd

	At acquisition £'000	*At balance sheet date* £'000	*Post-acquisition* £'000
Share capital	2,400	2,400	–
Accumulated profits	560	3,480	
Adjustments:			
FV	160	160	
PURP [W3]		(2)	
	3,120	6,038	2,918

[W3] Unrealised profits on intragroup

Chaf Ltd to Pip plc	£10,000	@25/125 = £2k
Pip plc to Seed Ltd	£10,000	@25/125 = £2k

[W4] Goodwill

Seed Ltd

	£'000
Cost of investment	3,200
Net assets acquired [60% × 3,200 (W2)]	(1,920)
	1,280
Less: Impairment	(1,280)
	nil

Chaf Ltd

	£'000
Cost of investment	2,820
Net assets acquired [75% × 3,120 (W2)]	(2,340)
	480
Less: Impairment	–
	480

[W5] Minority interests

Seed Ltd = 40% × £7,120 [W2] = £2,848k

Chaf Ltd = 25% × £6,038 [W2] = £1,509.5k

[W6] Consolidated accumulated profits c/f

	£'000
Pip plc	9,900
Less: Pip's own dividend	(720)
Add: Dividend receivable from Seed	240
Less: Unrealised profit	(2)
Seed Ltd [60% × 3,920 (W2)]	2,352
Chaf Ltd [75% × 2,918 (W2)]	2,188.5
Goodwill impairment	(1,280)
	12,678.5

[W7] Minority interests – Income statement

Seed Ltd = 40% × [3,960] = 1,584

Chaf Ltd = 25% × [1,680 − 2] = 419.5

[W8] Consolidated accumulated profits b/f

	£'000
Pip plc	7,500
Seed Ltd [60% × (1,560 − 1,200)]	216
Chaf Ltd [75% × (1,800 − 560)]	930
Goodwill impairment	(1,280)
	7,366

Question 2 – Liquid plc

Set out below is a summary of the financial statements of Liquid plc for the year ended 30 September 20X4.

Consolidated balance sheets as at 30 September 20X4

	20X4		20X3	
	£'000	£'000	£'000	£'000
Assets				
Non-current assets				
Property, plant and equipment		12,000		8,900
Intangibles		500		0
Investment in associates		300		250
		12,800		9,150
Current assets				
Inventory	9,800		8,150	
Receivables	7,100		6,050	
Cash	750		100	
		17,650		14,300
Total assets		30,450		23,450
Equity and liabilities				
Capital and reserves				
Ordinary share capital		11,750		11,500
Share premium		250		–
Accumulated profits		3,976		1,988
		15,976		13,488
Minority interests		400		300
		16,376		13,788
Non-current liabilities				
Loan		2,500		1,800
Current liabilities				
Payables	11,574		7,862	
		11,574		7,862
		30,450		23,450

Consolidated income statement for the year ended 30 September 20X4

	£'000
Revenue	10,000
Cost of sales	(5,600)
Gross profit	4,400
Selling and administration costs	(800)
Operating profit	3,600
Income from associates	90
Interest receivable	75
Interest payable	(70)
Profit before taxation	3,695
Taxation (includes £25,000 relating to associate)	(1,100)
Profit after taxation	2,595
Minority interests	(100)
	2,495

Further information

1 The statement of changes in equity reflects the following exchange gains that have occurred on retranslations and have been taken directly to accumulated profits.

	£'000
Inventory	120
Receivables	43
Payables	55

2 Current payables

	20X4	*20X3*
	£'000	£'000
Bank overdrafts	225	90
Trade payables	8,424	4,972
Taxation	2,150	1,900
Proposed dividends [declared in year]	725	900
Accrued interest	50	0
	11,574	7,862

3 Miffed Ltd

During the year (30 June 20X4) the company acquired the entire share capital of Miffed Ltd for a total consideration of £1,200,000. This comprised 250,000 £1 ordinary shares [Market value £2], with the balance in cash.

The fair value of the assets of Miffed Ltd was as follows

	£'000
Non-current assets	200
Inventory	110
Trade receivables	350
Trade payables	(105)
Cash	80
	635

Prior to the end of the accounting period the goodwill arising on this acquisition suffered a £65,000 impairment.

4 Non-current assets – net book value summary

	£'000
At 1 October 20X3	8,900
Additions	3,595
Disposals	(125)
Annual depreciation	(370)
	12,000

- The assets disposed of during the year generated a profit of £70,000.
- The additions include £300,000 of non-current assets acquired under finance leases. The first repayment is not due until 1 January 20X6.
- When preparing the financial statements the client has erroneously included finance lease liabilities within loans.

Requirement

Prepare the consolidated cash-flow statement for the year ended 30 September 20X4.

(25 marks)

Answer 2 – Liquid plc

Consolidated cash-flow statement for the year ended 30 September 20X4

	£'000	£'000
Cash flows from operating activities		
Operating profit	3,600	
Adjustments for		
Depreciation of PPE	370	
Profit on sale of PPE	(70)	
Impairment of intangible non-current assets	65	
Operating profit before working capital changes	365	
Increase in inventories [9,800 − 8,150 − 110 − 120]	(1,420)	
Increase in receivables [7,100 − 6,050 − 350 − 43]	(657)	
Increase in payables [8,424 − 4,972 − 105 + 55]	3,402	
Cash generated from operations	1,325	
Interest paid [70 − 50]	(20)	
Income taxes paid [W1]	(825)	
	(845)	
Net cash from operating activities		4,445
Cash flows from investing activities		
Purchase of PPE [3,595 − 200 − 300]	(3,095)	
Purchase of non-current investments [700 − 80]	(620)	
Proceeds from sale of PPE [125 + 70]	195	
Investment income	75	
Dividends from associates [W3]	15	(3,430)
Net cash (used in)/from investing activities		
Cash flows from financing activities		
Proceeds from issue of share capital [not issued for cash]	nil	
Proceeds from issue of long-term borrowings [2,500 − 1,800 − 300]	400	
Dividends paid	(900)	(500)
Net cash (used in)/from financing activities		
Net increase in cash and cash equivalents		515
Cash and cash equivalents at beginning of period [100 − 90]		10
Cash and cash equivalents at end of period [750 − 225]		525

Note 1: Acquisition of subsidiary

	£'000
Non-current assets	200
Inventory	110
Trade receivables	350
Trade payables	(105)
Cash	80
	635
Goodwill	565
	1,200
Consideration	
Equity shares [250k × £2]	500
Cash	700
	1,200

Note 2: Non-cash transactions

With respect to non-cash transactions, Liquid plc purchased Miffed Ltd on 30 June 20X4. Part of the consideration was £250,000 of £1 ordinary shares valued at £500,000.

The company entered into finance leases totaling £300,000 during the financial year.

Workings

[W1] Taxation

	£'000		£'000
		Bal b/f	1,900
Cash paid	825	P&L (excl associate)	1,075
Bal c/f	2,150		
	2,975		2,975

[W2] Minority interests

	£'000		£'000
		Bal b/f	300
Bal c/f	400	P&L	100
	400		400

[W3] Associates

	£'000		£'000
Bal b/f	250	% Tax	25
		Cash received	15
% PBT	90	Bal c/f	300
	340		340

Note: The shares issued in the year were exchanged as part of the consideration for the purchase of Miffed Ltd.

Question 3 – Pen plc

Pen plc was incorporated 15 years ago, and is now well known as an importer and seller of specialist cheeses from around the world. In recent years, the company has expanded its operations into the related sectors of yogurts and other dairy-based deserts; achieving this modest diversification via the acquisition of stakes in Quill Ltd and HB Ltd.

The balance sheets for all three companies as at 30 September 20X4 were as follows

	Pen plc		*Quill Ltd*		*HB Ltd*	
	£'000	£'000	£'000	£'000	£'000	£'000
Assets						
Non-current assets						
Property, plant and equipment		20,030		25,000		12,000
Investments						
In Quill [60%]		62,000		–		–
In HB [15%]		5,125		–		–
In HB [45%]		–		12,100		–
		87,155		37,100		12,000
Current assets						
Inventory	42,500		37,000		11,500	
Receivables	31,000		18,000		14,100	
Cash	1,200	74,700	2,750	57,750	200	25,800
Total assets		161,855		94,850		37,800
Equity and liabilities						
Capital and reserves						
Ordinary share capital		10,200		10,000		5,000
Share premium account		5,000		–		–
Accumulated profits		85,155		55,850		17,300
		100,355		65,850		22,300
Non-current liabilities						
Loan		20,000		–		–
Current liabilities						
Trade payables		41,500		29,000		15,500
		161,855		94,850		37,800

Further information

- Pen plc purchased its investments in Quill Ltd and HB Ltd in 20X1 when the accumulated profits of these two companies were £41 million and £5 million respectively.
- Quill Ltd had purchased its stake in HB Ltd several years earlier when the reserves of the latter were £1.5 million.
- The goodwill arising on Quill has suffered a 25% impairment during the current year. No previous grounds for impairment had been identified.
- Subsequent to the investments referred to above, neither Pen plc nor Quill Ltd have issued any further share capital.
- During the accounting period HB Ltd had made sales of £900,000 to Pen plc. This included as mark up on cost of 20%. Half of these items remain within the inventory of Pen plc at the balance sheet date.

- On 30 June 20X4 Pen plc sold plant and equipment to Quill Ltd for £2 million. The asset originally cost £1.8 million when purchased on 1 February 20X2, and the depreciation policy of the group is to depreciate over ten years straight line with a full year in the year of acquisition. Quill Ltd has already charged depreciation on this asset for the year ended 30 September 20X4.
- Both Pen plc and Quill Ltd declared a £1 million dividend prior to the year end, but neither has yet recorded these distributions in their financial statements (either receipts or payments).

Requirements

(a) Prepare the consolidated balance sheet for the year ended 30 September 20X4.

(17 marks)

(b) Discuss the advantages and disadvantages that arise from the preparation of consolidated financial statements.

(8 marks)
(Total = 25 marks)

Answer 3 – Pen plc

(a) Consolidated balance sheet as at 30 September 20X4

	£'000	£'000
Assets		
Non-current assets		
Intangibles [W4]		31,735
Property, plant and equipment		56,720
		88,455
Current assets		
Inventory [after PURP]	90,925	
Receivables	63,100	
Cash	4,150	158,175
Total assets		246,630
Equity and liabilities		
Capital and reserves		
Ordinary share capital		10,200
Share premium account		5,000
Accumulated profits [W6]		90,039.5
		105,239.5
Minority interests [W5]		33,990.5
		139,230
Non-current liabilities		
Loan		20,000
Current liabilities		
Trade payables		86,000
Dividends payable by Pip plc		1,000
Dividends payable to minority interests		400
		246,630

(b) Advantages and disadvantages of preparing consolidated financial statements.

Consolidated financial statements are an example of commercial substance prevailing over legal form. Each company that comprises the group is a separate legal entity and hence if strict legal form was applied each equity investment would be recorded in the balance sheet of the acquirer at cost; subject to any impairment. This is acceptable if the size of the investment gives neither influence nor control over the other entity, but when this is obtained then it would be useful to the investors in the lead company to have a clearer picture of the assets and liabilities they control.

Consequently many argue that consolidated financial statements give a fairer view to the stakeholders that use them, enabling improved decision-making. For example, the consolidation process eliminates intra-group transactions that would otherwise give an inflated view of performance and position.

In most groups there will be clear division between the shareholders who own the parent company and the management team responsible for day-to-day operations.

The consolidated financial statements help improve corporate governance allowing the shareholders to look at the detail of the equity investments made on their behalf.

However, many managers would claim that the time and expense dedicated towards the consolidation process could be better employed in the commercial development of the underlying business. It is also a process little understood by non-specialist users of the accounts who may wrongly believe that they are looking at the results of a single entity.

Consolidation also necessitates the calculation of goodwill. This is always a subjective exercise, and the subsequent impairment of this intangible asset introduces an element of volatility to the reported profits.

The claim that consolidation may prevent users from seeing the underlying assets and liabilities of individual business streams is also frequently heard, but this can easily be rectified by the use of segmental reporting disclosures.

Conclusion

The benefits associated with the consolidation process and group financial statements greatly outweigh the potential drawbacks, and this is reflected in their acceptance and widespread use throughout the world. When subjectivity does exist, the IASB constantly strives to minimise or eliminate these issues as evidenced by the prohibition now being implemented on merger accounting.

Workings

[W1] Group structure

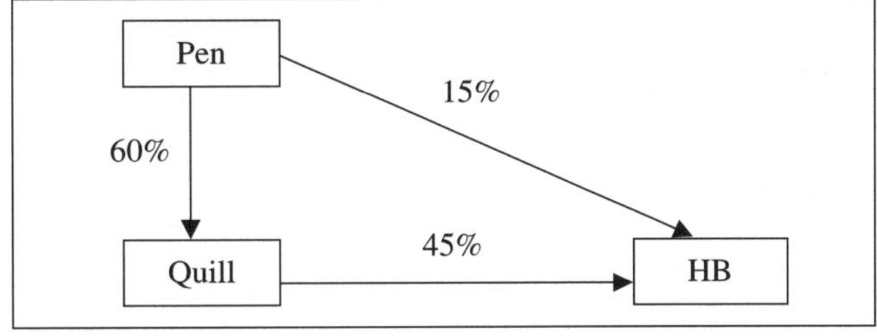

hence

Quill is a 60% subsidiary.

HB is a subsidiary in which the control percentage is 60%, but the effective percentage is 42%.

[W2] Net assets

Quill Ltd

	At acquisition £'000	*At balance sheet date* £'000	*Post-acquisition* £'000
Share capital	10,000	10,000	
Accumulated profits	41,000	55,850	
Adjustments			
Declared dividend		(1,000)	
	51,000	64,850	13,850

HB Ltd

	At acquisition [by Pen] £'000	*At acquisition [by Quill]* £'000	*At balance sheet date* £'000	*Post-acquisition (see note)*
Share capital	5,000	5,000	5,000	
Accumulated profits	5,000	1,500	17,300	
Adjustments				
PURP			(75)	
	10,000	6,500	22,225	12,225

[W3] Unrealised profit on non-current assets

NBV of asset transferred at 1 October 20X3 = £1,800k × [8/10] = £1,440k

Hence, profit on transfer = £2,000k − £1,440k = £560k

NBV currently in the books of Quill = £2,000 × [7/8] = £1,750k

Therefore adjustment to be made for unrealised profit = £1,750k − £1,440k = £310k

[W4] Goodwill

Quill Ltd

	£'000
Cost of investment	62,000
Net assets acquired [60% × 51,000 (W2)]	(30,600)
	31,400
Less: Impairment (25%)	(7,850)
	23,550

Pen in HB

	£'000
Cost of investment [60% × 12,100] + 5,125	12,385
Net assets acquired [42% × 10,000 (W2)]	(4,200)
	8,185
Less Impairment	–
	8,185

Note: The goodwill in HB has all been calculated from the date that Quill was brought into the group. Prior to this the 15% direct stake in HB would have given neither control nor influence.

[W5] Minority interests

In Quill = 40% × 64,850k [W2] = £25,940k

In HB = [58% × 22,225] − [40% × 12,100] = £8,050.5

[W6] Consolidated accumulated profits

	£'000
Pen plc	85,155
Less: Pen's own dividend	(1,000)
Add: Dividend receivable from Quill	600
Less: Unrealised profit	(310)
Quill Ltd [60% × 13,850 (W2)]	8,310
Chaf Ltd [42% × 12,225 (W2)]	5,134.5
Goodwill impairment	(7,850)
	90,039.5

Question 4 – Soapbox plc

John Temple, the new finance director of Soapbox plc, has been undertaking some background reading on the IASB and the development of a globally accepted GAAP. He has just joined the company from a small unlisted competitor who used local GAAP, and hence this is his first practical encounter with the implementation of IAS.

John is aware that the international rules have undergone a period of rapid development and that the knowledge he gained whilst qualifying as an accountant is now woefully outdated. He is determined to never let this happen again, and he was intrigued by the following paragraph he had encountered in a technical journal.

> Since its approval in 1989 by the IASC Board, and subsequent adoption by the IASB [International Accounting Standards Board] in 2001 the IASB Framework has been a cornerstone in the development of new accounting standards. It has helped to create a previously unseen consistency in accounting practice, and will continue to do so in the years ahead.

In an email to your office John queries if by understanding the IASB Framework he will have grasped the engine room of future accounting development.

Requirements

(a) Briefly explain how the IASB is assisted by the Framework, and how it may impact upon other stakeholder groups.

(5 marks)

(b) Prepare notes for a forthcoming meeting with John Temple at which you will discuss the query raised regarding the status of the IASB Framework in the future development of international accounting.

(10 marks)

(c) The Board of Soapbox plc has been investigating methods by which they can reward their key staff, and retain their services, without draining the cash resources of the company. Several of the directors are convinced that the most appropriate method is to award these employees options in the company that can only be exercised if the employees concerned continue in their current roles for a further three years after the options are granted.

The Marketing Director, Helen Carpenter, summarised the consensus with other directors as follows

> Soapbox plc is heavily reliant on the services of several key staff and the idea of locking these employees into the business via the issue of options is a clever ploy. The company will not have to pay a penny in cash or give away assets of any kind. Hence there is no cost or liability to be recognised by the business.
>
> My brother who completed an accounting module as part of his degree several years ago informs me that the only impact will be the figure disclosed for diluted earnings per share; which will fall. As this has no impact on the income statement or the balance sheet it strikes me that the issue of options is a cost free method of incentivising our staff!

Other details of the proposed plan are

- 100,000 options would be issued on 1 January 20X4, and give the recipients the right to subscribe for an equivalent number of ordinary shares for £2.40 between 1 January 20X7 and 31 December 20X8.
- The individuals must remain employed by Soapbox plc for the three period from the grant date.
- Using established option valuation models the fair value of the options have been estimated as

31 December 20X4	70p
31 December 20X5	85p
31 December 20X6	95p

Comment on the appropriateness of not recognising the options in the financial statements in the light of best international accounting practice supporting your arguments with numerical illustrations based on the scheme proposed by Soapbox plc.

(10 marks)
(Total = 25 marks)

Answer 4 – Soapbox plc

(a) The conceptual Framework

The IASB Framework describes the basic concepts by which financial statements are prepared under international accounting guidance. Consequently it assists the IASB in both the development of new accounting standards and in the review of standards already in issue.

One of the goals of any standard setting body is to get congruence of accounting practice in the recognition, measurement and presentation of accounting information within published financial statements. This improved consistency then promotes comparability and reliability. The Framework provides guidance on definitions, reduces the number of allowed accounting treatment alternatives, and hence makes a significant contribution to the goals described.

By influencing the accounting practice used in the preparation of published financial statements it can justifiably be argued that the Framework influences every stakeholder group from shareholders to tax collection agencies and governments!

Although the Framework is not an International Financial Reporting Standard and does not contain specific guidance on any particular accounting issue (e.g. pensions, deferred taxation), its range of influence is considerable.

- Auditors will use the Framework when determining if financial statements conform to International Accounting Standards.
- When developing local GAAP that is consistent with international principles, reference will be made to the Framework.

(b) The conceptual Framework and the future development of international accounting

The IASB Framework defines the objective of financial statements and the qualitative characteristics that make them useful, together with the elements that comprise them. Hence many would see the Framework as a common backbone to the development of all new accounting standards leading to consistency in financial statement preparation.

The objective of financial statements

The Framework perceives that the objective of financial statements is to enable a wide range of users to make economic decisions about the financial performance, financial position and changes in financial position of an entity.

It is difficult to criticise the basis of these objectives, but some observers would note that the Framework cannot be "all things to all men". It is designed for general purpose financial statements, and may not always be ideal for special purpose financial reports such as those produced for governmental regulatory authorities.

Qualitative characteristics of financial statements

The Framework identifies four principal qualitative characteristics that make financial statements useful

1 *Understandability* – by those with a reasonable knowledge of business and economic activities
2 *Relevance* – helping users evaluate past, present and future events
3 *Reliability* – free from material error and bias
4 *Comparability* – to enable users to identify trends in financial position and performance.

All of these are desirable, but it must be recognised that compromise is inevitable. For example, the generation of relevant information for future decision-making may require the use of less reliable data.

The elements of financial statements

By ensuring the usage of common definitions for element such as assets, liabilities, income and expenditure the Framework has eliminated a major cause of disparity between standards and provides a common platform for future development. However, there will always be items that create a challenge to the practical interpretation of these terms.

The term asset is defined as

> An asset is a resource controlled by the enterprise as a result of past events and from which future economic benefits are expected to flow to the enterprise.

When considering potential assets such as human intellectual capital, there is much debate on whether they can be recognised. There is a strong argument that control does not exist as the individual can always resign.

The future of the Framework itself

In the same way that new accounting standards are developed encapsulating the principles of the Framework so the Framework must itself come under regular scrutiny. This is currently occurring as the IASB has launched a project on *Revenue Recognition, Liabilities and Equity: Concepts*.

Conclusion

On balance John Temple's assertion that by becoming familiar with the IASB Framework he will have a good grasp of the driving force behind future IAS is true. However, he must be aware that aspects of the Framework itself may evolve and that the generalised nature of the Framework is both a benefit and a drawback. Whilst understanding core principles is essential, he will still need to look at the issues specific to the subject of each individual standard before he could apply them in his own accounts preparation work.

(c) Recognition of options

The argument put forward by the Marketing Director goes against best current practice as described by IFRS 2 *Share-based Payment*; although some of Helen's comments such as the issue of options will lead to a potential dilution of earnings per share are correct.

The key employees are providing a service to Soapbox plc, and if this had been rewarded by an increase in their salaries then this cost would have been recognised as an expense in the income statement. Hence the services provided clearly have a value, and this should be recognised irrespective of the method by which this is achieved. The value is deemed to equate to the fair value of the options issued and should be recognised over the period that benefit accrues. Namely the three years from the grant date to the date that the employees become unconditionally entitled to exercise the options (the vesting date).

The impact on the income statement of Soapbox plc over the three-year period ended 31 December 20X6 would be

Year		£	£
20X4	100,000 options @ 70p × 1/3		23,333
20X5	100,000 options @ 85p × 1/3	28,333	
	Plus backlog		
	100,000 @ (85p – 70p) × 1/3	5,000	33,333
20X6	100,000 options @ 95p × 1/3	31,667	
	Plus backlog		
	100,000 @ (95p – 85p) × 2/3	6,667	38,334

Further adjustments may be required in 20X7 depending on when the employees elect to exercise their options.

It should be noted that IFRS 2 remains a contentious accounting standard with some commentators as difficulties remain with the practical application of option pricing models. Furthermore, others argue that services do not usually meet the definition criteria of an asset, but the IASB Framework makes it clear that the term asset is not limited to resources that can be recognised as an asset in the balance sheet. Services to be received in the future definitely do not meet the definition of an asset, but services are assets when received.

Question 5 – David Raine

David Raine is a financial analyst for a large investment bank and has been clearing his desk before leaving for some long overdue holiday. He has stacked issues to be dealt with in different trays and is now about to tackle the final tray marked "Earnings and Performance".

He identifies that there are three separate tasks to be dealt with.

1 An internal memorandum from Sue Daye, a new starter at the bank, asking if he could provide some clarification on the significance of movements in the price/earning ratio, and any potential limitations in the use of this indicator.

She also mentions that one of her first tasks was to review price/earnings relatives (see below) and was curious to know if there was a preferred outcome to this analysis.

$$\text{Price/earnings relative} = \frac{\text{P/E [Company]}}{\text{P/E [Market]}}$$

2 DFG plc, a client of David's, is currently undertaking due diligence work on a target company it is considering purchasing. The target company has undergone several changes to its capital structure in the most recent financial period, but financial statements are yet to be completed. DFG plc has informed David that it would like some early soundings on certain key indicators and would like him to calculate basic and diluted EPS figures based on the draft financial information available.

Information available is as follows

- At 31 December 20X4 the company had 600,000 ordinary shares in issue.
- During the year ended 31 December 20X4 three capital transactions had been completed.

28 February 20X4	40,000 new ordinary shares were issued at full market price
30 June 20X4	A 1:4 bonus issue was completed
31 October 20X4	A 1:11 rights issue was completed with all the rights being fully taken up. The rights price was £4.50, whilst the cum-rights price was £5.5

- Net profits attributable to ordinary shareholders for the period £800,000.
- The company also had in issue throughout the period
  - 80,000 options with an exercise price of £4
  - 500,000 convertible preference shares that pay an annual dividend of £1. The terms of conversion are five preference shares convert into four ordinary shares
  - £10 million 2% convertible bonds. Every £1,000 bond is convertible into 25 ordinary shares
- The applicable tax rate for the period was 30%.
- The average fair value of an ordinary share during the period was £5.

3 Another of David's clients, ZXC plc, has declared dividends for the preceding three years as follows

	Total dividend (£)
20X1	200,000
20X2	210,000
20X3	225,000

However, for the year 20X4 it has announced a dividend of £1,200,000 although its overall profit levels have increased only modestly. At the same time a share consolidation was announced by which the £1 ordinary shares would be consolidated on a 3:2 basis.

The date of the dividend announcement was two months prior to the balance sheet date, and the number of ordinary shares in issue prior to the consolidation was 9 million.

The company's profit attributable to ordinary shareholders for 20X4 was £2.2 million.

Requirements

(a) Outline the points to be included in David Raine's response to Sue Daye.

(4 marks)

(b) Calculate the basic and diluted EPS for DFG plc for the year ended 31 December 20X4.

(16 marks)

(c) Comment on the impact on EPS of the events described for ZXC plc; illustrating your answer with illustrative figures.

(5 marks)

(Total = 25 marks)

Answer 5 – David Raine

(a) The price/earnings ratio [P/E ratio]

This ratio is calculated by dividing the market price of ordinary shares by the EPS. Consequently it is a ratio that is made up of a component that reflects market expectations about the future earnings of a company, and a component that reflects the earnings available for each ordinary share based on the results of the most recent accounting period.

Increases in the P/E ratio are usually perceived as a measure of confidence in the future of the business. Investors are prepared to pay a higher multiple of current earnings suggesting that either

- they believe that the current level of earnings will be sustained for a longer period or
- the earnings of the business will grow in real terms.

As with all financial indicators there are limitations; most notably the wide variety of commercial factors that influence trading on the financial exchanges many of which may have little direct bearing on the ability of a specific company to maintain or improve its own financial performance.

The price/earnings relative

The formula for this indicator highlights that it is a simple comparison of an entity's P/E ratio with a market average. Hence an outcome of exactly one would indicate that the company was exactly mirroring the overall market.

If the result exceeds one then the company may be a market leader or other factors have resulted in its share price being overvalued.

An improved variant of the price/earnings relative would be to make a comparison with a specific market sector instead of the market as a whole.

(b) DFG plc – basic and diluted EPS

Basic EPS = 800,000/556,641 = 143.7p

Diluted EPS = 106p (see below)

Calculation of basic EPS

Weighted average number of ordinary shares.

	Actual no.	*Time*	*Bonus fraction*	*Rights fraction*	*Weighted average*
1 January	400,000	2/12	5/4	5.5/5.42	84,563
Issue at full market price	40,000				
	440,000	4/12	5/4	5.5/5.42	186,039
Bonus issue [1:4]	110,000				
	550,000	4/12		5.5/5.42	186,039
Rights issue [1:11]	50,000				
	600,000	2/12			100,000
					556,641

To generate the rights fraction it is necessary to calculate the theoretical ex-rights price (TERPs).

TERPs = [(11 × £5.5) + (1 × £4.5)]/[(11 + 1)] = £5.42

Calculation of the diluted EPS

The new earnings and maximum increase to the number of ordinary shares must be calculated for each diluting factor.

	Increase to earnings (£)	*Increase to number of ordinary shares*	*"Individual" EPS*
Options	nil	80,000	nil
Convertible preference shares	500,000 × £1 = £500,000	400,000	125p
4% Convertible bonds	10,000,000 × 2% = 200,000 Less taxation at 30% = £140,000	250,000	56p

The basic EPS must be adjusted by the most diluting factor and then the next and so on, until no further dilution is possible.

Calculation of incremental EPS

	Profit (£)	*Ordinary shares*	*EPS* (p)
Basic	800,000	556,641	143.7
Options	0	80,000	
	800,000	636,641	125.6
4% Convertible bonds	140,000	250,000	
	940,000	886,641	106

The convertible preference shares are not a diluting factor and hence must be excluded from the calculation.

(c) ZXC plc

ZXC plc has paid a special dividend and consolidated its ordinary share capital on the same date.

The payment of the dividend depletes the resources of the company and hence impacts on its earnings potential. Consequently the EPS calculation for the year prorates the number of shares in issue for the year. This is not the equivalent of a bonus issue which is assumed to be in issue throughout the period because it does not affect the earning capability of the entity. For similar reasons the transactions undertaken by ZXC plc will not result in an amendment to their EPS for the previous accounting period.

The EPS for the current period will be 2,200,000/8,500,000 = 25.9p.

The weighted average number of shares is calculated as below

Ten months to dividend declaration	9,000,000 × 10/12	7,500,000
Two months to year end	6,000,000 × 2/12	1,000,000
		8,500,000

Question 6 – Greener plc

Greener plc has been producing an operating and financial review statement for several years. Extracts from the report for the year ended 31 December 20X4 are given below

Description of the Business

The business was established in 1962 to extract and process clay in preparation for conversion into building materials, and has shown strong growth to reach its current status. It now has two very distinct operating subsidiaries which have been allowed to develop their own corporate brand:

Bricktar Ltd – Responsible for the extraction of clay and its conversion into building bricks.

Techno Search Ltd – Incorporated in 20X2 this company comprises a small research and development team plus administrative support. It is involved in the development of new waterproofing additives that extend the life expectancy of cements exposed to the weather.

Business objectives/Management strategy

To become the European market leader by 20X8 in the supply of building bricks; capturing more than 15% of the market by volume.

This growth is based on the successful registration of patents for waterproofing building bricks that will provide a unique building product. Techno Search Ltd have already developed and patented similar technology for cements, and techno-cement will be commercially produced from September 20X5 onwards.

The company secretary of Greener plc is preparing the agenda for the AGM at which the 20X4 financial statements are to be approved and is aware that two questions have been scheduled by shareholder groups for response by the Board. He has summarised the key points in an internal memorandum to the Chief Executive Officer and the Finance Director.

To: Susan Nailer, Jeff Finch

From: Scott Bridges

Date: 22 March 20X5

Re: Matters to be Raised at the AGM

Although our financial position and performance as reported in the 20X4 financial statements is strong, and I am sure will be endorsed by the members, I think you should be aware that the AGM may not be an entirely smooth ride. In particular you will need to give consideration to the following questions which have been included in the running schedule.

1 The inclusion of an operating and financial review statement in the published accounts provides a useful insight to the Board's philosophy on moving the business forward. However, for reasons that elude us the contents are not comparable to the equivalent

document of Highrise plc the company's major competitor. What is supposed to be the purpose of this document, and why does the Board not use comparable formats for this report when they do for the balance sheet and income statement?

2 During 20X4 the company was one of several named in a report produced by a leading environmental group on the erosion of top soils caused by the extraction of clay and peat. We are aware that such criticism is unjustified as the company invested considerable amounts in the restoration of mining sites, but surely it would be preferable that such adverse publicity is nipped in the bud as evidenced by the 4% fall in share price immediately following the criticism.

What is the view of the Board on the adoption of the Global Reporting Initiative to promote the environmental credentials of Greener plc?

Let me know if you like these to be put on the agenda of the pre-AGM board meeting.

Regards

Requirements

(a) Discuss the issues raised by the two questions to be put to the Board at the AGM of Greener plc.

(16 marks)

(b) In the week prior to the AGM, the Board of Greener plc received a tentative enquiry from Highrise plc regarding the possibility of acquiring Techno Search Ltd. This was dismissed immediately as the work of this subsidiary represents the platform on which the group as a whole will grow. However, the approach did draw attention to the value of this business as the offer represented six times the balance sheet net assets with the caveat that all development staff would sign a lock-in clause for two years.

What do you understand by the term intellectual capital, and why might it prove challenging for Techno Search Ltd to recognise this on its balance sheet?

(9 marks)
(Total = 25 marks)

Answer 6 – Greener plc

(a) Discussion of issues arising from questions to be raised at the AGM

Q1: The operating and financial review statement

The operating and financial review statement is aimed primarily at investors, and hence the observation from the shareholders putting forward the question that they find it a useful insight would be the response hoped for by the Board.

Although the report contains some numerical disclosures, its primary aim is to give a narrative-based analysis on the performance of the business for the period and give added insight on issues that could impact on future objectives. Typical information provided would include details of

- Research projects
- Development of new products and services
- Branding
- Treasury policy.

The operating and financial review has been strongly promoted in the UK, and changes to Company Law in that country intend to make this a mandatory disclosure in the published financial statements on companies above a specified size limit. However, at present it remains a voluntary disclosure and consequently variability remains over the exact presentation given by those entities that decide to include it within their financial statements.

This contrasts with the balance sheet and income statement which are mandatory disclosures, and for which more precise guidance is given, either via IAS 1 *Presentation of Financial Statements* or local legislation.

Although it would be unfair to pass judgement on the report produced by the board of Greener plc, it is not possible for these individuals to ensure that the same scrupulous attention is given to the preparation of the equivalent report of its competitors. It is the desired intention of those who advocate this voluntary disclosure that it would contain an unbiased view of both good and bad aspects of performance, but the danger exists that some may elect to restrict disclosures to those that show the entity in a positive light.

The fact that the shareholders feel strongly enough to raise a question at the AGM may also suggest that they are placing undue reliance on this report. Whilst its purpose is to be both interesting and informative to corporate and individual investors alike there was never any intent that it should be considered as the sole primary disclosure.

Conclusion

The operating and financial review statement adds a valuable extra tier of disclosure to published financial statements that should enhance decision-making and provide an additional basis for comparison between entities. It is a valid criticism that until established as a mandatory disclosure the danger exists that it may fall short of these aspirations, but as the demand for wider ranging disclosures that go beyond pure financial data increase its inclusion is to be encouraged.

Q2: The global reporting initiative;

Established in 1997 this initiative resulted in the release and subsequent update of sustainability reporting guidelines.

Sustainability reporting looks at environmental, social and economic aspects of an entity's performance. The long-term aim is to achieve global consistency in the disclosures given on these matters by all organisations that impact these issues. Hence it would not be restricted to large listed companies, but smaller companies and not-for-profit organisations.

Key components of the report would include:

- an overview of the organisation to provide context
- the scope of the report
- details of the key performance indicators used
- a discussion of the strategy/vision by which the entity intends to integrate economic, environmental and social performance
- an overview of governance structure and management systems
- reporting on economic, environmental and social performance including trends and unusual items. The period reviewed should cover, as a minimum, the current year and the two previous years, and discuss a broad range of issues from emissions and health and safety to human rights.

The development of the Global Reporting Initiative is an important step towards broader stakeholder reporting, but at present it remains a voluntary code. As such it will be seen as an additional cost burden by many entities, and as with the operating and financial review statement runs the risk of giving a rose-tinted view on environmental and social issues as only those entities with a positive image to promote will adopt it.

However, Greener plc cannot ignore that the Global Reporting Initiative is one part of an increasing avalanche of voluntary guidance on environmental issues.

For example,

- The United Nations have issued a report titled "Environmental Financial Accounting, and Reporting at the Corporate Level".
- The ACCA has itself issued a guide to environmental and energy reporting.

The watershed in environmental accounting will arrive when reporting of these issues becomes a mandatory requirement; although the qualitative nature of some aspects of this information will result in greater flexibility in the disclosure to be given. This would be further consolidated by such reporting being subject to independent scrutiny, and the European Union's development of the eco-audit scheme represents an early step towards this objective.

Conclusion

The Global Reporting Initiative represents an important benchmark in environmental and social reporting. The early adoption by Greener plc would be commendable, but the initiative has only been field tested by a small number of international companies, and it might be appropriate to await feedback from these trials.

(b) Intellectual capital

The recognition of intellectual capital within financial statements represents a significant challenge to those developing international financial reporting as its intangible nature makes it difficult to measure. However, intangibles largely determine a company's value and growth prospects, and it is not a coincidence that knowledge intensive entities have the largest differential between market value and book value.

Intellectual capital represents knowledge that can be used to create value, and can take many forms:

- *Human resources* – the skill and knowledge of the employees.
- *Intellectual assets* – drawings, computer programs, etc.
- *Intellectual property* – intellectual assets which can be legally protected such as patents.

The operating and financial review statement of Greener plc clearly identifies that the group does possess intellectual property in the form of patents, but it is unclear what value has been assigned to these. However, it seems unlikely that this represents the primary reason for the large differential between balance sheet net assets and the substantially higher price offered by Highrise plc. The value appears to be associated with the unique skills of its research team as evidenced by the lock in clauses that would have formed part of the deal.

Many would argue that the value of these human resources should be recognised on the balance sheet as a non-current asset. This creates significant accounting difficulties as evidenced by the definition of an asset as described by the IASB's *Framework for the Preparation and Presentation of Financial Statements*:

> An asset is a resource controlled by the entity as a result of past events and from which future economic benefits are expected to flow to the entity.

Key questions arising from this definition are:

- Does a company ultimately have control over its employees as they have the right to resign?
- Can the contribution from employees be separated and measured from other assets of the business? . . . it is probably too simplistic to claim that the benefit obtained is directly proportionate to the salary and benefits given.

The inclusion of intellectual property on the balance sheet is clearly desirable as it supports the goal of enhancing shareholder value, and many claim that "what gets measured gets managed". A few pioneering companies have started to develop mechanisms by which to achieve this objective:

- A Swedish insurance company has developed a balance scorecard approach, and publishes intellectual capital supplements alongside its financial statements.
- The Intellectual Capital Research Centre in Zagreb has developed the "Value Added Intellectual Coefficient".

Conclusion

If Greener plc and its subsidiaries are to recognise intellectual capital in their financial statements then they will need to develop an awareness and understanding of the complex issues involved. Key indicators will need to be identified and a measurement system designed.

The cost of this work would be considerable, but if successful would make a positive contribution to user understanding about issues such as the rejected bid by Highrise plc.

Tutorial note: This answer is substantially longer than would be expected under exam conditions, but is designed as a learning tool for this important discussion topic.

Question 7 – MonAmi plc

MonAmi plc manufactures carrier bags for a range of well-known high street retail chains; the bags being customised with promotional material as requested by the customer. The market sector is very competitive and the directors of MonAmi plc have decided that further growth can only be achieved through complementary products rather than expansion of their existing business.

Following a successful rights issue two years previously the company has a cash rich balance sheet, and has decided that the quickest route to expansion is through acquisition. Negotiations have been started with Sedge plc which manufacture designer wrapping paper for the same retail chains, and as part of the acquisition process MonAmi plc have initiated a due diligence review of Sedge plc's financial position.

The latest published financial statements for Sedge plc are set out below:

Sedge plc: Balance Sheet as at 31 December 20X4

	20X4	*20X4*	*20X3*	*20X3*
	£m	£m	£m	£m
Assets				
Non-current assets				
Property, plant and equipment		252		172
Investments		5		5
		257		177
Current assets				
Inventory	72		49	
Receivables	340		96	
Cash	–	412	30	175
Total assets		669		352
Equity and liabilities				
Capital and reserves				
Ordinary share capital [£1 shares]		60		60
Share premium account		15		15
Accumulated profits		48		101
		123		176
Non-current liabilities		120		70
Current liabilities				
Trade payables	300		88	
Other creditors	16		18	
Bank	110	426	–	106
		669		352

Sedge plc: Income statement for the year ended 31 December 20X4

	20X4	*20X3*
	£m	£m
Revenue [almost exclusively on credit]	1,158	498
Cost of sales	(1,049)	(350)
Gross profit	109	148
Selling and administration costs	(80)	(38)
Operating profit	29	110
Finance expense	(23)	(7)
Profit before taxation	6	103
Taxation	(15)	(25)
Profit after taxation	(9)	78

Further information available:

1 Land is included in the property, plant and equipment at a carrying value of £18m; this has been unchanged for several years. The remaining non-current assets include some assets held under finance leases.

	20X4	*20X3*
	£m	£m
Owned assets	80	61
Leased assets	154	93

2 During 20X4 Sedge plc initiated a long-term price promise to its customers guaranteeing that it would always undercut a competitor's price for an equivalent product. To complement this deal they allowed long-term customers with a proven payment record, an added incentive for orders above a specified size either a 14-day extension to credit or 5% extra discount on the sales price.

Extra discount given during the year to 31 December 20X4 was £5m which has been included within selling and administration costs.

3 Dividends declared and paid during the year amounted to £20m (20X3 = £12m).

4 On 1 April 20X4 Sedge plc signed a contract with a new paper mill to secure its supply chain for the next 5 years. The new supplier has a reputation for high quality and efficiency.

5 Sedge plc has also provided some ad hoc balance sheet information for the year ended 31 December 20X2.

	£m
Inventory	47
Receivables	66
Trade payables	(50)

Requirements

(a) Write a letter to the directors of MonAmi plc commenting on the financial position and performance of Sedge plc.

(21 marks)

(b) List key questions you would like to ask the management team of Sedge plc to improve your understanding.

(4 marks)
(Total = 25 marks)

Answer 7 – MonAmi plc

(a)

XYZ & Co,
Princes Row,
London.

To
The Board,
MonAmi plc,
Chelmsford,
Essex.

x/x/20X5

Dear Sirs,

Re: Financial Position and Performance of Sedge plc

We have undertaken a review of the financial information provided to us on Sedge plc, and we detailed our comments below (supporting numerical analysis is given in the appendix attached to this letter).

Profitability

Both return on capital employed and the return on shareholders funds have shown a marked deterioration in 20X4. This can be explained by considering both the margins being achieved by the company and the efficiency with which it uses its assets to generate sales.

The company appears to have adopted an aggressive policy to increase its market share, and this has dramatically increased the absolute value of sales made in the period. This increase in volume has allowed the company to use its assets more efficiently as evidenced by asset turnover increasing from 2.9 to 4.6.

However, although the company's strategy has worked in quantitative terms there has been a knock-on effect for margins. The gross profit margin has fallen to below 10%. Furthermore, the overheads have also increased substantially for several reasons

- Some of the overheads will be variable and hence increase pro-rata to increased manufacturing activity.
- The massive increase in volumes may also have resulted in some overheads previously categorised as fixed becoming variable.
- Cash discounts to key customers.
- An increase in non-current assets increasing the depreciation burden.

As a result of these changes the operating margin has fallen from 22% to 2.5% leaving little scope for financing costs or reinvestment within the business.

To help fund its strategy Sedge plc has increased its long-term borrowing leading to higher interest costs. It should be noted that interest has increased by a higher proportion than the underlying debt; presumably due to interest charges on its overdrawn bank position. Interest cover has fallen from a multiple of almost 16 to less than 2 giving cause for concern as interest repayments will have to be met unless new terms could be negotiated with the provider of finance.

Liquidity

Current and quick ratios are notoriously difficult to interpret as they are very industry specific, but it is clear that Sedge plc's position has worsened with insufficient current assets to cover current liabilities.

A closer investigation of working capital identifies that inventory turnover has increased in spite of higher year inventory. The latter emphasises the increase in trading volumes which would require higher inventory levels to avoid the danger of stock outs.

The company policy of offering long-term customers increased credit terms has increased receivable days to more than 2 months. It is unclear if the increase is exclusively attributable to this policy change as the proportion of total sales to these key customers is unknown. The ultimate collection of these funds does not seem to be in question, but the delayed receipts do impact the cash position.

Sedge plc is showing many of the classic signs of overtrading, but unusually payables days have fallen whereas it would have been expected to rise as the company used trade payables as a form of short-term finance (although this is not something we would encourage!). However, it seems probable that the new paper mill contract requires prompt payment terms, and without this basic raw material the company would rapidly cease to trade.

As a result of the conflicting movements referred to above the working capital cycle has altered little between the two years, but factors such as cash discounts, dividends and finance costs have taken their toll on the cash position.

Solvency

The gearing has worsened between the two years and would have deteriorated further had the bank overdraft have been included as part of debt.

The increased output of the company has also required a significant increase in non-current assets. The poor cash position appearing to necessitate that a large proportion of these assets are acquired under finance leases; the annual lease rental being substantially less than an absolute cash payment in 20X4.

Insufficient information has been provided to know the split of lease creditors within liabilities.

Conclusion

Sedge plc has undertaken a disastrous strategy to grow the business. Margins have been cut to generate sales volumes but the increases obtained have been insufficient to prevent either a net profit in 20X3 falling to a loss, or the bank position becoming overdrawn. Serious doubts exists about their management team who in spite of this worsening position increased dividend payments by two-thirds.

The lack of interest cover, and the contractual constraints imposed by lease agreements and a new arrangement with a principle supplier give the business little opportunity to reduce the financial pressure. Furthermore, it is difficult to persuade customers that new benefits given to them should now be taken away!

An investment in Sedge plc would appear to be very risky. It is true that their sales indicate a product range that is attractive to the market, and if the growth created was to continue then a short-term injection of cash to the business plus the benefits of synergy might look attractive. However, the strategy they have set in motion will be difficult to reverse, and hence Sedge plc could drain the cash reserves of the new group.

We hope this analysis has provided you with the information required, but should you have any queries please contact us at your earliest opportunity.

Yours faithfully,

XYZ & Co

(b) Key questions for management

- Has the strategy to undercut competitors and offer other inducements increased the market share in 20X4?
- Do they have independently validated market analysis to prove their case?
- What has happened to the overall size of the market in 20X4 compared to previous periods?
- What is the proportion of fixed to variable overheads?
- What is the depreciation policy of the company?
- What proportion of total sales is made to key customers to whom you offer special terms?
- What is the impact of seasonal factors, such as Christmas, on the balance sheet position?
- What are the terms and conditions of the new leases?

[Any sensible request for information will be given merit, but it must be relevant to the scenario given.]

Appendix

	20X4	*20X3*
Profitability/Efficiency ratios	8.2%	44.7%
Return on capital employed (ROCE)		
$\frac{\text{Profit before interest and tax}}{\text{Capital employed}} \times 100 = x\%$		
Capital employed includes share capital, reserves, loans and overdrafts. No adjustment has been made for the investments as they remain constant and are immaterial.		
Return on shareholders' funds	negative	44.3%
Profit after tax Shareholders' funds (i.e. share capital and reserves)		
Gross profit %/Margin	9.4%	29.7%
$\frac{\text{GP}}{\text{Turnover}} \times 100 = x\%$		
Operating profit %/Margin	2.5%	22%
$\frac{\text{Operating profit}}{\text{Turnover}} \times 100 = x\%$		
Asset turnover	4.6 times	2.9 times
$\frac{\text{Turnover}}{\text{Non-current assets}} \times 100 = x \text{ times}$		
Investments have been excluded from the asset total		
Inventory turnover	17.3 times [= 21 days]	7.3 times [= 50 days]
$\frac{\text{Cost of sales}}{\text{Inventory [average]}} = x \text{ times}$		
Receivables days	69 days	59 days
$\frac{\text{Trade receivables}}{\text{Credit sales}} \times \text{No. of days in period} = x \text{ days}$		
Payables days	66 days	71 days
$\frac{\text{Trade payables}}{\text{Credit purchases}} \times \text{No. of days in period} = x \text{ days}$		
It has been assumed that all purchases have been made on credit terms		

	20X4	*20X3*
Liquidity/Solvency ratios		
Current ratio	0.96	1.65
$\frac{\text{Current assets}}{\text{Current liabilities}} = \text{x times}$		
Quick (acid test) ratio	0.79	1.18
$\frac{\text{Current assets less inventory}}{\text{Current liabilities}} = \text{x times}$		
Interest cover	1.26 times	15.7 times
$\frac{\text{Profit before interest}}{\text{Interest}} = \text{x times}$		
Gearing		
$\frac{\text{Long-term debt}}{\text{Shareholders funds} + \text{LT debt}} \times 100 = \text{x\%}$	49.3%	28.4%

Question 8 – Financial instruments aptitude testing

Jashita Singh works in the equity markets division of a large finance company, and has been asked to prepare an induction test for employees looking to transfer to the division. The test is to assess their current aptitude and knowledge, and Jashita has received an email from the head of department informing her that the first applicants have been given interview dates.

Before sending the induction test for printing Jashita noticed that answers were missing for a number of the questions, and with other commitments pressing she has asked you to work through them and "fill in the gaps"!

There are four questions for which answers are missing

1 On 1 January 20X4 ABC plc issued bonds with a par value of $2,000,000. The bonds carry a 4% coupon rate, and are convertible into equity shares at any time over their four-year life. The terms of conversion are that a $1,000 par value bond would convert to 800 ordinary shares.

At the date of issue government statistics showed that the market interest rate for equivalent debt lacking conversion rights was 6%.

Other information

- At 1 January 20X4 the market price of an ordinary share was $3.
- Each ordinary share is expected to distribute dividends of 12 cents over the four-year bond term.

Calculate the split between debt and equity for this hybrid instrument.

(5 marks)

2 On 1 April 20X4 QWE plc issues a $1,000,000 stepped bond for $980,000 which is to be redeemed in five years for $1,200,000. The coupon rate was stepped as follows:

Year	*Rate*
1	4%
2	5%
3	6%
4	7%
5	8%

Direct issue costs of $14,646 were incurred, and the rate of interest implicit to the bond is 10%.

Calculate the interest expense to be taken against profit in each year of the bond's five year existence.

(7 marks)

3 BNM plc enters into a forward contract to buy two million Australian dollars at Aus$2.4 = £1. The contract is initiated on 31 October 20X4 with a purchase date six months later.

At the balance sheet date, 31 December 20X4, the exchange Australian dollar had weakened against sterling to Aus$2.5 = £1, and this trend continued into 20X5 such that at the contract settlement date (30 April) the exchange rate had become Aus$2.55 = £1.

Comment on the accounting treatment of this derivative illustrating your response with calculations that show the gain or loss to be recorded in the financial statements of BNM plc for this derivative at its balance sheet date and the accounting treatment at the settlement date.

(7 marks)

4 IAS 39 *Financial Instrument: Recognition and Measurement* permits companies to use hedge accounting.

Outline the circumstances in which this would be allowed and the accounting mechanism by which it would be accomplished.

(6 marks)
(Total = 25 marks)

Answer 8 – Financial instruments aptitude testing

Q1 – Hybrid instrument:

IAS 32 requires split accounting for hybrid instruments with the debt component being calculated based on interest rates attributable to similar, but non-convertible debt, and the equity component "dropping out" as the balancing figure.

	$
Present value of the principal:	
\$2,000,000 discounted at 6% [2,000,000/(1.06)^4]	1,584,187
Present value of the interest:	
\$80,000 × (1/1.06) + (1/1.06^2) + (1/1.06^3) + (1/1.06^4)	277,208
	1,861,395
Equity component [balancing figure]	138,605
	2,000,000

Q2 – Stepped bond:

Year ended 31 March	*b/f* $	*Finance cost* [10%] $	*Payment* $	*c/f* $
20X5	965,354	96,536	(40,000)	1,021,890
20X6	1,021,890	102,189	(50,000)	1,074,079
20X7	1,074,079	107,408	(60,000)	1,121,487
20X8	1,121,487	112,149	(70,000)	1,163,636
20X9	1,163,636	116,364	(80,000)	1,200,000

↑ Charge against profits

Note: Direct issue costs have been netted off the opening position to give net proceeds.

Q3 – Derivative:

IAS 39 *Financial Instruments: Recognition and Measurement* requires that all derivatives are accounted for on the balance sheet irrespective of whether they are used as part of a hedging relationship.

At the date the forward contract is initiated it has cost BNM plc zero as it represents a promise to pay in the future.

However, as the exchange rate moves so the fair value of the derivative changes and this must be recorded in the financial statements.

At 31 December 20X4:

At this date the fair value of the derivative is 2,000,000/2.5 = £800,000, whereas the amount to be settled under the terms of the contract is 2,000,000/2.4 = £833,333. Hence the weakening Australian dollar is not working to the advantage of BNM plc as it have to settle for an amount larger than would be required in the currency markets at 31 December 20X4. This loss must be charged against profit:

DR	Income statement (loss)	Aus\$33,333
CR	Derivative liability	Aus\$33,333

At 30 April 20X5:

In the period to settlement of the contract the Australian dollar has continued to weaken further changing the fair value of the derivative (2,000,000/2.55 = £784,314) and crystallising an additional loss.

DR	Income statement (loss)	Aus$15,686
CR	Derivative liability	Aus$15,686

At 30 April 20X5 the derivative ceases and must be removed from the books.

DR	Derivative liability	Aus$49,019
DR	Australian dollar cash a/c	Aus$784,314
CR	Cash	Aus$833,333

Q4 – Hedge accounting:

Hedge accounting is an allowed option under IAS 39 *Financial Instruments: Recognition and Measurement*.

For a hedging relationship to exist three elements must be present.

1 *Hedged item* – the item the enterprise is protecting through hedging. Examples would include
   - a recognised asset or liability
   - an unrecognised firm commitment.
2 *Hedged risk* – the hedge must be for specific risks (i.e. micro-hedging) such as foreign exchange risk.
3 *Hedging instruments* – The derivative (usually) or other instrument taken out to offset gains or losses on the hedged item.

However, for hedging to be allowed there are two additional provisos:

1 The hedging relationship must be formally designated and documented. The formal documentation should include the enterprises risk management objective, identification of the hedging instrument/hedged item and how effectiveness of the hedge will be assessed.

2 There must be an expectation that the hedge will be highly effective – the gain or loss on the hedged item is offset by an opposite gain or loss on the hedging instrument for between 80 and 125% of the gain and loss on the hedged item.

IAS 39 identifies three types of hedge and each has its own unique accounting treatment.

Fair value hedge: Any gain or loss on remeasuring the hedging instrument and the hedged item are recognised in the income statement for the period.

Cash flow hedge: A hedge in which the cash flows of the item being hedged change as the market price changes. The gain or loss on the hedging instrument is recognised directly in the reserves, but controversially if the instrument being hedged subsequently results in the recognition of an asset or liability the gain or loss should be recycled as part of the cost of that asset or liability.

Foreign investment hedge: The gain or loss on the hedging instrument should be recognised directly in reserves to match against the gain or loss on the hedge instrument.

Question 9 – Rook plc

Rook plc is a non-trading parent company with wholly owned subsidiaries involved in the manufacture and sale of a diverse product portfolio. Until 1 January 20X3 all of these operations were based in the United Kingdom, but at that date the group acquired a 90% stake in Pawn GbmH in an attempt to establish a foothold in new markets.

At 31 December 20X4 summary financial statements are available as follows

Balance sheets

	Rook group £'000	*Pawn GmbH* €'000
Assets		
Non-current assets		
Property, plant and equipment	400	100
Investment in Pawn GmbH	96	–
	496	100
Net current assets	304	45
Total assets	800	145
Equity and liabilities		
Capital and reserves		
Ordinary share capital	100	40
Accumulated profits	450	75
	550	115
Non-current liabilities		
Loan	250	30
	800	145

Income statements

	Rook group £'000	*Pawn GbmH* €'000
Revenue	2,000	1,200
Cost of sales	(1,500)	(750)
Gross profit	500	450
Selling and administration costs	(100)	(280)
Operating profit	400	170
Interest payable	(20)	(10)
Profit before taxation	380	160
Taxation	(120)	(90)
Profit after taxation	260	70

Statement of changes in equity

	Rook group £'000	*Pawn GbmH* €'000
Balance at start of period	450	45
Profit for the period	260	70
Dividends	(160)	–
Balance at end of the period	550	115

At the date of the investment the accumulated profits on Pawn GbmH were €20,000, and due to a long-term reinvestment plan it has not paid a dividend since that date. The cost of the investment was €120,000.

There have been no impairments to goodwill since the date of acquisition.

Relevant rates of exchange are as follows

	Euro to £1
1 January 20X3	1.25
31 December 20X3	1.3
Average for 20X4	1.32
31 December 20X4	1.4

Requirements

(a) Prepare the consolidated balance sheet for Rook plc as at 31 December 20X4.

(7 marks)

(b) Prepare the consolidated income statement for the year ended 31 December 20X4.

(5 marks)

(c) Prepare the consolidated statement of changes in equity for the year ended 31 December 20X4.

(7 marks)

(d) Demonstrate that the foreign exchange movement for the year arising on the translation of Pawn GbmH can be verified.

(6 marks)

(Total = 25 marks)

[Work to the nearest €100]

Answer 9 – Rook plc

(a) Consolidated balance sheet as at 31 December 20X4

	£'000
Assets	
Non-current assets	
Intangibles [W1]	47.1
Property, plant and equipment	471.4
	518.5
Current assets	336.1
Total assets	854.6
Equity and liabilities	
Capital and reserves	
Ordinary share capital	100
Accumulated profits	475
	575
Minority interests [W3]	8.2
Non-current liabilities	
Loan	271.4
	854.6

Workings

W1:

Goodwill

	€'000	€'000
Cost of investment [96 × €1.25]		120
Share capital at acquisition	40	
Reserves at acquisition	20	
	60	
90% stake		(54)
		66
Translated at the closing rate [£1 = €1.4]		€47.1

W2:

Translation of Pawn's balance sheet

Balance sheet

	€'000	*Rate*	£'000
Assets			
Non-current assets			
Property, plant and equipment	100	1.4	71.4
	100		71.4
Net current assets	45	1.4	32.1
Total assets	145		103.5

	€'000	*Rate*	£'000
Equity and liabilities			
Capital and reserves			
Ordinary share capital	40	1.25	32
Pre-acquisition reserves	20	1.25	16
Post-acquisition reserves	55	Bal	34.1
	115		82.1
Non-current liabilities			
Loan	30	1.4	21.4
	145		103.5

W3:

Minority interest

10% × 82.1 [W2] = €8.2k

(b) Consolidated income statement for the year ending 31 December 20X4

	£'000
Revenue	2,909.1
Cost of sales	(2,068.2)
Gross profit	840.9
Selling and administration costs	(312.1)
Operating profit	528.8
Interest payable	(27.6)
Profit before taxation	501.2
Taxation	(188.2)
Profit after taxation	313.0
Minority interest [10% × 53]	(5.3)
Profit attributable to the shareholders of Rook plc	307.7

W4:

Translation of Pawn GbmH income statement

Income statement	*Pawn GbmH* €'000	*Rate*	£'000
Revenue	1,200	1.32	909.1
Cost of sales	(750)	1.32	(568.2)
Gross profit	450		340.9
Selling and administration costs	(280)	1.32	(212.1)
Operating profit	170		128.8
Interest payable	(10)	1.32	(7.6)
Profit before taxation	160		121.2
Taxation	(90)	1.32	(68.2)
Profit after taxation	70		53.0

(c) Consolidated statement of changes in equity for the year ended 31 December 20X4

	£'000
Brought forward at 1 January 20X4 [W5]	436
Profit for the period	307.7
Dividend (Rook plc)	(160)
Exchange loss (balancing figure)	(8.7)
Carried forward at 31 December 20X4	575

W5:

Consolidated equity brought forward

	£'000
Rook plc	450
90% Post-acquisition of Pawn GbmH [W6]	(12)
Exchange movement on goodwill	(2)
@ acquisition = 52.8	
@ 31 December 20X3 (66/1.3) = 50.8	
Hence exchange loss = 2.0	
	436

W6:

Pawn GbmH post-acquisition profits

	£'000
Opening equity (45,000/1.3)	34.6
Share capital (per translated balance sheet)	(32)
Pre-acquisition reserves (per translated balance sheet)	(16)
	(13.4)

(d) Proof of foreign exchange movement for the year

	£'000	£'000	
Opening net assets @ opening rate [45/1.3]	34.6		
Opening net assets @ closing rate [45/1.4]	32.1	2.5	loss
Profit @ average rate [70/1.32]	53		
Profit @ closing rate [70/1.4]	50	3	loss
		5.5	loss
@ 90%		5	loss
Goodwill @ opening rate [66/1.3]	50.8		
Goodwill @ closing rate [66/1.4]	47.1	3.7	loss
		8.7	loss

Question 10 – Illusion Ltd

Illusion Ltd is a car dealership with 17 outlets in the North West of the United Kingdom. The ambition of the directors has always been to float the company, and to use this as a vehicle by which to fund expansion into mainland Europe.

The company's financial advisers, Peacock & Co, have stated that the company would need to show positive earnings and dividend growth, and a strong balance sheet over a five year period to facilitate a successful flotation. Every year the directors of Illusion Ltd attend a meeting with Peacock & Co to discuss methods by which the financial performance and position of the company can be enhanced whilst maintaining good corporate governance.

For the year ended 30 June 20X4 the directors have asked that the scheduled meeting should commence with a slide presentation from the financial advisers on two issues that have caused particular confusion:

1 Knowing that a strong cash flow position is important the directors entered into an agreement with a factoring company to "sell" their existing receivable accounts and then to outsource the management of receivables. The factoring company has an excellent reputation, and the directors of Illusion perceive that the "sale" will lead to a substantial cash inflow without changing the net asset position, and will shorten the working capital cycle thereafter.

   The confusion has arisen after a comment from the auditors of the company who suggested that it might be inappropriate to remove the receivables from the balance sheet, and that a liability would also need to be recognised.

   Other details of the factoring agreement are:

   - Illusion Ltd would receive an upfront payment for existing receivables equivalent to 75% of face value less an administration charge of 2% of face value. These funds were successfully negotiated by the directors of Illusion Ltd who were able to demonstrate the credit worthiness of their receivables portfolio.
   - After 4 months the factor pays the remaining outstanding balance to Illusion Ltd less an interest charge equivalent to 1% per month based on the value of the receivables that have yet to be collected on that date.
   - There is a ceiling on the ultimate amount paid by the factor to Illusion Ltd set at 98% of the face value of the portfolio on the date of transfer.
   - If any receivable balance ultimately proves uncollectible the factor has the right to reclaim 20% of its value from Illusion Ltd.

   The value of the receivables portfolio on the date of transfer was £1,000,000.

2 The Illusion Ltd dealerships sell only one brand of vehicle with monthly deliveries to each dealership from the manufacturer.

   The price charged by the manufacturer is calculated based on the wholesale price at the delivery date. Illusion can return vehicles in excess of their needs at any time, but are charged a penalty by the manufacturer of 1% per month based on cost price.

   The manufacturer also insists that Illusion bear the cost of insurance from the time the vehicles are offloaded onto the forecourts.

   Each year the directors of Illusion Ltd are split as to the treatment of the vehicles remaining unsold at the dealerships; some believing they should be included in inventory whilst others would prefer to have them excluded. Although the directors have always followed the advice of their advisers on the most appropriate treatment the annual debate has become tiresome, and they would like the issue resolved to the satisfaction of the entire board.

Requirements

(a) Explain the concept of commercial substance prevailing over legal form.

(4 marks)

(b) Prepare slides for the presentation to the Board of Illusion Ltd on the two issues highlighted (a maximum of two slides for each) with accompanying notes for the speaker on the recommended accounting treatment.

(12 marks)

(c) The directors of Illusion plc are aware that an essential component of their expansion plan is the retention of key staff. Consequently they decided to retain the company's defined benefit pension scheme, unlike many of their competitors who had switched to defined contribution schemes, although they realised that a downturn in the financial markets could result in the scheme showing a substantial deficit.

Relevant information on the scheme for the year ended 30 June 20X4 includes:

	20X3 £'000	*20X4* £'000
Present value of obligations at 30 June		
Fair value of plan assets at 30 June		
Current service cost	n/a	
Contributions received	n/a	
Benefits paid	n/a	

- The discount rate applicable to both years was 8%.
- The expected return on scheme assets was 11% for the year ended 30 June 20X3 and 10% for 20X4.
- The expected average remaining service lives of employees in the scheme is 12 years.
- Net cumulative unrecognised actuarial gains at 1 July 20X1 were £75,000.

Calculate the impact of the scheme on the profits of Illusion plc for the year ended 30 June 20X4.

Comment on the potential impact of your calculations on the reported profits for the year ended 30 June 20X5.

(9 marks)
(Total = 25 marks)

Answer 10 – Illusion Ltd

(a) The concept of commercial substance over legal form

One of the overriding requirements associated with published financial statements is that the information contained therein should be fairly presented. This should enable stakeholders to make appropriate decisions about the performance and position of the entity.

Fair presentation will not always be achieved by adhering to strict legal form if this prevents the financial statements from disclosing the true commercial substance of the underlying transactions. There are many high profile examples of this principle:

- When an asset is leased under a finance lease the asset is recorded in the books of the lessee because they are exposed to the risks and rewards of ownership even though they do not have legal title.
- Group financial statements are an example of substance over form as each member company of a group is a separate legal entity, but application of the single entity concept results in consolidated accounts reflecting position and performance of the constituent entities as if they were a single company.

The concept of substance over legal form is often prevalent in cases of window dressing or creative accounting; several linked transactions may be separated to conceal their true purpose.

There is no specific IAS on substance over form although IAS 1 does set out the basic principle that substance should prevail.

> Management should develop policies to ensure that the financial statements provide information that is . . . reliable in that they reflect the economic substance of events and transactions and not merely the legal form

Further guidance is given by IAS 18 *Revenue* and IAS 39 *Financial Instruments: Recognition and Measurement*.

When determining substance the key is usually to determine whether or not a sale should be recognised and the related asset(s) derecognised. This can be achieved by identifying the assets and liabilities recognised in the balance sheet before and after the transaction; the substance of the transaction is a function of the changes in these items.

(b) Board presentation

(i) Factoring receivables

Slide 1: Factoring agreement
• 98% payment ceiling • Amounts received in advance • Administration charge • Finance charge.

Comments

- The 98% ceiling effectively means that the remaining 2% should be treated as a bad debt expense and written off as it will never be received by Illusion Ltd.
- Of the 75% received at the start of the agreement a proportion [55% of face value] is effectively received without recourse. Illusion Ltd is no longer exposed to any of the risks and rewards and hence £550,000 should be derecognised.

  However £200,000 of the funds may have to be repaid in the receivables prove uncollectible. It can be argued that the "sale" of the receivables is not complete as the final outcome is not known, and hence linked presentation will be appropriate.

  The £200,000 received with recourse should be recognised within payables as the possibility exists that it may have to be repaid to the factor.

- Both the administration fee and the monthly finance fee should be recognised in the income statement as the costs are incurred.
- Key extracts of balance sheet disclosure would be:

	£	£
Current assets		
Trade receivables [1,000,000 × 98%]	980,000	
Less: Non returnable proceeds [75% − 20%]	(550,000)	
		430,000
Cash		750,000
		1,180,000
Current liabilities		
Amounts subject to recourse		200,000

(ii) Consignment inventory

Slide 2: Consignment inventory

- Transfer price based on delivery date
- Right of return
- Penalty fee
- Insurance costs.

Comments

- Basing the pricing on the wholesale price at the delivery date suggests that the risks and rewards of ownership have passed to Illusion Ltd on that date. If the price rises after delivery then Illusion will be protected from these increases, but if the price falls they will still have to pay the earlier higher price.
- If Illusion had an unfettered right to return the vehicles at any time to the manufacturer without penalty this would indicate that the risk of obsolescence effectively lies with the manufacturer. However, the penalty of 1% per month suggests that risk has been transferred to the dealership.
- Illusion Ltd bears the cost of insurance again suggesting it has the costs associated with ownership of the inventory.

- All evidence available indicates that the risks associated with the vehicles has transferred to the dealerships, and Illusion Ltd should recognise the inventory and purchases within its financial statements.

(c) Impact of defined benefit scheme on reported profits

	£'000
Impact on reported profits for the year ended 30 June 20X4:	
Current Service Cost [operating expense]	(140)
Interest on opening scheme liabilities [900 × 8%]	(72)
Return on scheme assets [820 × 10%]	82
Overall effect	(130)

There is no impact from actuarial gains or losses as these do not fall outside the 10% corridor [see below].

Workings:

Actuarial gains and losses

	£'000
Present value of plan assets at 1 July 20X3	820
Contributions	70
Expected return on assets [820 × 10%]	82
Benefits paid	(130)
Actuarial gains [Balance]	23
Present value of plan assets at 30 June 20X4	865

	£'000
Present value of plan liabilities at 1 July 20X3	900
Current service cost	140
Finance cost [900 × 8%]	72
Benefits paid	(130)
Actuarial gains [Balance]	(13)
Present value of plan liabilities at 30 June 20X4	995

Actuarial gains and losses only have to be recognised in the income statement if the net cumulative unrecognised actuarial gain/loss at the end of the previous accounting period exceeds the greater of:

- 10% of the present value of the plan obligation.
- 10% of the fair value of the plan assets.

Hence the corridor at 1 July 20X3 is £90,000 [10% × 900k]. Consequently there is no actuarial gain or loss to recognise in the income statement as the actuarial gain brought forward does not exceed this barrier.

Profits for the year ended 30 June 20X5

The 10% corridor as at 1 July 20X4 will be £99,500 [10% × £995k]. The actuarial gain brought forward to this date of £140k clearly exceeds this threshold, and the excess of £40.5k will be recognised in the income statement over the average remaining lives of employees in the scheme.

Income statement impact for year ended 30 June 20X5 = £3,375 [£40,500/12 years].

Question 11 – Bata Ltd

Bata Ltd is a successful company involved in the making safe of hazardous waste from the energy sector. Its Managing Director, Henry Bata, has always been seen as a forward thinker, and has become concerned that the financial statements of the company do not adequately reflect the true value of the transactions that lie behind them. To investigate his concerns Henry has decided to focus on the performance of a subsidiary company, Nuvo Ltd, which was incorporated and commenced trading on 1 January 20X4.

To improve his understanding of the impact of changing prices on the performance and position of his business Henry asked his financial manager to collect data on changes in both general market prices and those specific to Bata Ltd. He has just received the summary he requested.

	1 January 20X4	*31 December 20X4*	*Average for the year*
Specific indices from trade journals			
Inventory	112	136	127
Property, plant and equipment	142	188	158
General price index	132	160	147

A summary of the most recent financial information, as at 31 December 20X4, is given below:

Income statement for the year ended 31 December 20X4

	£
Revenue	694,740
Cost of sales	(396,700)
Gross profit	298,040
Selling and administration costs	(96,800)
Net profit	201,240

Further information:

- An initial purchase of inventory (£27,500) was made on 1 January 20X4.
- Non-current assets were acquired and paid for at the same time as the initial inventory. The full cost was £810,000 and depreciation incurred during 20X4 was £20,200.
- Selling and administration costs include depreciation of £20,200.

Balance sheet as at 31 December 20X4

	£	£
Assets		
Non-current assets		
Property		514,800
Plant and equipment		285,000
		799,800
Current assets		
Inventory	19,400	
Receivables	202,800	
Cash	872,240	
		1,094,440
Total assets		1,894,240

	£	£
Equity and liabilities		
Capital and reserves		
Ordinary share capital [50p shares]		1,200,000
Accumulated profits		201,240
		1,401,240
Non-current liabilities		
Loan		400,000
Current liabilities		
Trade payables	93,000	
		93,000
		1,894,240

Further information.

- The property plant and equipment cost £240,000 at 1 January 20X4 (payment being made on this date) and is being depreciated to a nil residual value straight line over six years.

Requirements

(a) Discuss the problems associated with the use of historic cost, and the underlying concepts behind the current cost accounting and current purchasing power methodologies. [There is no requirement to illustrate your answer with calculations, and the discussion should be given in simple terms.]

(12 marks)

(b) Restate the financial statements using the principles associated with the current purchasing power methodology for reflecting price changes.

(13 marks)
(Total = 25 marks)

Answer 11 – Bata Ltd

(a) Problems of historic cost accounting

Historic cost accounting is the traditional measurement base used in financial statements although many businesses do elect to revalue their non-current assets. It is a traditional method used for more than six centuries since its introduction by Venetian merchants, and its enduring popularity cannot be dismissed. Particular attributes include:

- *Objectivity* – entries to the financial statements are largely supported by documentary evidence such as invoices, cheques and bank statements.
- *Understandability* – its wide use across the world means it represents a universal language.
- *Factual* – the figures are beyond dispute.

However, some of these benefits are not as persuasive as they first appear. Historic cost financial statements include provisions for bad debts, depreciation, etc. all of which require estimation and hence undermine objectivity. Similarly historic cost is not always the exact figure expected . . . inventory is valued at the lower of cost and net realisable value, but "cost" may vary depending on the system of valuation used (e.g. FIFO, weighted average, etc.).

In the income statement current revenues are matched against historic costs leading to the over-estimation of true profit. Similarly the inclusion of assets and liabilities in the balance sheet at their historic cost conceals the true value of the business, and when this is combined with the historic profits from the income statement it implies that ratio analysis and interpretation could lead to poor management decisions.

Advocates of change away from historic cost accounting point to the fact that the balance sheet is a mishmash of different values with some elements such as inventory being closer to a reflection of current cost than others such as property, plant and equipment. It is true that some entities elect to revalue the latter on a regular basis, but this policy is one of choice, and hence not adopted by all; thereby leading to less comparability.

Current cost accounting and current purchasing power

To overcome the issues associated with historic cost accounting we need a new concept of value, and new concept of income (more usually referred to as capital maintenance). Assuming positive inflation the following journals would be needed to reflect price changes:

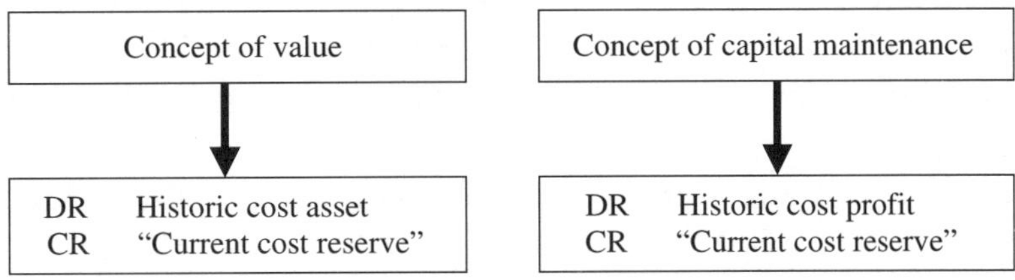

The difficulty is in identifying the appropriate numerical entry for this adjustment, and several different methods have been developed to address this.

Current purchasing power accounts for inflation by adjusting the values of non-monetary items for changes in a general economic price index. The information required is easily available (e.g. the retail price index in the United Kingdom), and is widely recognised making it more understandable to non-specialist users of the financial statements.

Current cost accounting focuses more closely on the impact of inflation specific to a particular entity. This "value to the business" approach considers the current value of an asset to be the lower of replacement cost and recoverable amounts, where the latter is the higher of the net realisable value and the value in use (i.e. discounted value of future cash flows that are expected to be generated by the asset).

The historic cost profit is adjusted for:

- Cost of sales adjustment [COSA]
- Depreciation adjustment [DA]
- Monetary working capital adjustment [MWCA]
- Gearing adjustment [GA].

Unlike current purchasing power the identification of price changes to a specific business can be very time consuming and subjective, and the concept of capital maintenance employed (operating capital maintenance) is not one easily grasped by a non-specialist user of financial information.

Conclusion

The problems associated with historic cost accounting, and proposed schemes for its replacement have been a recurring theme over many years. The flaws associated with historic cost accounting are not disputed, but the subjectivity of alternatives means they have never gained a foothold outside of a few specialised industries.

The IASB recognises the issues, but revisiting the impact of price changes is not in the current wave of international accounting developments.

(b) Restatement using current purchasing power

Income statement for the year ended 31 December 20X4

	£		£
Revenue	694,740	160/147	756,180
Cost of sales			
Opening inventory	(27,500)	160/132	(33,333)
Purchases	(388,600)	160/147	(422,966)
Closing inventory	19,400	160/160	19,400
Gross profit	298,040		319,281
Selling and administration costs	(76,600)	160/147	(83,374)
Depreciation	(20,200)	160/132	(24,484)
Net profit	201,240		211,423

Note: Assumption made that closing inventory acquired on 31 December 20X4

Balance sheet as at 31 December 20X4

	£	£		£
Assets				
Non-current assets				
Property, plant and equipment		799,800	160/132	969,455
		799,800		969,455
Current assets				
Inventory	19,400		160/160	19,400
Receivables	202,800			202,800
Cash	872,240			872,240
		1,094,440		
Total assets		1,894,240		2,063,895
Equity and liabilities				
Capital and reserves				
Ordinary share capital [50p shares]		1,200,000	160/132	1,454,545
Accumulated profits		201,240	W1	116,350
		1,401,240		1,570,895
Non-current liabilities				
Loan		400,000		400,000
Current liabilities				
Trade payables	93,000			93,000
		93,000		
		1,894,240		2,063,895

[W1] Gain/Loss on monetary items

	£	£	£
Change in receivables			202,800
Change in payables			(493,000)
Change in cash		872,240	
Received at 1 January via capital	1,200,000		
Less: Initial purchase of inventory and non-current assets	(847,500)	(352,500)	519,740
			229,540

Loss on holding monetary assets as occurring during the period:

229,540 × [(160 − 147)/147] = 20,300

Loss on holding the opening cash balance during the period:

352,500 × [(160 − 132)/132] = 74,773

Hence total movement to take to reserves = £95,073

Reserves = Profit [211,423] − 95,073 = £116,350.

May 2005 Questions and Commentary

23

Financial Analysis (Paper P8)

Published separately on the CIMA website (www.cimaglobal.com) from the end of September 2005 is a Post Examination Guide for this paper, which provides much valuable and complementary material including indicative mark information.

Financial Management Pillar

Managerial Level Paper

P8 – Financial Analysis

24 May 2005 – Tuesday Afternoon Session

Instructions to candidates

You are allowed three hours to answer this question paper.
You are allowed 20 minutes reading time **before the examination begins** during which you should read the question paper and, if you wish, make annotations on the question paper. However, you will **not** be allowed, **under any circumstances**, to open the answer book and start writing or use your calculator during this reading time.
You are strongly advised to carefully read the question requirement before attempting the question concerned. The question requirements for questions in Sections B and C are highlighted in a dotted box.
Answer the ONE compulsory question in Section A. This is comprised of eight sub-questions on pages 282 to 284.
Answer ALL THREE compulsory sub-questions in Section B on pages 285 to 287.
Answer TWO of the three questions in Section C on pages 288 to 293.
Maths Tables and Formulae are provided on pages 294 to 296.
Write your full examination number, paper number and the examination subject title in the spaces provided on the front of the examination answer book. Also write your contact ID and name in the space provided in the right-hand margin and seal to close.
Tick the appropriate boxes on the front of the answer book to indicate which questions you have answered.

SECTION A – 20 MARKS

[indicative time for answering this section is 36 minutes]

ANSWER *ALL* EIGHT SUB-QUESTIONS

Instructions for answering Section A:

The answers to the eight sub-questions in Section A should ALL be written in your answer book.

Your answers should be clearly numbered with the sub-question number and ruled off, so that the markers know which sub-question you are answering.

For sub-question **1.8** you should show your workings, as marks are available for the method you use to answer this sub-question.

? Question One

1.1 The FG group of entities comprises FG and its subsidiaries, HI and JK.

FG acquired 80% of HI's ordinary shares on 31 December 2001, when the reserves of HI stood at $10,000,000, and the reserves of JK stood at $7,600,000.

HI acquired 75% of JK's ordinary shares on 31 December 2000, when the reserves of JK stood at $7,000,000.

At 31 December 2004, HI's reserves stood at $12,200,000, and JK's reserves stood at $10,600,000.

There have been no other acquisitions and disposals in the group, and no impairments of goodwill or intra-group trading adjustments have been recorded.

How much profit has been added to consolidated reserves in the FG group in respect of the investments in HI and JK between acquisition and 31 December 2004?

A $3,560,000
B $3,920,000
C $4,010,000
D $4,460,000

(2 marks)

1.2 On 1 March 2005, PB, a listed entity, acquired 80% of 3,000,000 issued ordinary shares of SV. The consideration for each share acquired comprised a cash payment of $1.20, plus two ordinary shares in PB. The market value of a $1 ordinary share in PB on 1 March 2005 was $1.50, rising to $1.60 by the entity's year end on 31 March 2005. Professional fees paid to PB's external accountants and legal advisers in respect of the acquisition were $400,000.

What is the fair value of consideration in respect of this acquisition, for inclusion in PB's financial statements for the year ended 31 March 2005?

A $10,080,000
B $10,480,000
C $10,560,000
D $10,960,000

(2 marks)

1.3 Where the purchase price of an acquisition is less than the aggregate fair value of the net assets acquired, which ONE of the following accounting treatments of the difference is required by IFRS 3 *Business Combinations*?

A Deduction from goodwill in the consolidated balance sheet.
B Immediate recognition as a gain in the statement of changes in equity.
C Recognition in the income statement over its estimated useful life.
D Immediate recognition as a gain in the income statement.

(2 marks)

1.4 On 1 March 2004, NS acquired 30% of the shares of TP. The investment was accounted for as an associate in NS's consolidated financial statements. Both NS and TP have an accounting year end of 31 October. NS has no other investments in associates.

Net profit for the year in TP's income statement for the year ended 31 October 2004 was $230,000. It declared and paid a dividend of $100,000 on 1 July 2004. No other dividends were paid in the year.

What amount will be shown as an inflow in respect of earnings from the associate in the consolidated cash flow statement of NS for the year ended 31 October 2004?

A $20,000
B $26,000
C $30,000
D $46,000

(2 marks)

1.5 Which of the following statements, in respect of foreign currency translation, are correct according to IAS 21 *The Effects of Changes in Foreign Exchange Rates?*

(i) The functional currency of an entity is selected by management.
(ii) The presentation currency of an entity is selected by management.
(iii) The functional currency of an entity is identified by reference to circumstances of the business.
(iv) The presentation currency of an entity is identified by reference to circumstances of the business.

A (i) and (ii) only
B (iii) and (iv) only
C (i) and (iv) only
D (ii) and (iii) only

(2 marks)

1.6 During the financial year ended 28 February 2005, MN issued the two financial instruments described below. For EACH of the instruments, identify whether it should be classified as debt or equity, **explaining in not more than 40 words each** the reason for your choice. In each case you should refer to the relevant International Accounting Standard or International Financial Reporting Standard.

(i) Redeemable preferred shares with a coupon rate of 8%. The shares are redeemable on 28 February 2009 at a premium of 10%.

(2 marks)

(ii) A grant of share options to senior executives. The options may be exercised from 28 February 2008.

(2 marks)
(Total = 4 marks)

1.7 The following statement contains a missing word:

"Current purchasing power accounting is based upon the concept of_____capital maintenance."

Which ONE of the following is the missing word?

A Real
B General
C Physical
D Cash-based

(2 marks)

1.8 On 1 February 2004, BJ sold a freehold interest in land to a financing institution for $7.2 million. The contractual terms require that BJ repurchase the freehold on 31 January 2007 for $8.82 million. BJ has the option to repurchase on 31 January 2005 for $7.7 million, or on 31 January 2006 for $8.24 million. Prior to the disposal, the land was recorded at its carrying value of $6 million in BJ's accounting records. The receipt of $7.2 million has been recorded with a corresponding credit to suspense account. No other accounting entries have been made in respect of this transaction.

At 31 January 2005, BJ's directors decide not to take up the option to repurchase.

Briefly explain the substance of this transaction, and prepare journal entries to record it correctly in the accounting records of BJ for the year ended 31 January 2005.

(4 marks)
(Total marks for Section A = 20)

SECTION B – 30 MARKS

[indicative time for answering this section is 54 minutes]

ANSWER *ALL* THREE QUESTIONS

? Question Two

On 1 February 2004, CB, a listed entity, had 3,000,000 ordinary shares in issue.

On 1 March 2004, CB made a rights issue of 1 for 4 at $6.50 per share. The issue was completely taken up by the shareholders.

Extracts from CB's financial statements for the year ended 31 January 2005 are presented below:

CB: Extracts from income statement for the year ended 31 January 2005

	$'000
Operating profit	1,380
Finance cost	(400)
Profit before tax	980
Income tax expense	(255)
Profit for the period	725

CB: Extracts from summarised statement of changes in equity for the year ended 31 January 2005

	$'000
Balance at 1 February 2004	7,860
Issue of share capital	4,875
Surplus on revaluation of properties	900
Profit for the period	725
Equity dividends	(300)
Balance at 31 January 2005	14,060

Just before the rights issue, CB's share price was $7.50, rising to $8.25 immediately afterwards. The share price at close of business on 31 January 2005 was $6.25.

At the beginning of February 2005, the average price earnings (P/E) ratio in CB's business sector was 28.4, and the P/E of its principal competitor was 42.5.

Requirements

(a) Calculate the earnings per share for CB for the year ended 31 January 2005, and its P/E ratio at that date.

(6 marks)

(b) Discuss the significance of P/E ratios to investors and CB's P/E ratio relative to those of its competitor and business sector.

(4 marks)
(Total = 10 marks)

? Question Three

RW holds 80% of the 1,000,000 ordinary shares of its subsidiary, SX. Summarised income statements of both entities for the year ended 31 December 2004 are shown below:

	RW	*SX*
	$'000	$'000
Revenue	6,000	2,500
Operating costs	(4,500)	(1,700)
Profit before tax	1,500	800
Income tax expense	(300)	(250)
Profit for the period	1,200	550

RW purchased 800,000 of SX's $1 shares in 2003 for $3.2 million, when SX's reserves were $2.4 million. Goodwill has been carried at cost since acquisition, and there has been no subsequent impairment.

On 1 July 2004, RW disposed of 200,000 shares in SX for $1 million. SX's reserves at 1 January 2004 were $2.9 million, and its profits accrued evenly throughout the year. RW is liable to income tax at 30% on any accounting profits made on the disposal of investments.

The effects of the disposal are not reflected in the income statements shown above.

Requirement

Prepare the summarised consolidated income statement for RW for the year ended 31 December 2004.

(Total = 10 marks)

? Question Four

During its financial year ended 31 December 2004, an entity, PX, entered into the transactions described below:

In November 2004, having surplus cash available, PX made an investment in the securities of a listed entity. The directors intend to realise the investment in March or April 2005 in order to fund the planned expansion of PX's principal warehouse.

PX lent one of its customers, DB, $3,000,000 at a variable interest rate pegged to average bank lending rates. The loan is scheduled for repayment in 2009, and PX has provided an undertaking to DB that it will not assign the loan to a third party.

PX added to its portfolio of relatively small investments in the securities of listed entities. PX does not plan to dispose of these investments in the short term.

Requirements

In accordance with IAS 39 *Financial Instruments: Recognition and Measurement*

(a) Identify the appropriate classification of these three categories of financial asset and briefly explain the reason for each classification.

(6 marks)

(b) Explain how the financial assets should be measured in the financial statements of PX at 31 December 2004.

(4 marks)

(Total = 10 marks)

(Total marks for Section B = 30)

SECTION C – 50 MARKS

[indicative time for answering this section is 90 minutes]

ANSWER *TWO* QUESTIONS OUT OF THREE

? Question Five

DM, a listed entity, has just published its financial statements for the year ended 31 December 2004. DM operates a chain of 42 supermarkets in one of the six major provinces of its country of operation. During 2004, there has been speculation in the financial press that the entity was likely to be a takeover target for one of the larger national chains of supermarkets that is currently under-represented in DM's province. A recent newspaper report has suggested that DM's directors are unlikely to resist a takeover. The six board members are all nearing retirement, and all own significant minority shareholdings in the business.

You have been approached by a private shareholder in DM. She is concerned that the directors have a conflict of interests and that the financial statements for 2004 may have been manipulated.

The income statement and summarised statement of changes in equity of DM, with comparatives, for the year ended 31 December 2004, and a balance sheet, with comparatives, at that date are as follows:

DM: Income statement for the year ended 31 December 2004

	2004 $m	2003 $m
Revenue, net of sales tax	1,255	1,220
Cost of sales	(1,177)	(1,145)
Gross profit	78	75
Operating expenses	(21)	(29)
Profit from operations	57	46
Finance cost	(10)	(10)
Profit before tax	47	36
Income tax expense	(14)	(13)
Profit for the period	33	23

DM: Summarised statement of changes in equity for the year ended 31 December 2004

	2004 $m	2003 $m
Opening balance	276	261
Profit for the period	33	23
Dividends	(8)	(8)
Closing balance	301	276

DM: Balance sheet at 31 December 2004

	2004		2003	
	$m	$m	$m	$m
Assets				
Non-current assets				
Property, plant and equipment	580		575	
Goodwill	100		100	
		680		675
Current assets				
Inventories	47		46	
Trade receivables	12		13	
Cash	46		12	
		105		71
Total assets		785		746
Equity and liabilities				
Equity				
Share capital	150		150	
Accumulated profits	151		126	
		301		276
Non-current liabilities				
Interest-bearing borrowings	142		140	
Deferred tax	25		21	
		167		161
Current liabilities				
Trade and other payables	297		273	
Short-term borrowings	20		36	
		317		309
		785		746

Notes:

1 DM's directors have undertaken a reassessment of the useful lives of non-current tangible assets during the year. In most cases, they estimate that the useful lives have increased and the depreciation charges in 2004 have been adjusted accordingly.
2 Six new stores have been opened during 2004, bringing the total to 42.
3 Four key ratios for the supermarket sector (based on the latest available financial statements of twelve listed entities in the sector) are as follows:

  (i) Annual sales per store: $27.6m
  (ii) Gross profit margin: 5.9%
  (iii) Net profit margin: 3.9%
  (iv) Non-current asset turnover (including both tangible and intangible non-current assets): 1.93

Requirements

(a) Prepare a report, addressed to the investor, analysing the performance and position of DM based on the financial statements and supplementary information provided above. The report should also include comparisons with the key sector ratios, and it should address the investor's concerns about the possible manipulation of the 2004 financial statements.

(20 marks)

(b) Explain the limitations of the use of sector comparatives in financial analysis.

(5 marks)

(Total = 25 marks)

Question Six

AJ is a law stationery business. In 2002, the majority of its board of directors was replaced. The new board decided to adopt a policy of expansion through acquisition. The balance sheets at 31 March 2005 of AJ and of two entities in which it holds substantial investments are shown below:

	AJ		*BK*		*CL*	
	$'000	$'000	$'000	$'000	$'000	$'000
Assets						
Non-current assets						
Property, plant and equipment	12,500		4,700		4,500	
Investments	18,000		–		1,300	
		30,500		4,700		5,800
Current assets						
Inventories	7,200		8,000		–	
Trade receivables	6,300		4,300		3,100	
Financial assets	–		–		2,000	
Cash	800		–		900	
		14,300		12,300		6,000
		44,800		17,000		11,800
Equity and liabilities						
Equity						
Called up share capital ($1 shares)		10,000		5,000		2,500
Reserves		14,000		1,000		4,300
		24,000		6,000		6,800
Non-current liabilities						
Loan notes		10,000		3,000		–
Current liabilities						
Trade payables	8,900		6,700		4,000	
Income tax	1,300		100		600	
Short-term borrowings	600		1,200		400	
		10,800		8,000		5,000
		44,800		17,000		11,800

NOTES TO THE BALANCE SHEETS

Note 1 – Investment by AJ in BK
On 1 April 2002, AJ purchased $2 million loan notes in BK at par.

On 1 April 2003, AJ purchased 4 million of the ordinary shares in BK for $7.5 million in cash, when BK's reserves were $1.5 million.

At the date of acquisition of the shares, BK's property, plant and equipment included land recorded at a cost of $920,000. At the date of acquisition, the fair value of the land was $1,115,000. No other adjustments in respect of fair value were required to BK's assets and liabilities upon acquisition. BK has not recorded the fair value in its own accounting records.

Note 2 – Investment by AJ in CL
On 1 October 2004, AJ acquired 1 million shares in CL, a book distributor, when the reserves of CL were $3.9 million. The purchase consideration was $4.4 million. Since the acquisition, AJ has had the right to appoint one of the five directors of CL. The remaining shares in CL are owned principally by three other investors.

No fair value adjustments were required in respect of CL's assets or liabilities upon acquisition.

Note 3 – Goodwill on consolidation
Since acquiring its investment in BK, AJ has adopted the requirements of IFRS 3 *Business Combinations* in respect of goodwill on consolidation. During March 2005, it conducted an impairment review of goodwill. As a result, the goodwill element of the investment in CL is unaltered, but the value of goodwill on consolidation in respect of BK is now $1.7 million.

Note 4 – Intra-group trading
BK supplies legal books to AJ. On 31 March 2005, AJ's inventories included books purchased at a total cost of $1 million from BK. BK's mark-up on books is 25%.

Requirements

(a) Explain, with reasons, how the investments in BK and CL will be treated in the consolidated financial statements of the AJ group.

(5 marks)

(b) Prepare the consolidated balance sheet for the AJ group as at 31 March 2005. Full workings should be shown.

(20 marks)
(Total = 25 marks)

Question Seven

FW is a listed entity involved in the business of oil exploration, drilling and refining in three neighbouring countries, Aye, Bee and Cee. The business has been consistently profitable, creating high returns for its international shareholders. In recent years, however, there has been an increase in environmental lobbying in FW's three countries of operation. Two years ago, an environmental group based in Cee started lobbying the government to take action against FW for alleged destruction of valuable wildlife habitats in Cee's protected wetlands and the displacement of the local population. At the time, the directors of FW took legal advice on the basis of which they assessed the risk of liability at less than 50%. A contingent liability of $500 million was noted in the financial statements to cover possible legal costs, compensation to displaced persons and reinstatement of the habitats, as well as fines.

FW is currently preparing its financial statements for the year ended 28 February 2005. Recent advice from the entity's legal advisers has assessed that the risk of a successful action against FW has increased, and must now be regarded as more likely than not to occur. The board of directors has met to discuss the issue. The directors accept that a provision of $500 million is required, but would like to be informed of the effects of the adjustment on certain key ratios that the entity headlines in its annual report. All of the directors are concerned about the potentially adverse effect on the share price, as FW is actively engaged in a takeover bid that would involve a substantial share exchange. In addition, they feel that the public's image of the entity is likely to be damaged. The chief executive makes the following suggestion:

> Many oil businesses now publish an environmental and social report, and I think it may be time for us to do so. It would give us the opportunity to set the record straight about what we do to reduce pollution, and could help to deflect some of the public attention from us over this law suit. In any case, it would be a good public relations opportunity; we can use it to tell people about our equal opportunities programme. I was reading about something called the Global Reporting Initiative [GRI]. I don't know much about it, but it might give us some help in structuring a report that will get the right message across. We could probably pull something together to go out with this year's annual report.

The draft financial statements for the year ended 28 February 2005 include the following information relevant for the calculation of key ratios. All figures are before taking into account the $500 million provision. The provision will be charged to operating expenses.

	$m
Net assets (before long-term loans) at 1 March 2004	9,016
Net assets (before long-term loans) at 28 February 2005	10,066
Long-term loans at 28 February 2005	4,410
Share capital + reserves at 1 March 2004	4,954
Share capital + reserves at 28 February 2005	5,656
Revenue	20,392
Operating profit	2,080
Profit before tax	1,670
Profit for the period	1,002

The number of ordinary shares in issue throughout the years ended 29 February 2004 and 28 February 2005 were 6,000 million shares of 25¢ each.

FW's key financial ratios for the 2004 financial year (calculated using the financial statements for the year ended 29 February 2004) were:

• Return on equity (using average equity)	24.7%
• Return on net assets (using average net assets)	17.7%
• Gearing (debt as a percentage of equity)	82%
• Operating profit margin	10.1%
• Earnings per share	12.2¢ per share

Requirements

In your position as assistant to FW's Chief Financial Officer, produce a briefing paper that

(a) analyses and interprets the effects of making the environmental provision on FW's key financial ratios. You should take into account the possible effects on the public perception of FW.

(12 marks)

(b) identifies the advantages and disadvantages to FW of adopting the chief executive's proposal to publish an environmental and social report.

(7 marks)

(c) describes the THREE principal sustainability dimensions covered by the GRI's framework of performance indicators.

(6 marks)
(Total = 25 marks)

Present value table

Present value of £1 i.e. $(1 + r)^{-n}$ where r = interest rate; n = number of periods until payment or receipt.

Periods (n)	Interest rates (r)																			
	1%	2%	3%	4%	5%	6%	7%	8%	9%	10%	11%	12%	13%	14%	15%	16%	17%	18%	19%	20%
1	0.990	0.980	0.971	0.962	0.952	0.943	0.935	0.926	0.917	0.909	0.901	0.893	0.885	0.877	0.870	0.862	0.855	0.847	0.840	0.833
2	0.980	0.961	0.943	0.925	0.907	0.890	0.873	0.857	0.842	0.826	0.812	0.797	0.783	0.769	0.756	0.743	0.731	0.718	0.706	0.694
3	0.971	0.942	0.915	0.889	0.864	0.840	0.816	0.794	0.772	0.751	0.731	0.712	0.693	0.675	0.658	0.641	0.624	0.609	0.593	0.579
4	0.961	0.924	0.888	0.855	0.823	0.792	0.763	0.735	0.708	0.683	0.659	0.636	0.613	0.592	0.572	0.552	0.534	0.516	0.499	0.482
5	0.951	0.906	0.863	0.822	0.784	0.747	0.713	0.681	0.650	0.621	0.593	0.567	0.543	0.519	0.497	0.476	0.456	0.437	0.419	0.402
6	0.942	0.888	0.837	0.790	0.746	0.705	0.666	0.630	0.596	0.564	0.535	0.507	0.480	0.456	0.432	0.410	0.390	0.370	0.352	0.335
7	0.933	0.871	0.813	0.760	0.711	0.665	0.623	0.583	0.547	0.513	0.482	0.452	0.425	0.400	0.376	0.354	0.333	0.314	0.296	0.279
8	0.923	0.853	0.789	0.731	0.677	0.627	0.582	0.540	0.502	0.467	0.434	0.404	0.376	0.351	0.327	0.305	0.285	0.266	0.249	0.233
9	0.914	0.837	0.766	0.703	0.645	0.592	0.544	0.500	0.460	0.424	0.391	0.361	0.333	0.308	0.284	0.263	0.243	0.225	0.209	0.194
10	0.905	0.820	0.744	0.676	0.614	0.558	0.508	0.463	0.422	0.386	0.352	0.322	0.295	0.270	0.247	0.227	0.208	0.191	0.176	0.162
11	0.896	0.804	0.722	0.650	0.585	0.527	0.475	0.429	0.388	0.350	0.317	0.287	0.261	0.237	0.215	0.195	0.178	0.162	0.148	0.135
12	0.887	0.788	0.701	0.625	0.557	0.497	0.444	0.397	0.356	0.319	0.286	0.257	0.231	0.208	0.187	0.168	0.152	0.137	0.124	0.112
13	0.879	0.773	0.681	0.601	0.530	0.469	0.415	0.368	0.326	0.290	0.258	0.229	0.204	0.182	0.163	0.145	0.130	0.116	0.104	0.093
14	0.870	0.758	0.661	0.577	0.505	0.442	0.388	0.340	0.299	0.263	0.232	0.205	0.181	0.160	0.141	0.125	0.111	0.099	0.088	0.078
15	0.861	0.743	0.642	0.555	0.481	0.417	0.362	0.315	0.275	0.239	0.209	0.183	0.160	0.140	0.123	0.108	0.095	0.084	0.074	0.065
16	0.853	0.728	0.623	0.534	0.458	0.394	0.339	0.292	0.252	0.218	0.188	0.163	0.141	0.123	0.107	0.093	0.081	0.071	0.062	0.054
17	0.844	0.714	0.605	0.513	0.436	0.371	0.317	0.270	0.231	0.198	0.170	0.146	0.125	0.108	0.093	0.080	0.069	0.060	0.052	0.045
18	0.836	0.700	0.587	0.494	0.416	0.350	0.296	0.250	0.212	0.180	0.153	0.130	0.111	0.095	0.081	0.069	0.059	0.051	0.044	0.038
19	0.828	0.686	0.570	0.475	0.396	0.331	0.277	0.232	0.194	0.164	0.138	0.116	0.098	0.083	0.070	0.060	0.051	0.043	0.037	0.031
20	0.820	0.673	0.554	0.456	0.377	0.312	0.258	0.215	0.178	0.149	0.124	0.104	0.087	0.073	0.061	0.051	0.043	0.037	0.031	0.026

Cumulative present value of £1

This table shows the Present Value of £1 per annum. Receivable or Payable at the end of each year for n years $\frac{1 - (1 + r)^{-n}}{r}$

Periods (n)	Interest rates (r)																			
	1%	2%	3%	4%	5%	6%	7%	8%	9%	10%	11%	12%	13%	14%	15%	16%	17%	18%	19%	20%
1	0.990	0.980	0.971	0.962	0.952	0.943	0.935	0.926	0.917	0.909	0.901	0.893	0.885	0.877	0.870	0.862	0.855	0.847	0.840	0.833
2	1.970	1.942	1.913	1.886	1.859	1.833	1.808	1.783	1.759	1.736	1.713	1.690	1.668	1.647	1.626	1.605	1.585	1.566	1.547	1.528
3	2.941	2.884	2.829	2.775	2.723	2.673	2.624	2.577	2.531	2.487	2.444	2.402	2.361	2.322	2.283	2.246	2.210	2.174	2.140	2.106
4	3.902	3.808	3.717	3.630	3.546	3.465	3.387	3.312	3.240	3.170	3.102	3.037	2.974	2.914	2.855	2.798	2.743	2.690	2.639	2.589
5	4.853	4.713	4.580	4.452	4.329	4.212	4.100	3.993	3.890	3.791	3.696	3.605	3.517	3.433	3.352	3.274	3.199	3.127	3.058	2.991
6	5.795	5.601	5.417	5.242	5.076	4.917	4.767	4.623	4.486	4.355	4.231	4.111	3.998	3.889	3.784	3.685	3.589	3.498	3.410	3.326
7	6.728	6.472	6.230	6.002	5.786	5.582	5.389	5.206	5.033	4.868	4.712	4.564	4.423	4.288	4.160	4.039	3.922	3.812	3.706	3.605
8	7.652	7.325	7.020	6.733	6.463	6.210	5.971	5.747	5.535	5.335	5.146	4.968	4.799	4.639	4.487	4.344	4.207	4.078	3.954	3.837
9	8.566	8.162	7.786	7.435	7.108	6.802	6.515	6.247	5.995	5.759	5.537	5.328	5.132	4.946	4.772	4.607	4.451	4.303	4.163	4.031
10	9.471	8.983	8.530	8.111	7.722	7.360	7.024	6.710	6.418	6.145	5.889	5.650	5.426	5.216	5.019	4.833	4.659	4.494	4.339	4.192
11	10.368	9.787	9.253	8.760	8.306	7.887	7.499	7.139	6.805	6.495	6.207	5.938	5.687	5.453	5.234	5.029	4.836	4.656	4.486	4.327
12	11.255	10.575	9.954	9.385	8.863	8.384	7.943	7.536	7.161	6.814	6.492	6.194	5.918	5.660	5.421	5.197	4.988	4.793	4.611	4.439
13	12.134	11.348	10.635	9.986	9.394	8.853	8.358	7.904	7.487	7.103	6.750	6.424	6.122	5.842	5.583	5.342	5.118	4.910	4.715	4.533
14	13.004	12.106	11.296	10.563	9.899	9.295	8.745	8.244	7.786	7.367	6.982	6.628	6.302	6.002	5.724	5.468	5.229	5.008	4.802	4.611
15	13.865	12.849	11.938	11.118	10.380	9.712	9.108	8.559	8.061	7.606	7.191	6.811	6.462	6.142	5.847	5.575	5.324	5.092	4.876	4.675
16	14.718	13.578	12.561	11.652	10.838	10.106	9.447	8.851	8.313	7.824	7.379	6.974	6.604	6.265	5.954	5.668	5.405	5.162	4.938	4.730
17	15.562	14.292	13.166	12.166	11.274	10.477	9.763	9.122	8.544	8.022	7.549	7.120	6.729	6.373	6.047	5.749	5.475	5.222	4.990	4.775
18	16.398	14.992	13.754	12.659	11.690	10.828	10.059	9.372	8.756	8.201	7.702	7.250	6.840	6.467	6.128	5.818	5.534	5.273	5.033	4.812
19	17.226	15.679	14.324	13.134	12.085	11.158	10.336	9.604	8.950	8.365	7.839	7.366	6.938	6.550	6.198	5.877	5.584	5.316	5.070	4.843
20	18.046	16.351	14.878	13.590	12.462	11.470	10.594	9.818	9.129	8.514	7.963	7.469	7.025	6.623	6.259	5.929	5.628	5.353	5.101	4.870

Formulae

Annuity

Present value of an annuity of £1 per annum receivable or payable for n years, commencing in one year, discounted at r% per annum:

$$PV = \frac{1}{r}\left[1 - \frac{1}{[1 + r]^n}\right]$$

Perpetuity

Present value of £1 per annum, payable or receivable in perpetuity, commencing in one year, discounted at r% per annum:

$$PV = \frac{1}{r}$$

Growing perpetuity

Present value of £1 per annum, receivable or payable, commencing in one year, growing in perpetuity at a constant rate of g% per annum, discounted at r% per annum:

$$PV = \frac{1}{r - g}$$

Review of May 2005 paper

Section A

Exactly half the marks available were based on the groups section of the syllabus with the remainder used to get syllabus coverage. The one notable omission related to financial analysis, but this is a topic better suited to longer questions where candidates have a greater opportunity to demonstrate their interpretative skills.

There was a balance between written and computational questions, and it would have been important to manage time efficiently; particularly as some questions would need in excess of their designated time whilst others were a straight selection based on knowledge. It would have been useful to have included a 10 mark time check as part of your exam technique to avoid missing potentially easy marks.

Section B

Question 2: Examined core skills in relation to basic EPS, but did not require knowledge on dilution. The question cleverly used this as a springboard into interpretation by requiring computation of the P/E ratio and a brief discussion on its relative merits.

The inclusion of discussion requirements is likely to be a recurring theme as it allows the demonstration of professional skills and commercial awareness in addition to pure knowledge.

Question 3: This was deceptive question as the volume of information provided looked modest, but as part of the preparation of a consolidated income statement candidates were required to calculate goodwill and the profit/loss arising on disposal. This was a question which played into the hands of those who had undertaken considerable question practice as part of their preparation, and they will have looked to score heavily.

Question 4: Candidates should have been expecting a question on financial instruments, and this was a very fair examination of their knowledge, requiring no complex computations.

The brevity of the accredited answer shows that the examiner had allowed some thinking time, and this is to be commended as it allows differentiation between those who tried to rote learn this subject, and those who could apply their knowledge.

Section C

Question 5: Part (a) of this question represented classic financial analysis requiring the calculation of ratios and incisive commentary on the story they told. The key skills need to perform well in this section included

- Ensuring adequate time allocated to writing the report
- Adding value rather than simply observing that indicators have increased/decreased . . . remember the investor would be paying you to tell them something they do not already know!

Part (b) looking at weaknesses in financial analysis was straightforward providing time had been set aside to tackle it.

Question 6: A benchmark question on consolidation with both written and numerical sections. There was plenty to do in the time with associates and intra-group trading featuring prominently. This is a question a majority of candidates would have been expected to select, and should have been a major contributor to the overall exam mark.

Question 7: An interesting question combining interpretation with social and environmental accounting issues. There was a lot of information to absorb for Part (a), and many will have elected not to do the question for this reason. However, for those that did grasp the thistle the remaining two requirements tested core knowledge on social and environmental reporting. This is a topic that can be expected to feature regularly in the exam as it one of the growth areas of modern financial reporting

Overall

The first exam using the new syllabus was a fair test which concentrated on the subjects of groups and interpretation, and had few nasty surprises. Candidates should have been well prepared, and those that held their nerve and maintained good exam technique will have been rewarded.

November 2005 Questions and Answers

24

Financial Analysis (Paper P8)

The answers published here have been written by the Examiner and should provide a helpful guide for both tutors and students.

Published separately on the CIMA website (www.cimaglobal.com) from the end of February 2006 is a Post Examination Guide for this paper, which provides much valuable and complementary material including indicative mark information.

Financial Management Pillar

Managerial Level Paper

P8 – Financial Analysis

22 November 2005 – Tuesday Afternoon Session

Instructions to candidates

You are allowed three hours to answer this question paper.
You are allowed 20 minutes reading time **before the examination begins** during which you should read the question paper and, if you wish, make annotations on the question paper. However, you will **not** be allowed, **under any circumstances**, to open the answer book and start writing or use your calculator during this reading time.
You are strongly advised to carefully read ALL the question requirements before attempting the question concerned (that is, all parts and/or sub-questions). The question requirements for questions in Section B and C are highlighted in a dotted box.
Answer the ONE compulsory question in Section A. This is comprised of seven objective test questions on pages 301 to 303.
Answer ALL THREE questions in Section B on pages 304 to 305.
Answer TWO of the three questions in Section C on pages 306 to 312.
Maths Tables are provided on pages 313 to 315.
Write your full examination number, paper number and the examination subject title in the spaces provided on the front of the examination answer book. Also write your contact ID and name in the space provided in the right hand margin and seal to close.
Tick the appropriate boxes on the front of the answer book to indicate which questions you have answered.

SECTION A – 20 MARKS

[the indicative time for answering this section is 36 minutes]

ANSWER *ALL* SEVEN SUB-QUESTIONS

Instructions for answering Section A:

The answers to the seven sub-questions in Section A should ALL be written in your answer book.

Your answers should be clearly numbered with the sub-question number and then ruled off, so that the markers know which sub-question you are answering. For multiple choice questions, you need only write the sub-question number and the letter of the answer option you have chosen. You do not need to start a new page for each sub-question.

For sub-questions **1.1** and **1.2**, you should show your workings as marks are available for method for these sub-questions.

? Question One

1.1 FAL owns 75% of the issued ordinary share capital and 25% of the issued irredeemable preferred shares in PAL. The share capital and accumulated profits of PAL at 31 March 2005, the FAL group's year end, were:

	$
Ordinary share capital	60,000
7% preferred share capital	20,000
	80,000
Accumulated profits	215,000
	295,000

Upon acquisition of FAL's interests in PAL, which took place on 30 September 2004, the fair values of PAL's net assets were the same as book values, with the exception of an item of plant. The carrying value of the plant at 30 September 2004 was $10,200, and its fair value was $15,600. Its estimated remaining useful life at that date was 4 years. Depreciation is charged for each month of ownership. No adjustment was made in PAL's own accounting records for the increase in fair value.

Calculate the minority interest in PAL at 31 March 2005 for inclusion in the group's consolidated balance sheet (to the nearest $).

(4 marks)

1.2 AB owns a controlling interest in another entity, CD, and exerts significant influence over EF, an entity in which it holds 30% of the ordinary share capital.

During the financial year ended 30 April 2005, EF sold goods to AB valued at $80,000. The cost of the goods to EF was $60,000. 25% of the goods remained in AB's inventory at 30 April 2005.

Which ONE of the following is the correct consolidation adjustment in respect of the inventory?

A DR Consolidated reserves $5,000, CR Inventory $5,000
B DR Consolidated reserves $1,500, CR Inventory $1,500
C DR Consolidated reserves $5,000, CR Investment in Associate $5,000
D DR Consolidated reserves $1,500, CR Investment in Associate $1,500

(3 marks)

1.3 Which ONE of the following describes the method of accounting preferred by IAS 31 *Interests in Joint Ventures* for jointly controlled entities?

A Trade investment with disclosure of share of assets by way of note.
B The equity method of consolidation.
C Proportionate consolidation.
D Acquisition accounting with deduction of a minority interest.

(2 marks)

1.4 IAS 29 *Financial reporting in hyperinflationary economies* lists characteristics of the economic environment of a country which tend to indicate that hyperinflation is a problem.

Identify TWO of these characteristics.

(4 marks)

1.5 On 1 January 2005, an entity issued a debt instrument with a coupon rate of 3.5% at a par value of $6,000,000. The directly attributable costs of issue were $120,000. The debt instrument is repayable on 31 December 2011 at a premium of $1,100,000.

What is the total amount of the finance cost associated with the debt instrument?

A $1,470,000
B $1,590,000
C $2,570,000
D $2,690,000

(2 marks)

1.6 XYZ operates a defined benefit pension plan for its employees. The present value of the plan's obligations on 1 September 2004 was $6,600,000, increasing to $7,200,000 by the entity's year-end on 31 August 2005. Benefits paid to members of the pension plan during the year were $650,000 and the current service cost for the financial year was $875,000. The increase in the present value of the pension plan's liabilities for the year was $540,000.

What was the actuarial gain or loss in respect of the plan's obligations for the year ended 31 August 2005?

A Gain of $165,000
B Loss of $285,000
C Gain of $1,465,000
D Loss of $1,585,000

(2 marks)

1.7 At its year end, 31 March 2005, entity JBK held 60,000 shares in a listed entity, X. The shares were purchased on 11 February 2005 at a price of 85¢ per share. The market value of the shares on 31 March 2005 was 87.5¢. The investment is categorised as held-for-trading.

Show the journal entries required in respect of both the initial acquisition of the investment and its subsequent remeasurement on 31 March 2005.

(3 marks)

(Section A = 20 marks)

SECTION B – 30 MARKS

[the indicative time for answering this section is 54 minutes]

ANSWER *ALL* THREE QUESTIONS

Question Two

DCB is a manufacturing and trading entity with several overseas operations. One of its subsidiaries, GFE, operates in a country which experiences relatively high rates of inflation in its currency, the crown. Most entities operating in that country voluntarily present two versions of their financial statements: one at historical cost, and the other incorporating current cost adjustments. GFE complies with this accepted practice.

Extracts from the income statement adjusted for current costs for the year ended 30 September 2005 are as follows:

	Crowns '000	*Crowns* '000
Historical cost operating profit		750
Current cost adjustments		
Cost of sales adjustment	65	
Depreciation adjustment	43	
Loss on net monetary position	16	
		124
Current cost operating profit		626

Requirements

(a) Explain the defects of historical cost accounting in times of increasing prices. **(4 marks)**

(b) Explain how EACH of the three current cost accounting adjustments in GFE's financial statements contributes to the maintenance of capital.

(6 marks)

(Total for Question Two = 10 marks)

Question Three

ABC is currently expanding its portfolio of equity interests in other entities. On 1 January 2005, it made a successful bid for a controlling interest in DEF, paying a combination of shares and cash in order to acquire 80% of DEF's 100,000 issued equity shares. The terms of the acquisition were as follows:

In exchange for each $1 ordinary share purchased, ABC issued one of its own $1 ordinary shares and paid $1.50 in cash. In addition to the consideration paid, ABC agreed to pay a further $1 per share on 1 January 2007, on condition that the profits of DEF for the year ended 31 May 2006 will exceed $6,000,000. ABC's directors consider that it is more likely than not that the additional consideration will be paid. The market value of a $1 share in ABC at 1 January 2005 was $3.50, rising to $3.60 at ABC's 31 May 2005 year end.

Total legal, administrative and share issue costs associated with the acquisition were $60,000: this figure included $20,000 paid to external legal and accounting advisers, an estimated $10,000 in respect of ABC's own administrative overhead and $30,000 in share issue costs.

The carrying value of DEF's net assets at 1 January 2005 was $594,000. Carrying value was regarded as a close approximation to fair value, except in respect of the following:

1. The carrying value of DEF's property, plant and equipment at 1 January 2005 was $460,000. Market value at that date was estimated at $530,000.
2. DEF had a contingent liability in respect of a major product warranty claim with a fair value of $100,000.
3. The cost of reorganising DEF's activities following acquisition was estimated at $75,000.
4. DEF's inventories included goods at an advanced stage of work-in-progress with a carrying value of $30,000. The sales value of these goods was estimated at $42,000 and further costs to completion at $6,000.

Requirement

Calculate goodwill on the acquisition of DEF, in accordance with the requirements of IFRS 3 *Business Combinations*, explaining your treatment of the legal, administrative, share issue and reorganisation costs.

(Total for Question Three = 10 marks)

? Question Four

At a recent staff seminar on Accounting Standards, a senior member of your firm's accounting staff made the following observation:

> "International Standards have now been adopted in many countries across the world. Unfortunately though, they can never be truly international because US GAAP will continue to dominate accounting in the USA and therefore in many multinational businesses."

Requirement

Explain the rationale for this observation, illustrating your explanation with examples of significant differences and similarities between US GAAP and International Accounting Standards.

(Total for Question Four = 10 marks)

(Section B = 30 marks)

SECTION C – 50 MARKS

[the indicative time for answering this section is 90 minutes]

ANSWER *TWO* QUESTIONS OUT OF THREE

? Question Five

You are assistant to the Finance Director (FD) of OPQ, a well-known retailer of music, video and games products. OPQ's profit margins are under increasing pressure because of the entry of online retailers into the market. As part of their response to this challenge, OPQ's directors have decided to invest in entities in the supply chain of their most popular products. They are currently considering the acquisition of the business that supplies some of its best-selling computer games, PJ Gamewriters (PJ). The FD has asked you, as a preliminary step, to examine the most recent financial statements of the entity.

PJ was established in 1999 by twin brothers, Paul and James, who had recently graduated in computing. Their first business success was a simulated empire building game; this has continued to bring in a large proportion of PJ's revenue. However, they have also been successful in a range of other games types such as combat simulations, golf and football management games. The business has grown rapidly from year to year, and by 2005 it employed ten full-time games writers. Manufacture and distribution of the software in various formats is outsourced, and the business operates from office premises in a city centre. PJ bought the freehold of the office premises in 2002, and its estimated market value is now $900,000, nearly $350,000 in excess of the price paid in 2002. Apart from the freehold building, the business owns few non-current assets.

The equity shares in PJ are owned principally by Paul, James and their parents, who provided the initial start-up capital. Paul and James are the sole directors of the business. A small proportion of the shares (around 8%) is owned by five of the senior software writers. PJ is now up for sale as the principal shareholders wish to realise the bulk of their investment in order to pursue other business interests. It is likely that about 90% of the shares will be for sale. The copyrights of the games are owned by PJ, but no value is attributed to them in the financial statements.

PJ's income statement and summarised statement of changes in equity for the year ended 31 July 2005, and balance sheet at that date (all with comparatives) are as follows:

PJ: Income statement for the year ended 31 July 2005

	2005	*2004*
	$'000	$'000
Revenue	2,793	2,208
Cost of sales (see note below)	(1,270)	(1,040)
Gross profit	1,523	1,168
Operating expenses	(415)	(310)
Profit from operations	1,108	858
Interest receivable	7	2
Profit before tax	1,115	860
Income tax expense	(331)	(290)
Profit for the period	784	570

Note: Cost of sales comprises the following:	*2005*	*2004*
	$'000	$'000
Games writers' employment costs	700	550
Production costs	215	160
Directors' remuneration	200	200
Other costs	155	130
	1,270	1,040

PJ: Summarised statement of changes in equity for the year ended 31 July 2005

	2005	*2004*
	$'000	$'000
Opening balance	703	483
Profit for the period	784	570
Dividends	(500)	(350)
Closing balance	987	703

PJ: Balance sheet at 31 July 2005

	2005		2004	
	$'000	$'000	$'000	$'000
Non-current assets				
Property, plant and equipment		610		620
Current assets				
Inventories	68		59	
Trade receivables	460		324	
Cash	216		20	
		744		403
		1,354		1,023
Equity				
Share capital	60		60	
Retained earnings	927		643	
		987		703
Current liabilities				
Trade and other payables	36		30	
Income tax	331		290	
		367		320
		1,354		1,023

Requirements

(a) Prepare a report on the financial performance and position of PJ Gameswriters, calculating and interpreting any relevant accounting ratios.

(17 marks)

(b) Explain the limitations of your analysis, identifying any supplementary items of information that would be useful.

(8 marks)

(Total for Question Five = 25 marks)

? Question Six

Extracts from the consolidated financial statements of the AH Group for the year ended 30 June 2005 are given below:

AH Group: Consolidated income statement for the year ended 30 June 2005

	2005
	$'000
Revenue	85,000
Cost of sales	(59,750)
Gross profit	25,250
Operating expenses	(5,650)
Profit from operations	19,600
Finance cost	(1,400)
Profit before disposal of property	18,200
Disposal of property (*note* 2)	1,250
Profit before tax	19,450
Income tax	(6,250)
Profit for the period	13,200

Attributable to	$'000
Minority interest	655
Group profit for the year	12,545
	13,200

AH Group: Extracts from statement of changes in equity for the year ended 30 June 2005

	Share capital	*Share premium*	*Consolidated revenue reserves*
	$'000	$'000	$'000
Opening balance	18,000	10,000	18,340
Issue of share capital	2,000	2,000	
Profit for period			12,545
Dividends			(6,000)
Closing balance	20,000	12,000	24,885

AH Group: Balance sheet, with comparatives, at 30 June 2005

	2005		2004	
ASSETS	$'000	$'000	$'000	$'000
Non-current assets				
Property, plant and equipment	50,600		44,050	
Intangible assets (*note 3*)	6,410		4,160	
		57,010		48,210
Current assets				
Inventories	33,500		28,750	
Trade receivables	27,130		26,300	
Cash	1,870		3,900	
		62,500		58,950
		119,510		107,160
EQUITY AND LIABILITIES				
Equity				
Share capital	20,000		18,000	
Share premium	12,000		10,000	
Consolidated revenue reserves	24,885		18,340	
		56,885		46,340
Minority interest		3,625		1,920
Non-current liabilities				
Interest-bearing borrowings		18,200		19,200
Current liabilities				
Trade payables	33,340		32,810	
Interest payable	1,360		1,440	
Tax	6,100		5,450	
		40,800		39,700
		119,510		107,160

Notes:

1. Several years ago, AH acquired 80% of the issued ordinary shares of its subsidiary, BI. On 1 January 2005, AH acquired 75% of the issued ordinary shares of CJ in exchange for a fresh issue of 2 million of its own $1 ordinary shares (issued at a premium of $1 each) and $2 million in cash. The net assets of CJ at the date of acquisition were assessed as having the following fair values:

	$'000
Property, plant and equipment	4,200
Inventories	1,650
Receivables	1,300
Cash	50
Trade payables	(1,950)
Tax	(250)
	5,000

2. During the year, AH disposed of a non-current asset of property for proceeds of \$2,250,000. The carrying value of the asset at the date of disposal was \$1,000,000. There were no other disposals of non-current assets. Depreciation of \$7,950,000 was charged against consolidated profits for the year.
3. Intangible assets comprise goodwill on acquisition of BI and CJ (2004: BI only). Goodwill has remained unimpaired since acquisition.

Requirement

Prepare the consolidated cash flow statement of the AH Group for the financial year ended 30 June 2005 in the form required by IAS 7 *Cash flow statements*, and using the indirect method. Notes to the cash flow statement are NOT required, but full workings should be shown.

(Total for Question Six = 25 marks)

Question Seven

One of your colleagues has recently inherited investments in several listed entities and she frequently asks for your advice on accounting issues. She has recently received the consolidated financial statements of STV, an entity that provides haulage and freight services in several countries. She has noticed that note 3 to the financial statements is headed "Segment information".

Note 3 explains that STV's primary segment reporting format is business segments of which there are three: in addition to road and air freight, the entity provides secure transportation services for smaller items of high value. STV's *Operating and Financial Review* provides further background information; the secure transport services segment was established only three years ago. This new operation required a sizeable investment in infrastructure which was principally funded through borrowing. However, the segment has experienced rapid revenue growth in that time, and has become a significant competitor in the industry sector.

Extracts from STV's segment report for the year ended 31 August 2005 are as follows:

	Road haulage		*Air freight*		*Secure transport*		*Group*	
	2005	*2004*	*2005*	*2004*	*2005*	*2004*	*2005*	*2004*
	$m	*$m*	*$m*	*$m*	*$m*	*$m*	*$m*	*$m*
Revenue	653	642	208	199	98	63	959	904
Segment result	169	168	68	62	6	(16)	243	214
Unallocated corporate expenses							(35)	(37)
Operating profit							208	177
Interest expense							(22)	(21)
Share of profits of associates	16	12					16	12
Profit before tax							202	168
Income tax							(65)	(49)
Profit							137	119
Other information								
Segment assets	805	796	306	287	437	422	1,548	1,505
Investment in equity method associates	85	84					85	84
Unallocated corporate assets							573	522
Consolidated total assets							2,206	2,111
Segment liabilities	345	349	176	178	197	184	718	711
Unallocated corporate liabilities							37	12
Consolidated total liabilities							755	723

Your colleague finds several aspects of this note confusing:

> "I thought I'd understood what you told me about consolidated financial statements; the idea of aggregating several pieces of information to provide an overall view of the activities of the group makes sense. But the segment report seems to be trying to disaggregate the information all over again: what is the point of doing this? Does this information actually tell me anything useful about STV? I know from talking to you previously that financial information does not always tell us everything we need to know. So, what are the limitations in this statement?"

Requirements

(a) Explain the reasons for including disaggregated information about business segments in the notes to the consolidated financial statements.

(5 marks)

(b) Analyse and interpret STV's segment disclosures for the benefit of your colleague, explaining your findings in a brief report.

(12 marks)

(c) Explain the general limitations of segment reporting, illustrating your answer where applicable with references to STV's segment report.

(8 marks)

(Total for Question Seven = 25 marks)

(Section C = 50 marks)

MATHS TABLES AND FORMULAE

Present value table

Present value of $1, that is $(1 + r)^{-n}$ where r = interest rate; n = number of periods until payment or receipt.

Periods (n)	Interest rates (r)									
	1%	2%	3%	4%	5%	6%	7%	8%	9%	10%
1	0.990	0.980	0.971	0.962	0.952	0.943	0.935	0.926	0.917	0.909
2	0.980	0.961	0.943	0.925	0.907	0.890	0.873	0.857	0.842	0.826
3	0.971	0.942	0.915	0.889	0.864	0.840	0.816	0.794	0.772	0.751
4	0.961	0.924	0.888	0.855	0.823	0.792	0.763	0.735	0.708	0.683
5	0.951	0.906	0.863	0.822	0.784	0.747	0.713	0.681	0.650	0.621
6	0.942	0.888	0.837	0.790	0.746	0.705	0.666	0.630	0.596	0.564
7	0.933	0.871	0.813	0.760	0.711	0.665	0.623	0.583	0.547	0.513
8	0.923	0.853	0.789	0.731	0.677	0.627	0.582	0.540	0.502	0.467
9	0.914	0.837	0.766	0.703	0.645	0.592	0.544	0.500	0.460	0.424
10	0.905	0.820	0.744	0.676	0.614	0.558	0.508	0.463	0.422	0.386
11	0.896	0.804	0.722	0.650	0.585	0.527	0.475	0.429	0.388	0.350
12	0.887	0.788	0.701	0.625	0.557	0.497	0.444	0.397	0.356	0.319
13	0.879	0.773	0.681	0.601	0.530	0.469	0.415	0.368	0.326	0.290
14	0.870	0.758	0.661	0.577	0.505	0.442	0.388	0.340	0.299	0.263
15	0.861	0.743	0.642	0.555	0.481	0.417	0.362	0.315	0.275	0.239
16	0.853	0.728	0.623	0.534	0.458	0.394	0.339	0.292	0.252	0.218
17	0.844	0.714	0.605	0.513	0.436	0.371	0.317	0.270	0.231	0.198
18	0.836	0.700	0.587	0.494	0.416	0.350	0.296	0.250	0.212	0.180
19	0.828	0.686	0.570	0.475	0.396	0.331	0.277	0.232	0.194	0.164
20	0.820	0.673	0.554	0.456	0.377	0.312	0.258	0.215	0.178	0.149

Periods (n)	Interest rates (r)									
	11%	12%	13%	14%	15%	16%	17%	18%	19%	20%
1	0.901	0.893	0.885	0.877	0.870	0.862	0.855	0.847	0.840	0.833
2	0.812	0.797	0.783	0.769	0.756	0.743	0.731	0.718	0.706	0.694
3	0.731	0.712	0.693	0.675	0.658	0.641	0.624	0.609	0.593	0.579
4	0.659	0.636	0.613	0.592	0.572	0.552	0.534	0.516	0.499	0.482
5	0.593	0.567	0.543	0.519	0.497	0.476	0.456	0.437	0.419	0.402
6	0.535	0.507	0.480	0.456	0.432	0.410	0.390	0.370	0.352	0.335
7	0.482	0.452	0.425	0.400	0.376	0.354	0.333	0.314	0.296	0.279
8	0.434	0.404	0.376	0.351	0.327	0.305	0.285	0.266	0.249	0.233
9	0.391	0.361	0.333	0.308	0.284	0.263	0.243	0.225	0.209	0.194
10	0.352	0.322	0.295	0.270	0.247	0.227	0.208	0.191	0.176	0.162
11	0.317	0.287	0.261	0.237	0.215	0.195	0.178	0.162	0.148	0.135
12	0.286	0.257	0.231	0.208	0.187	0.168	0.152	0.137	0.124	0.112
13	0.258	0.229	0.204	0.182	0.163	0.145	0.130	0.116	0.104	0.093
14	0.232	0.205	0.181	0.160	0.141	0.125	0.111	0.099	0.088	0.078
15	0.209	0.183	0.160	0.140	0.123	0.108	0.095	0.084	0.079	0.065
16	0.188	0.163	0.141	0.123	0.107	0.093	0.081	0.071	0.062	0.054
17	0.170	0.146	0.125	0.108	0.093	0.080	0.069	0.060	0.052	0.045
18	0.153	0.130	0.111	0.095	0.081	0.069	0.059	0.051	0.044	0.038
19	0.138	0.116	0.098	0.083	0.070	0.060	0.051	0.043	0.037	0.031
20	0.124	0.104	0.087	0.073	0.061	0.051	0.043	0.037	0.031	0.026

Cumulative present value of $1 per annum

Receivable or Payable at the end of each year for n years $\frac{1-(1+r)^{-n}}{r}$

Periods (n)	Interest rates (r)									
	1%	2%	3%	4%	5%	6%	7%	8%	9%	10%
1	0.990	0.980	0.971	0.962	0.952	0.943	0.935	0.926	0.917	0.909
2	1.970	1.942	1.913	1.886	1.859	1.833	1.808	1.783	1.759	1.736
3	2.941	2.884	2.829	2.775	2.723	2.673	2.624	2.577	2.531	2.487
4	3.902	3.808	3.717	3.630	3.546	3.465	3.387	3.312	3.240	3.170
5	4.853	4.713	4.580	4.452	4.329	4.212	4.100	3.993	3.890	3.791
6	5.795	5.601	5.417	5.242	5.076	4.917	4.767	4.623	4.486	4.355
7	6.728	6.472	6.230	6.002	5.786	5.582	5.389	5.206	5.033	4.868
8	7.652	7.325	7.020	6.733	6.463	6.210	5.971	5.747	5.535	5.335
9	8.566	8.162	7.786	7.435	7.108	6.802	6.515	6.247	5.995	5.759
10	9.471	8.983	8.530	8.111	7.722	7.360	7.024	6.710	6.418	6.145
11	10.368	9.787	9.253	8.760	8.306	7.887	7.499	7.139	6.805	6.495
12	11.255	10.575	9.954	9.385	8.863	8.384	7.943	7.536	7.161	6.814
13	12.134	11.348	10.635	9.986	9.394	8.853	8.358	7.904	7.487	7.103
14	13.004	12.106	11.296	10.563	9.899	9.295	8.745	8.244	7.786	7.367
15	13.865	12.849	11.938	11.118	10.380	9.712	9.108	8.559	8.061	7.606
16	14.718	13.578	12.561	11.652	10.838	10.106	9.447	8.851	8.313	7.824
17	15.562	14.292	13.166	12.166	11.274	10.477	9.763	9.122	8.544	8.022
18	16.398	14.992	13.754	12.659	11.690	10.828	10.059	9.372	8.756	8.201
19	17.226	15.679	14.324	13.134	12.085	11.158	10.336	9.604	8.950	8.365
20	18.046	16.351	14.878	13.590	12.462	11.470	10.594	9.818	9.129	8.514

Periods (n)	Interest rates (r)									
	11%	12%	13%	14%	15%	16%	17%	18%	19%	20%
1	0.901	0.893	0.885	0.877	0.870	0.862	0.855	0.847	0.840	0.833
2	1.713	1.690	1.668	1.647	1.626	1.605	1.585	1.566	1.547	1.528
3	2.444	2.402	2.361	2.322	2.283	2.246	2.210	2.174	2.140	2.106
4	3.102	3.037	2.974	2.914	2.855	2.798	2.743	2.690	2.639	2.589
5	3.696	3.605	3.517	3.433	3.352	3.274	3.199	3.127	3.058	2.991
6	4.231	4.111	3.998	3.889	3.784	3.685	3.589	3.498	3.410	3.326
7	4.712	4.564	4.423	4.288	4.160	4.039	3.922	3.812	3.706	3.605
8	5.146	4.968	4.799	4.639	4.487	4.344	4.207	4.078	3.954	3.837
9	5.537	5.328	5.132	4.946	4.772	4.607	4.451	4.303	4.163	4.031
10	5.889	5.650	5.426	5.216	5.019	4.833	4.659	4.494	4.339	4.192
11	6.207	5.938	5.687	5.453	5.234	5.029	4.836	4.656	4.486	4.327
12	6.492	6.194	5.918	5.660	5.421	5.197	4.988	7.793	4.611	4.439
13	6.750	6.424	6.122	5.842	5.583	5.342	5.118	4.910	4.715	4.533
14	6.982	6.628	6.302	6.002	5.724	5.468	5.229	5.008	4.802	4.611
15	7.191	6.811	6.462	6.142	5.847	5.575	5.324	5.092	4.876	4.675
16	7.379	6.974	6.604	6.265	5.954	5.668	5.405	5.162	4.938	4.730
17	7.549	7.120	6.729	6.373	6.047	5.749	5.475	5.222	4.990	4.775
18	7.702	7.250	6.840	6.467	6.128	5.818	5.534	5.273	5.033	4.812
19	7.839	7.366	6.938	6.550	6.198	5.877	5.584	5.316	5.070	4.843
20	7.963	7.469	7.025	6.623	6.259	5.929	5.628	5.353	5.101	4.870

FORMULAE

Annuity

Present value of an annuity of \$1 per annum receivable or payable for n years, commencing in one year, discounted at $r\%$ per annum:

$$PV = \frac{1}{r}\left[1 - \frac{1}{[1+r]^n}\right]$$

Perpetuity

Present value of \$1 per annum receivable or payable in perpetuity, commencing in one year, discounted at $r\%$ per annum:

$$PV = \frac{1}{r}$$

Growing Perpetuity

Present value of \$1 per annum, receivable or payable, commencing in one year, growing in perpetuity at a constant rate of $g\%$ per annum, discounted at $r\%$ per annum:

$$PV = \frac{1}{r-g}$$

The Examiner for Financial Analysis offers to future candidates and to tutors using this booklet for study purposes, the following background and guidance on the questions included in this examination paper.

Section A – Compulsory

Question one

1.1 Short question that required calculation of the minority interest in a recently acquired subsidiary, taking account of relevant fair value adjustments. This tested learning outcome A (iv).

1.2 OTQ that required identification of the correct accounting treatment for unrealised profit in inventory in respect of an associate's supply of goods to the investor entity. This tested learning outcome A (vi).

1.3 OTQ that required identification of the method of accounting for joint ventures preferred by IAS 31. This tested learning outcome A (vi).

1.4 Short question that required identification of two characteristics of the economic environment of a hyper-inflationary country with reference to IAS 29. This tested learning outcome B (ii).

1.5 OTQ that required calculation of the finance cost associated with a debt instrument. This tested learning outcome B (iv).

1.6 OTQ that required calculation of the actuarial gain or loss in respect of a pension plan's obligations. This tested learning outcome B (vi).

1.7 Short question that required candidates to show journal entries in respect of a financial asset. This tested learning outcome B (v).

Section B – Compulsory

Question Two required explanation of the defects of historical cost accounting in times of increasing prices, and explanations of three current cost adjustments shown in the extracts from the income statement of a subsidiary operating in a country with high rates of price inflation. This question tested learning outcome B (ii).

Question Three required the calculation of goodwill in respect of the acquisition of a subsidiary whose fair values differed from book values. Explanations were required in respect of the treatment of various costs of acquisition. This question tested learning outcome A (iv).

Question Four required explanation of the rationale for an observation about the enduring differences between international accounting standards and US GAAP. Candidates were required to demonstrate the application of knowledge by providing examples of significant differences and similarities between the two sets of standards. This question tested learning outcome D (vi).

Section C – Answer two from three questions

Question Five required preparation of a report on the financial performance and position of an unlisted entity. This involved the calculation, analysis and interpretation of the entity's balance sheet, summarised statement of changes in equity and income statement. Candidates were also required to identify the limitations of their analysis. This question tested learning outcomes C (i), (ii), (iii) and (iv).

Question Six required the preparation of a consolidated cash flow statement for a group of entities. One of the subsidiary entities had been acquired during the accounting period. This question tested learning outcome A (iii).

Question Seven required an explanation of the reasons for including disaggregated information in the form of segment reports in consolidated financial statements. Candidates were required to analyse and interpret extracts from a segment report provided in the question, and were also asked to explain the limitations of such reports. This question tested learning outcome C (v).

Examiner's Answers

SECTION A

Question One

1.1

	$	$	$
Minority share of preferred share capital: $20,000 × 75%			15,000
Ordinary share capital and reserves: $60,000 + $215,000		275,000	
Fair value uplift ($15,600 − 10,200)	5,400		
Less: Depreciation for 6 months: $5,400/4 × 6⁄12	(675)		
		4,725	
		279,725	
Minority share: 25%			69,931
Total minority share			84,931

1.2 B

Unrealised profit = ($80,000 − $60,000) × 25% = $5,000.

The group share of the figure is 30% : $1,500. The profit and inventory are located in the holding entity, so therefore the adjustment is to consolidated reserves and consolidated inventory.

1.3 C

1.4 Any TWO of the following characteristics, as listed in IAS 29:

- The general population prefers to keep its wealth in non-monetary assets or in a relatively stable foreign currency.
- The general population regards monetary amounts not in terms of the local currency, but in terms of a relatively stable foreign currency.
- Sales and purchases on credit take place at prices that compensate for the expected loss of purchasing power during the credit period, even if that period is short.
- Interest rates, wages and prices are linked to a price index.
- The cumulative inflation index over three years is approaching, or exceeds, 100%.

1.5 D

Total payable

	$
Interest 7 years × 3.5% × $6,000,000	1,470,000
Payable on redemption: $6,000,000 + $1,100,000	7,100,000
	8,570,000
Total received	
Debt instrument	6,000,000
Less: Issue costs	(120,000)
	5,880,000

Net amount = finance costs = $2,690,000

1.6 A

	$'000
Present value of obligations on 1 September 2004	6,600
Increase in the present value of the plan liabilities	540
Current service cost	875
Benefits paid	(650)
Actuarial gain on obligations (balancing figure)	(165)
Present value of obligations on 31 August 2005	7,200

1.7 Journal entry on initial acquisition:

11 February 2005

		$	$
DR	Held-for-trading investment (60,000 × 85¢)	51,000	
CR	Cash		51,000

(Being the acquisition of a held-for-trading investment in X.)

Journal entry at JBK's year end:

31 March 2005

DR	Held-for trading investment (60,000 × [87.5¢ − 85¢])	1,500	
CR	Income statement (gains on investment)		1,500

(Being the revaluation of the held-for-trading investment to fair value.)

SECTION B

Question Two

(a) In times of increasing prices, historical cost accounting displays the following defects:

(i) Revenues are stated at current values, but they tend to be matched with costs incurred at an earlier date. Therefore, profit is overstated.

(ii) Where historical cost accounting is applied consistently, asset values are stated at cost less accumulated depreciation. Current values of the assets may be considerably in excess of net book value, with the result that the historical cost depreciation charge does not constitute a realistic estimate of the value of the asset consumed.

(iii) By the time monetary liabilities are repayable, the amount of the outflow in current value terms is less than the original inflow. An entity can therefore gain by holding liabilities, but historical cost accounting does not recognise these gains. The opposite effect is experienced in respect of monetary assets.

(iv) Typically, in a time of rising prices, profits are likely to be overstated, and capital to be understated, thus giving rise to unrealistic measurements of return on capital employed.

(b) The cost of sales adjustment comprises the additional amount of value over and above value at historical cost that is consumed at current cost. It represents an additional charge against profits, thus tending to reduce distributable earnings and ensuring that the business conserves the resources that allow it to continue to trade at current levels.

The depreciation adjustment is the difference between the historical cost accounting and current cost depreciation charges. Current cost depreciation is the value of the non-current asset consumption that has taken place during the year. In a time of rising prices it is a more realistic representation of the asset consumption. It tends to reduce distributable profits thus contributing to capital maintenance.

In the case of GFE, there is a loss on net monetary position. As noted earlier in part (a) holding monetary liabilities in times of rising prices tends to give rise to gains, whereas holding monetary assets produces losses. GFE appears, therefore, to have an excess of monetary assets over monetary liabilities, as the net effect is a loss. The recognition of this loss produces a more realistic estimation of distributable profit, and thus contributes to capital maintenance.

Question Three

Calculation of goodwill on the acquisition of 80% of the equity shares in DEF:

	$'000	$'000
Fair value of consideration		
80,000 shares acquired for consideration of $5 each		
($1.50 in cash + $3.50 in shares)		400
Contingent consideration: $1 per share		80
Directly attributable costs of acquisition – legal fees		20
Total consideration		500
Fair value of net assets acquired		
Net assets at carrying value	594	
Adjustments for fair value:		
Property, plant and equipment ($530,000 − $460,000)	70	
Contingent liability	(100)	
Inventories (fair value of $36,000 less carrying value of $30,000)	6	
	570	
80% acquired (80% × $570,000)		456
Goodwill on acquisition		44

According to IFRS 3, directly attributable costs of acquisition should be included in the cost of acquisition. The amount of $20,000 payable to external advisers is therefore included. Neither general administrative expenses or the costs of issuing equity instruments are permitted by the standard to be included in the cost of acquisition.

Similarly, the Standard requires that, when allocating the cost of the combination, the acquirer should not recognise liabilities for future losses of costs expected to be incurred as a result of the business combination.

Question Four

International Standards have, indeed, been adopted in many countries across the world: for example, compliance with them is compulsory in companies listed on a Stock Exchange within the European Union, and their adoption in Australia and New Zealand is well under way.

Nevertheless, it is certainly the case that accounting in accordance with International Standards continues to differ from US GAAP in many respects. To this extent, the observation by the senior staff member has some validity. Examples of important areas of difference are

- Performance reporting: In the US a comprehensive income model is used whereas international practice has not, to date, developed performance reporting requirements beyond IAS 1. Performance reporting has been on the agenda of the IASB since 2001, but it has not yet published an exposure draft on the topic.
- Valuation: International accounting practice allows the option to value property, plant and equipment at either depreciated cost or fair value. US GAAP is more restrictive in this respect and reporting at depreciated cost is much more prevalent.

On the other hand, convergence between US and international practice is becoming increasingly common. For example, a significant area of difference in the past has been that of business combinations: it was common in the US until recently to account for many business combinations as pooling of interests. While international practice did not outlaw pooling of interests its use was far less common. However, developments in US and International Standards have now resulted in a position where pooling of interests accounting is no longer available.

The senior staff member does not mention the "Norwalk agreement", which established a formal convergence project between the IASB and its US counterpart, the Financial Accounting Standards Board (FASB). Under the terms of this agreement, the IASB and FASB agreed to work together to remove differences between their respective sets of Standards, and to co-ordinate their future programmes of work. The agreement has already resulted in a narrowing of differences: for example, IFRS 5 *Non-current assets held for sale and discontinued operations* brings international practice into line with US GAAP. The two boards are working together on a project on performance reporting which is likely to produce convergence in the form of a comprehensive income reporting requirement.

There is a great deal of work to be done before US GAAP and international practice can be described as "convergent". However, much has already been achieved in a short time. The view expressed by the senior staff member would have been widely regarded as valid until very recently, but it has been overtaken by events. The convergence project has undoubtedly been given additional impetus by the recent, spectacular, corporate and accounting failures in the USA. These have resulted in a period of introspection and self-criticism among US regulators and in a push towards significant improvement in financial reporting.

Traditionally, the US approach to accounting regulation has been "rules-based"; this has resulted in the production of very lengthy, detailed Accounting Standards. By contrast, International Accounting Standards have tended to be "principles-based". For example, instead of having a very detailed international Standard addressing substance over form, international accounting practice relies much more upon promulgation and acceptance of the general principle of substance over form. The recent US accounting scandals have led to a great deal of criticism of the "rules-based" approach and greater acceptance of the value of the "principles-based" approach.

On the other hand, international regulation appears to be moving to some extent in the opposite direction, as International Standards become lengthier and more prescriptive (for example, IAS 39 *Financial instruments: recognition and measurement*). Therefore, it seems likely that US and international regulators will find it easier to occupy common ground in their approach to Standard setting.

SECTION C

Question Five

(a)

REPORT

To: The Finance Director

From: Assistant

Subject: PJ Gameswriters

PJ Gameswriters is a very successful business. Between 2004 and 2005 its revenue increased by 26.5% and its gross profit by 30.4%. However, unusually, cost of sales includes directors' remuneration, presumably because the directors are directly involved in games writing. If directors' remuneration is excluded from the analysis, gross profit restated increased by 26.0%, that is, very much in line with the revenue increase.

Gameswriters' employment costs comprise a significant part of cost of sales (55.1% – 2004: 52.9%). If the business were to be taken over by OPQ this expense might change if new writers were brought in to replace Paul and James. Production costs have increased to 17% of cost of sales (2004: 15.4%). These costs are outsourced, and it may be worth considering whether it is cost effective to continue such arrangements. Distribution costs are, presumably, included within cost of sales, probably under the category "other costs".

Operating expenses have increased by 33.9% between 2004 and 2005, that is, at a faster rate than revenue. Given that some of these expenses might be expected to be fixed, this rate of increase would require further information and explanation. Despite this increase, net profit margin has increased slightly, helped by an increase in interest receivable.

Turning to the balance sheet, the position appears healthy. No cash flow statement is provided, but nevertheless, it is clear that the business generates substantial amounts of cash. During the 2004–05 financial year, PJ managed to pay substantial amounts of dividend, directors' remuneration and income tax, while increasing its cash balance by almost $200,000. The current ratio has improved by a large margin from 1.26 : 1 at the 2004 year-end to 2.03 : 1. There is little change to inventories which, in any case, constitute a relatively minor element in current assets, but trade receivables has increased sharply, representing 60.1 days of sales (2004 : 53.6 days). It might be possible to make a significant improvement in this collection period.

Return on equity is very substantial in both years. However, this ratio should be treated with caution. Equity has been increased by $350,000 (reflecting the potential revaluation of the office premises) for the purposes of the calculation in both years so as to produce a more realistic result. The figure of $350,000 is strictly applicable only in 2005, however, and the equivalent figure in 2004 might well have been lower. It should also be appreciated that a higher asset valuation would give rise to additional depreciation charges which would reduce profits. In addition, it is worth noting that the value of equity would almost certainly be substantially higher if the intangible asset of software copyrights were to be included.

Conclusion

PJ has expanded significantly while managing to maintain its margins and a sound financial position. The business is cash rich and has needed no external financing. It appears to be a good prospect for acquisition and further detailed investigation is recommended.

Appendix: calculations

1. Cost of sales analysis

	2005 $'000	*% of total*	*2004* $'000	*% of total*
Games writers' employment costs	700	55.1	550	52.9
Production costs	215	17.0	160	15.4
Directors' remuneration	200	15.7	200	19.2
Other costs	155	12.2	130	12.5
	1,270	100.0	1,040	100.0

2. Gross profit margin (excluding directors' remuneration from cost of sales)

	2005 $'000	*2004* $'000
Gross profit (as stated)	1,523	1,168
Add back: directors' remuneration	200	200
Gross profit restated	1,723	1,368
Gross profit margin	1,723/2,793 × 100 = 61.7%	1,368/2,208 × 100 = 62.0%

3. Operating expenses as a percentage of revenue

2005 : 415/2,793 × 100 = 14.9%
2004 : 310/2,208 × 100 = 14.0%

4. Net profit margin (excluding directors' remuneration from profit)

	2005 $'000	*2004* $'000
Net profit (as stated)	784	570
Add back: directors' remuneration	200	200
Net profit restated	984	770
Net profit margin	984/2,793 × 100 = 35.2%	770/2,208 × 100 = 34.9%

(*Note*: This adjustment ignores tax)

5. Current ratio

2005 : 744 : 367 = 2.03 : 1

2004 : 403 : 320 = 1.26 : 1

6. Trade receivables collection period

$$2005 : \frac{460}{2{,}793} \times 365 = 60.1 \text{ days}$$

$$2004 : \frac{324}{2{,}208} \times 365 = 53.6 \text{ days}$$

7. **Return on equity (including potential revaluation of $350,000):**

$$2005: \frac{1{,}115}{987 + 350} \times 100 = 83.4\%$$

$$2004: \frac{860}{703 + 350} \times 100 = 81.7\%$$

Directors' remuneration may not be relevant to the analysis here. ROE excluding directors' remuneration is:

$$2005: \frac{1{,}115 + 200}{987 + 350} \times 100 = 98.4\%$$

$$2004: \frac{860 + 200}{703 + 350} \times 100 = 100.7\%$$

(b) Financial analysis is almost always hampered by limitations. In the case of PJ, there are some specific limitations in respect of the scope of the information reported in the annual financial statements. The value of the software titles generated during the life of the business is likely to be a substantial sum. As noted in part (a), it is not possible to calculate a realistic return on equity figure without this information. If OPQ is going to enter into serious negotiations to purchase PJ, the value of the copyrights should be established at an early stage. A further limitation is that financial statements place no value on the human assets employed within the business. However, where a business like PJ is to be taken over, such elements should, in any event, be downplayed. Paul and James will, presumably, leave the business, and it may not be possible to retain the services of all of the software writers.

A more detailed breakdown of certain elements in the income statement would be helpful in analysing the performance of the business. Within cost of sales "other costs" constitute a significant item in both years, and the nature of operating expenses is obscure.

There are general limitations to the value of financial statements to the analyst. Some of the limitations relevant to PJ include the following:

(i) Financial statements are prepared for the common needs of most users. Where they are being used to assist in making a specific decision (such as whether or not to invest in an entity, as in this case) the information they contain is likely to be found wanting.
(ii) Timeliness is often a problem. PJ's financial statements have apparently been prepared within a quite reasonable timeframe. However, this is clearly a business experiencing rapid growth, and it is likely that more current information will be needed, perhaps in the form of management accounts, in order to make an informed decision.
(iii) It is usually helpful to have a more complete picture than that provided by a single set of financial statements. Also, it is important to obtain a full set of notes to the financial statements as these often contain useful information. In the case of PJ, complete sets of the financial statements since the business was founded would be helpful.

Question Six

AH Group: consolidated cash flow statement for the year ended 30 June 2005

	$'000	$'000	*Ref. to working*
Cash flows from operating activities			
Profit before taxation	19,450		
Adjustments for:			
Profit on disposal of property	(1,250)		
Depreciation	7,950		
Finance cost	1,400		
	27,550		
Decrease in receivables	470		1
(Increase) in inventories	(3,100)		1
(Decrease) in trade payables	(1,420)		1
Cash generated from operations	23,500		
Interest paid	(1,480)		2
Income taxes paid	(5,850)		2
Net cash from operating activities		16,170	
Cash flows from investing activities			
Acquisition of subsidiary (net of cash)	(1,950)		3
Purchase of property, plant and equipment	(11,300)		4
Proceeds from sale of property	2,250		
Net cash used in investing activities		(11,000)	
Cash flows from financing activities			
Repayment of interest-bearing borrowings	(1,000)		
Dividends paid by AH	(6,000)		
Dividends paid to minority	(200)		5
Net cash used in financing activities		(7,200)	
Net decrease in cash		(2,030)	
Cash at beginning of period		3,900	
Cash at end of period		1,870	

Working 1 – Working capital changes

	Receivables $'000	*Inventories* $'000	*Trade payables* $'000
Closing balance	(27,130)	(33,500)	(33,340)
Less: Acquired with CJ	1,300	1,650	1,950
	(25,830)	(31,850)	(31,390)
Opening balance	26,300	28,750	32,810
Decrease/increase/decrease	470	(3,100)	1,420

Working 2 – Interest and income taxes

	Interest $'000	*Income taxes* $'000
Liability brought forward	1,440	5,450
Liability acquired with CJ	-	250
Charge to income statement	1,400	6,250
Liability carried forward	(1,360)	(6,100)
Balance: Amount paid	1,480	5,850

Working 3 – Acquisition of subsidiary

	$'000
Cash element of consideration	2,000
Less: Cash acquired with CJ	(50)
	1,950

Working 4 – Purchase of property, plant and equipment

	$'000
Balance brought forward	44,050
Acquired with CJ	4,200
Disposal at net book value	(1,000)
Depreciation for year	(7,950)
Less: Balance carried forward	(50,600)
Balance: Purchased	(11,300)

Working 5 – Dividend paid to minority

	$'000
Balance brought forward	1,920
Profit attributable to minority	655
Acquired with CJ ($5,000 × 25%)	1,250
Less: Balance carried forward	(3,625)
Balance: Dividend paid	200

Question Seven

(a) The overall objective of financial statements is to provide information about the financial position, performance and changes in financial position of an entity that helps users in making economic decisions. In the case of a group of companies, consolidated financial statements help users to see the overall performance of businesses that are often disparate in nature. It is, additionally, helpful to users to see aggregated results for businesses which are under common control, as it permits them to make judgements about the effectiveness of senior management. However, different types of product or service may be subject to differing rates of return, opportunities for growth, future prospects and risk. Segment reporting allows users to make better informed assessments of the risk profile of a business by examining the performance and position of different major business segments. Users can identify those segments (geographical and/or business segments) that are performing well or badly, and those that are inherently more risky because, for example, they are located in an unstable economic environment. It may thus become clear, for example, that one segment significantly outperforms others, and that it helps to compensate for poor performance in other areas.

(b) **Report on the segment information of STV for the year ended 31 August 2005**

The group result as a percentage of revenue shows a sound improvement from 23.7% in 2004 to 25.3% in 2005. However, this hides significant variations which are revealed once the segment result is analysed. The result as a percentage of revenue has fallen slightly in the road haulage segment and has improved slightly in the air freight segment. However, the really significant change has been in the secure transport segment which has turned from loss to profit during the year. Similarly, asset turnover is little changed in the two established segments, but has improved significantly in secure transport. However, asset turnover is very low in secure transport compared to the other two segments, suggesting that the business is only just starting to recoup the significant investment that it made in this segment three years ago. In terms of investment in assets, the investment in secure transport is far greater than that made in air freight, and it seems likely that this segment of the business is expected to grow in importance in the near future.

The best return on investment (measured by segment result as a percentage of net assets) is made by the air freight segment. The move from loss into profit results in a big improvement in this measure in the secure transport segment. However, this segment's overall contribution to group result remains relatively insignificant.

There has been no significant additional investment in the road haulage segment, and its results are slightly worse in 2005 than in 2004. It is possible that the segment's assets are ageing, and/or that competition is eroding margins. STV's management may have decided that it therefore makes sense to diversify its operations and this could explain the move into secure transport services. Nevertheless, road haulage continues at the moment to be the dominant segment, accounting for 68% of total group revenue in 2005.

The return on investments in associates is good in both years. The share of net profits in associates in 2005 accounts for almost 8% of profit before tax.

In summary, STV appears to be performing fairly well. If current trends were to continue, the secure transport segment could become a very important contributor to overall profitability, and could help to make up for slowly declining profitability in the road haulage segment.

Appendix: key ratios

	Road haulage	*Air freight*	*Secure transport*	*Group*
Segment result as a percentage of revenue				
2005	169/653 × 100 = 25.9%	68/208 × 100 = 32.7%	6/98 × 100 = 6.1%	243/959 × 100 = 25.3%
2004	168/642 × 100 = 26.2%	62/199 × 100 = 31.1%	(16)/63 × 100 = (25.4%)	214/904 × 100 = 23.7%
Profit before tax as a percentage of revenue				
2005				202/959 × 100 = 21.1%
2004				168/904 × 100 = 18.6%
Asset turnover (revenue/segment assets)				
2005	653/805 = 0.81	208/306 = 0.68	98/437 = 0.22	959/1,548 = 0.62
2004	642/796 = 0.81	199/287 = 0.69	63/422 = 0.15	904/1,505 = 0.60
Segment net assets				
2005	805 − 345 = 460	306 − 176 = 130	437 − 197 = 240	
2004	796 − 349 = 447	287 − 178 = 109	422 − 184 = 238	
Segment result as a percentage of segment net assets				
2005	169/460 × 100 = 36.7%	68/130 × 100 = 52.3%	6/240 × 100 = 2.5%	
2004	168/447 × 100 = 37.6%	62/109 × 100 = 56.9%	(16)/238 × 100 = (6.7%)	

Return on investments in associates

2005 16/85 × 100 = 18.8%
2004 12/84 × 100 = 14.3%

Contribution of each segment to group revenue and results

	2005	*%*	*2004*	*%*
Revenue – haulage	653/959 × 100	68%	642/904 × 100	71%
Revenue – freight	208/959 × 100	22%	199/904 × 100	22%
Revenue – secure	98/959 × 100	10%	63/904 × 100	7%
Result – haulage	169/243 × 100	70%	168/214 × 100	79%
Result – freight	68/243 × 100	28%	62/214 × 100	29%
Result – secure	6/243 × 100	2%	(16)/214 × 100	(8%)

(c) Most groups of entities have problems in defining segments and in allocating assets and liabilities to them. It is common to find that segment information includes amounts for unallocated expenses, assets and liabilities, and STV is no exception. The unallocated items in STV's segment information are significant, especially in the case of assets. Unallocated assets account for 26.0% of total assets in 2005 (24.7% in 2004). If the unallocated items were, in reality, found to belong to one or more of the segments, this could significantly alter the accounting ratios based on asset values. Also, of course, unscrupulous managers could classify items as "unallocated" in order to manipulate the picture presented by the segment information.

IAS 14 *Segment reporting* does not require the allocation of interest expense between segments. In STV's case, it would be informative to see such an allocation; we are told that the sizeable investment in the infrastructure required for the secure transport operation was funded principally through borrowing. However, we do not know how much borrowing was required, and how much of the group interest charge relates to it.

Other general limitations in segment reporting include the definition of segments, which is a matter of judgement on the part of the directors. Also, there may be quite genuine difficulties and ambiguities in allocating elements such as assets to different segments. A further general problem lies in comparability between businesses. Comparisons between STV's segment report and that of another haulage and freight business could be misleading if the segments have been defined differently.

Order Form

For CIMA Official Study Materials for 2006 Exams

Qty	Title	Author	ISBN	ISBN 13	Price	Total
	CIMA Official Study Systems					
	Management Accounting Fundamentals	Walker	0750667087	9780750667081	£33.00	
	Financial Accounting Fundamentals	Lunt	0750667044	9780750667043	£33.00	
	Business Mathematics	Peers	0750667052	9780750667050	£33.00	
	Economics for Business	Adams	0750667060	9780750667067	£33.00	
	Business Law	Sagar	0750667079	9780750667074	£33.00	
	Performance Evaluation	Scarlett	0750667117	9780750667111	£33.00	
	Decision Management	Wilks	0750667125	9780750667128	£33.00	
	Risk and Control Strategy	Collier	0750667168	9780750667166	£33.00	
	Organisational Management and Information Systems	Perry	0750667095	9780750667098	£33.00	
	Integrated Management	Harris	0750667109	9780750667104	£33.00	
	Business Strategy	Botten	0750667184	9780750667180	£33.00	
	Financial Accounting and Tax Principles	Rolfe	0750667133	9780750667135	£33.00	
	Financial Analysis	Gowthorpe	0750667141	9780750667142	£33.00	
	Financial Strategy	Ogilvie	075066715X	9780750667159	£33.00	
	TOP CIMA	Barnwell	0750667176	9780750667173	£33.00	
	CIMA Official Exam Practice Kits					
	Management Accounting Fundamentals	Allan	0750665807	9780750665803	£14.99	
	Financial Accounting Fundamentals	Allan	0750665831	9780750665834	£14.99	
	Business Mathematics	Allan	0750665866	9780750665865	£14.99	
	Economics for Business	Allan	075066584X	9780750665841	£14.99	
	Business Law	Benton	0750665858	9780750665858	£14.99	
	Performance Evaluation	Barnett	0750669322	9780750669320	£14.99	
	Decision Management	Barnett	0750669292	9780750669290	£14.99	
	Risk and Control Strategy	Robertson	0750669373	9780750669375	£14.99	
	Organisational Management & Information Systems	Robertson	0750669306	9780750669306	£14.99	
	Integrated Management	dalton	0750669314	9780750669313	£14.99	
	Business Strategy	Allan	0750669365	9780750669368	£14.99	
	Financial Accounting and Tax Principles	Patel	0750669330	9780750669337	£14.99	
	Financial Analysis	Rodgers	0750669349	9780750669344	£14.99	
	Financial Strategy	Allan	0750669357	9780750669351	£14.99	
	TOPCIMA	Little	0750666277	9780750666275	£14.99	
	CIMA Revision Cards					
	Management Accounting Fundamentals	Walker	0750664770	9780750664776	£6.99	
	Financial Accounting Fundamentals	Holland	0750664762	9780750664769	£6.99	
	Business Mathematics	Peers	0750664800	9780750664806	£6.99	
	Economics for Business	Adams	0750664789	9780750664783	£6.99	
	Business Law	Sagar	0750664797	9780750664790	£6.99	
	Performance Evaluation	Scarlett	0750664819	9780750664813	£6.99	
	Decision Management	Avis	0750664827	9780750664820	£6.99	
	Risk and Control Strategy	Harris	0750664835	9780750664837	£6.99	
	Organisational Management and Information Systems	Perry	0750664843	9780750664844	£6.99	
	Integrated Management	Harris	0750664851	9780750664851	£6.99	
	Business Strategy	Botten	075066486X	9780750664868	£6.99	
	Financial Accounting and Tax Principles	Rolfe	0750664878	9780750664875	£6.99	
	Financial Analysis	Gowthorpe	0750664886	9780750664882	£6.99	
	Financial Strategy	Ogilvie	0750664894	9780750664899	£6.99	
					P+P (£)	2.95
					Total (£)	

Post this form to:
CIMA Publishing Customer Services
Elsevier
FREEPOST (OF 1639)
Linacre House, Jordan Hill
OXFORD, OX2 8DP, UK

Or FAX +44 (0)1865 474 010
Or PHONE +44 (0)1865 474 014

Email: cimaorders@elsevier.com

www.cimapublishing.com

Name: ______

Organisation: ______

Invoice Address: ______

Postcode: ______

Phone number: ______

Email: ______

Delivery Address if different:

FAO: ______

Address: ______

Postcode: ______

Please note that all deliveries must be signed for

1. Cheques payable to Elsevier.
2. Please charge my:

Visa ☐ ☐ MasterCard

Amex ☐ ☐ Switch Issue No.______

Card No: ______

Expiry Date: ______

Cardholder Name: ______

Signature: ______

Date: ______

CIMA Official *Study Systems*

These comprehensive ring-binders are the only texts written and endorsed by the CIMA Faculty. As writers of the new 2006 syllabus and exams, nobody is better qualified to explain how to pass.

- Step-by-step subject coverage directly linked to CIMA's learning outcomes
- Extensive question practice throughout
- Complete revision section
- Pilot papers on the new syllabus, complete with examiner's solutions
- Two mock exams for Certificate subjects

CIMA Official *Revision Cards*

- Pocket-sized books for learning all the key points – especially for students on the move
- Relevant, succinct and compact reminders of all the bullet points and diagrams needed for the new CIMA 2006 exams
- Break down the syllabus into memorable bite-size chunks

CIMA Official *Exam Practice Kits*

Supplement the Study Systems with a bank of additional questions focusing purely on applying what has been learnt to passing the exam. Ideal for independent study or tutored revision courses. Prepare with confidence for exam day, and pass the new syllabus first time.

- Practice applying and displaying knowledge so CIMA examiners can award you marks
- Avoid common pitfalls with fully worked model answers which include analysis of typical incorrect answers
- Type and weighting of questions match the format of the exam by paper, helping you prepare by giving you the closest available preview of the exam
- Certificate subjects include 200 exam standard multiple choice questions. All have detailed explanations or calculations to show how to arrive at the correct answer
- Written by an outstanding team of freelance tutors with established reputations for success. The only materials endorsed by CIMA.

CIMA *Introduction to Business Taxation*

We continue to publish the authors of the syllabus with this first CIMA CPD product. Chris Jones is Tax Training Director at Lexis Nexis UK, with 10 years experience in training on tax issues. He prepared both the syllabus and this Official study manual.

Fully equips those studying for the new CIMA Certificate in Business Taxation. There is only one paper to be examined and one book for the course – this one.

Each chapter has full explanation of the rules and calculations as required by the Finance Act 2005. Short summaries then provide a "pocket digest" and together form a comprehensive overview of the syllabus. Each chapter contains examples questions to assess knowledge ahead of the CBA.

CIMA Publishing is an imprint of Elsevier
Registered Office:
The Boulevard, Langford Lane, Kidlington, Oxford OX5 1GB, UK
Registered in England: 3099304, VAT 494 627212